HUMAN DISABILITY AND THE SERVICE OF GOD

HUMAN DISABILITY AND THE SERVICE OF GOD

REASSESSING RELIGIOUS PRACTICE

NANCY L. EIESLAND
AND DON E. SALIERS, EDITORS

ABINGDON PRESS
Nashville

HUMAN DISABILITY AND THE SERVICE OF GOD
Reassessing Religious Practice

Library of Congress Cataloging-in-Publication Data

Eiesland, Nancy L., 1964–
    Human disability and the service of God: reassessing religious
practice/Nancy L. Eiesland and Don E. Saliers.
        p.   cm.
    Papers presented at a conference funded by the Louisville
Institute.
    Includes bibliographical references and index.
    ISBN 0-687-27316-1 (pbk.: alk. paper)
        1. Church work with the handicapped—Congresses.   2. Handicapped—
Religious aspects—Christianity—Congresses   I. Saliers, Don E.,
1937–   .   II. Title.
BV4460.E35   1998
261.8'324—dc21   98-12288
                                                                                                              CIP

98 99 00 01 02 03 04 05 06 07 —10 9 8 7 6 5 4 3 2 1

MANUFACTURED IN THE UNITED STATES OF AMERICA

To

William A. Hall, Jr.
Who lacks neither wit
Nor courage,
Nor friendship,
From whom we continue to learn.

CONTENTS

ACKNOWLEDGMENTS

W e owe a debt of gratitude to a number of individuals who have assisted us throughout the process of compiling this volume. Thanks are particularly due to all the chapter contributors for their cooperation and enthusiasm for this project. Our colleagues at Candler School of Theology at Emory University have provided good advice and valuable suggestions.

This volume was born of a conference also entitled "Human Disability and the Service of God." Funding for both the conference and this volume was provided by the Louisville Institute. We wish to thank James W. Lewis, Executive Director of the Institute, who offered advice and encouragement from the outset.

Dinah Shelly single-handedly organized the conference that brought scholars, ministers, laypersons, and interested others together to discuss the works presented here. Her competence and good cheer were essential in bringing this project to completion. The volume was strengthened by participants at the conference. We valued the opportunity to converse with people from multiple perspectives as we considered how the disciplines of theological education might more fully incorporate the experiences, insights, and gifts of people with disabilities.

As the papers of the conference were crafted into chapters, Karen VanderMeulen provided vital technical and editorial support. Karen Thorkilsen also offered sound editorial advice. Our editor at Abingdon Press guided us helpfully throughout, with competence and commitment to the volume's topic.

Thanks also to Terry Eiesland and Jane Saliers for their steadfast support through this and other projects. As editors, we treasure the friendship and common commitments that have made this collaborative work possible and gratifying.

CONTRIBUTORS

Hector Avalos is Assistant Professor of Religious Studies and Chair of the U.S. Latino Studies Program at Iowa State University, Ames, Iowa, where he was named the 1996 Professor of the Year. He is the author of *Illness and Health Care in the Ancient Near East: The Role of the Temple in Greece, Mesopotamia, and Israel* and numerous articles on health care in the ancient world. His next book will focus on the role of health care in the rise of Christianity.

Helen R. Betenbaugh earned M.Div. and D.Min. degrees from Perkins School of Theology, Southern Methodist University, Dallas, Texas, where her work involved biblical studies from the perspective of disability. Following a lengthy career as a distinguished church musician, she is now a priest in the Episcopal Diocese of Dallas. A frequent speaker, workshop leader, and prolific author, she has used a wheelchair for more than twenty years.

Nancy L. Eiesland is Assistant Professor of Sociology of Religion at the Candler School of Theology at Emory University, Atlanta, Georgia. The author of *The Disabled God: Toward a Liberatory Theology of Disability,* Eiesland has published numerous articles and chapters in the area of physical disability, religion, and social status. Other areas of research include work on religious response to exurban change.

Colleen C. Grant is Assistant Professor of New Testament at Methodist Theological School in Ohio. Other research interests include literary criticism and gender studies.

11

Ulrike Guthrie is academic books editor with Abingdon Press.

Albert Herzog received his doctorate in sociology from Ohio State University and serves as Executive Director of the Center for Persons with Disabilities in the Life of the Church. He is an ordained United Methodist minister.

Simon Horne is an Anglican priest in parish ministry in Basingstoke, U.K. After completing a classics degree at Oxford, he trained and worked as a nurse specializing in physical and mental disability. Upon marrying Mel, a disability rights activist and a wheelchair user, he taught for three years in a rural mission in Zimbabwe. He is presently completing a doctorate at the University of Birmingham in the uses of disability in the Bible and in the writings of the early Church.

Adele B. McCollum is Professor of Philosophy and Religion at Montclair State University where she has taught for more than twenty years. Her writing includes articles on marginalized groups, including English utopian communities, the Church of Jesus Christ of Latter Day Saints (Mormons), gay and lesbian groups, people with AIDS, and people with disabilities. Her most recent research interests concern women in evangelical Protestantism and fundamentalist Judaism.

Sarah J. Melcher is a doctoral candidate at Emory University, finishing a dissertation on sexual practice and bodily purity in the book of Leviticus. Other interests include a study of denominational affiliation and its influence on Pentateuchal criticism.

Jürgen Moltmann is emeritus Professor of Systematic Theology on the Protestant Faculty at the University of Tübingen and a prolific author.

Vereene Parnell is a doctoral student and adjunct instructor at Drew University and the Program Coordinator for the Resource Center for Women in Summit, New Jersey. In addition to lecturing broadly in feminist liberation theologies, ethics and cultural theory, she has worked as an activist for the past twenty years on issues relating to women, the environment, and international affairs. Her dissertation, currently in progress, is entitled, "Stranger Fruit: The Strategic Iconographies of the Cross."

Barbara A. B. Patterson ("Bobbi") is a faculty member in the Religion Department of Emory University. Her degrees are from Smith College, Harvard Divinity School, and Emory University. Her fields of study include theology, symbolic anthropology, and feminist theory. Much of her work focuses on the Christian tradition and the experiences of women. She is especially interested in contemporary practices of spiritual formation and how they relate to traditional and non-traditional spiritual and ethical practices.

Marjorie Procter-Smith is LeVan Professor of Worship and Preaching at Perkins School of Theology, Southern Methodist University, in Dallas, Texas. She is the author of *In Her Own Rite: Constructing Feminist Liturgical Tradition* and *Praying With Our Eyes Open: Engendering Feminist Liturgical Prayer,* and is co-editor, with Janet Walton, of *Women at Worship: Interpretations of North American Diversity.*

Jan B. Robitscher holds a Bachelor of Music degree from DePauw University, an M.A. in Liturgy from the University of Notre Dame and an M.Div. from Nashotah House Episcopal Seminary. Since 1991, she has been an instructor in music and liturgy at the School for Deacons of the Episcopal Diocese of California. The author of several articles, she is most recently a contributor to the Diocese of California Commission on Accessibility Awareness *Handbook on Accessibility in Our Churches* and also to *Grotto Stories from the Heart of Notre Dame.*

Don E. Saliers is Franklin Nutting Parker Professor of Theology and Worship, and director of the Masters in Sacred Music Program at Emory University. Widely known for ecumenical work in liturgy and spirituality, his most recent books include *Worship as Theology* and *Worship Come to Its Senses.*

Harold Dean Trulear is Professor of Church and Society at New York Theological Seminary. He has contributed articles to *The Journal of Religious Thought, Liturgy, American Baptist Quarterly,* and *Prism: A*

13

Journal of Evangelicals for Social Action. He serves on the national board of Intervarsity Christian Fellowship and credits his interest in human disability to his father, retired special educator Harold Holland Trulear, and to the late Douglas Sullivan.

Brett Webb-Mitchell is Assistant Professor of Christian Nurture at Duke Divinity School, Durham, North Carolina, and is an ordained minister in the Presbyterian Church (USA). He has published *God Plays the Piano, Too: The Spiritual Lives of Disabled Children*; *Unexpected Guests at God's Banquet: Welcoming People with Disabilities into the Church*; *Dancing with Disabilities: Opening the Church to All God's Children*; and *Christly Gestures* (forthcoming). He is past president of the Religion Division of the American Association on Mental Retardation.

PREFACE

Nancy L. Eiesland and Don E. Saliers

In recent years major changes in the religious landscape have emerged and have encouraged scholars to consider the changing context within which they work. Numerous signs across the nation point to these changes, including the increased presence and visibility of minority and ethnic groups in religious life. Among these groups are the more than forty-eight million Americans with disabilities (approximately one in every five) who are increasingly taking part in public life, and hence in public worship.[1]

Within the past two decades the context for people with disabilities has changed rapidly. Advances in technology, new civil rights protections, the AIDS pandemic, a generation of "mainstreamed" students, disability and Deaf studies, new group consciousness, and political activism have increased the social participation and improved social understanding of the experiences and situation of people with disabilities. A growing literature by people with disabilities has emerged as they begin to write their own history, create their own images in literature and art, and develop their own theories of disability. These recent developments among people with disabilities are beginning to be integrated into teaching and scholarship in religion and theology. Scholars of disability issues in religion are countering the prevailing sentiment that the religious practices of the able-bodied constitute the only relevant spiritual pulse and that whatever is outside this ambit is of little if any religious significance. However, multi-disciplinary theological interpretations of human disability and their challenge and promise for religious communities in the Christian tradition in North America have not yet been adequately addressed.

15

This volume seeks to respond to that deficit. This work is the result of a conference funded by the Louisville Institute, that brought together and related scholars and writers who belong to different disciplines in order to explore, generally and specifically, the broad working question: *What implications are or ought to be raised by the full participation of people with disabilities in the life of the Christian church?* Further, we asked what questions, insights, and perspectives would be advanced if people with disabilities, in all their diversity, were placed at the center of theological education rather than at the periphery— to which they have too often been relegated. These questions, we deemed, were best posed to each discipline implicated in theological education, rather than to theological faculties as a whole. Thus we developed the model of this book.

The introductory essay serves a dual purpose. On the one hand, it seeks to show how liturgical theology bears upon and learns from the new awareness of human disability. Understanding worship practices requires attending to ritual analysis and spiritual formation of the Christian assembly. On the other, the essay places persons with disabilities at the center of what deepening our yearning for God requires.

The following chapters show the ways various disciplines and approaches in theological education converge to bring new levels of understanding to liturgy and the life of Christian communities. Part I addresses the question: How does the participation of people with disabilities reframe biblical interpretation of the Hebrew Bible and the New Testament? Authors address the question by exploring the historical variety of healing rituals, engaging textual analysis of ritual purity codes in Leviticus and healing narratives in the Gospels, and interpreting the multiple construals of disability and impairment within the New Testament. Part II revisits historical theological themes raised by the incorporation of people with disabilities, highlighting new emphases arising from their full participation. Liberationist perspectives, eschatological analysis, and pastoral theology are engaged as elements of the theological visions necessary to include more fully people with disabilities in Christian life. Part III offers greater insight into the changed cultural context of the church and people with disabilities. Here analysis of folklore, the experiences of ministers with disabilities, the emergence of the disability rights movement, and the often tense relationship between activists and traditional religious bodies highlight the social context within which people with disabilities press for full inclusion. Part IV explores how worship, in all its social-cultural idioms, is a theological act. The focus in this section is on the cultural communication of liturgical innovations inclusive of people with disabilities and their prophetic critique of liturgy and culture.

These essays display varying angles of vision and intensities of response to issues confronting theology and practice. This diversity is intentional. At present we find ourselves at the beginning stages of a long and complex set of discussions. We have not tried to "standardize" terminology or tone. Our discussions as well as these essays reflect the struggle to find an appropriate and adequate language to do justice to questions of disability related to liturgy and theological reflection. The diversity of voices in this volume represents in brief compass the status of work begun but unfinished.

At the same time, the work of acknowledging, including, and learning from persons with disabilities in religious life and Christian ministry is immensely promising. Honest admission of ambivalence toward this work is required, both on the part of able-bodied church members and on the part of persons with disability who have been relegated to the margins or even neglected by churches. Real anxieties and fears must be faced.

Authentic inclusivity will be contextual, and cannot be legislated by abstract, universal principles. Real social transformation occurs and can be nurtured by careful attention to particular social contexts. Not all religious communities will be able to do large-scale, dramatic things. Beginning with asking "with whom among us and in our wider community do we begin?" is crucial. In some cases, people with hearing loss will be present; in others, physically disabled; in others, attention must focus on individuals with mental disabilities. In all cases the religious institutions are challenged to think and act in ways simultaneously relevant and truthful. So, too, people with disabilities, both within religious groups and outside of them, are invited to engage local congregations and theological disciplines as potential, if not yet fully realized, allies in the struggle for societal inclusion.

We invite you, as readers, to use this book as a resource for further study and reflection. Our principal concern is to foster a conversation about the interrelatedness of informed awareness and patterns of intentional practice required to make a difference. The authors, each

17

with his or her distinctive area of interpretation and concern, wish to contribute to the next steps along the way toward a more humane, faithful, and graciously liberating community of the people of God for the sake of the world.

1. U.S. Bureau of Census, *Americans with Disabilities: 1991-1992.*

TOWARD A SPIRITUALITY OF INCLUSIVENESS

Don E. Saliers

Saint John's Abbey in south central Minnesota is a large Benedictine monastery known for its ecumenical and liturgical work. One evening several years ago, during one of my times of summer teaching there, a group of us was invited to attend a special evening gathering for prayer. We were told that many of the older monks who now resided in the monastic infirmary would be present. Taking one of my accustomed places with others in the great curved choir of the Abbey church designed by Marcel Breuer, I noticed an inner circle of chairs with spaces between them. As we gathered, there occurred an informal procession of walkers and wheelchairs bearing members of the community, most of whom I had not met before.

Following the singing of psalms and a few brief prayers and a reading, vessels of oil were brought forward for the Abbot's prayer of blessing. As this rite of anointing was about to begin, something totally unexpected occurred. Abbot Jerome (now of blessed memory) invited all of us, not just the designated deacons, to come forward and lay hands on those in the center. As the blessed oils were applied to those hands and those foreheads, the rest of us followed by touching with a simple word of blessing the whole circle of those elders. This took time. A slow adagio dance. A remarkable circle. The silence was music given pitch and tone by the human and gentle exchange of words of blessing. As I approached Father Alfred, with whom I had been on retreat many years before, placing my tentative hand on his, he reached out with his good palsied hand to touch my face. As we circled amongst the chairs, the double anointing continued likewise

19

with others—many of whom I did not know—and the tears intermingled with the fragrance of the oil and the rhythm of this luminous dance of blessing.

Who anointed whom? Who were those there for others to pray for? Who were the pray-ees and who the pray-ers? The simple liturgy concluded and we moved on into the evening. The ones in the center went back to their infirmary rooms and their spaces, the rest of us walking out under the stars. The tears, a friend and I observed to one another days later, were not of sympathy, not of some felt pity, but of *recognition*—that in the midst of that community disability and ability, illness and health, strength and weakness comingled. In that unexpected space and place and time, I rediscovered what liturgy reveals in and through the pain and beauty of human bodies assembled. All are meant for such inclusion.

In a society whose marketing engines and projected fantasies in the mass media focus on the forever youthful, the ideally attractive, the highly mobile, and the physically strong, such an experience of liturgy is profoundly countercultural. It is the opening up of what is there all the time beneath the bright glitz and glaze of these projected images of our humanity, these projected ideals. Against the oppressive iconography and the mythology of the perfect body, something needs to be revealed of another way of doing, and another way of being. At one and the same time, that simple rite of prayer and anointing with oil and human hands, with the touch of faces and foreheads, was both prophetic and priestly. To use nonchurchly terms, the physical action in that assembly was both critical and generative. A critical and generative sign—a complex of signs—against the indignity of our noninclusive practices. Yet such a ritual action is also a sign of grace and liberation simultaneously.

Persons with disabilities comprise an increasingly active and critically reflective body of participants in Christian communities of worship. Moreover, the spiritual pulse and the gifts such persons bring to churches and synagogues—a way of seeing things long obscured and neglected—raise important theological and spiritual questions about the nature and quality of our worshiping assemblies.

I propose that our common task is to raise questions and enjoin a much needed new level of conversation about the relation of human disability to every gathering of two or three around the book, the font, and the Lord's table. How could liturgy as inclusive be a critical *generative* sign to the oppressive madness of the projected humanity of our mass media?

My concern is with specific ways in which Christian liturgy can be inclusive, and why it must be. I will explore four questions:

- First, what is liturgy about?
- Second, what are the human languages and models of inclusion of persons of disability?
- Third, how does liturgy form and express a spirituality that might lead us forward toward mutuality?
- Finally, what does disability have to do with the integrity of worship?

WHAT IS LITURGY ABOUT?

The root of *liturgy*—the Greek word *leitourgia*—is a secular word meaning a common work, something done by a gathered community. This particular root meaning has fortunately been retrieved in the theology and anthropology of worship in the last half-century. Liturgy is not something done *to* the congregation but something done *by* the whole assembly with certain persons leading, prompting, and evoking. Liturgy in its root meaning has to do with the gathered assembly—with its memory and hope, with its singing and praying, with eating and drinking together, with blessing one another, with anointing one another and being anointed. At root, liturgy is that common work in which the community assembles about the book of memory and hope, the font of the water of life, and the table of the word and the meal. It implicitly is for all humanity. I suggest three definitions of liturgy because any one definition is insufficient because it stresses something and leaves out something else. The first definition of liturgy is disarming: speaking, touching, singing, and acting in God's name.[1] This definition starts with human phenomena: speaking—something we do every day, yet in worship it is addressed to God; touching—not only physical touching as in gestures of greeting and blessing, but touching also in the sense of coming close, being present to one another. We take leave of one another and the touching is tinged with "Is this the last time?" We greet one another and the touching is "We've been restored! We're connected again." We all have images of such greetings and farewells.

The speaking extends itself into singing. Why do we sing? What's there to sing about? Why hum in the shower? Why do people sing their laments? Why do people raise a song at a birthday? on a festival? Why was it that when my wife and I lived in the inner city for those seven years, we could always count on the children gathering with the two jumping ropes—not just one—and the rhythmic song from the children spontaneously, "Miss Mary Mack, Mack, Mack . . . All dressed in black, black, black . . . " Why? Because singing is indigenous to being alive. Singing praise and lament and thanksgiving to God is the profoundly human dimension of worship. So speaking and touching and singing and enacting—the whole notion of converging in a place around a table, breaking bread, listening and responding—that is the stuff of liturgy. Each dimension contains the others. Some persons who cannot sing can touch. Some persons who have difficulty moving may speak.

Consider a second, more classic definition: "Christian liturgy is the glorification of God and the sanctification of what is human." The glorification of God and the sanctification (or the rendering holy) of all things. Worship does not make things holy by magic, but reveals and discloses what has already been rendered holy, what is already intrinsically holy by the grace of God in creation and redemption. This definition shows that in one and the same activity we can praise and thank and glorify and bless the divine source of life, and in so doing discover something about who we are. Authentic liturgy sanctifies and reveals the dignity and sanctity of not only what it is to be human but more fully of everything that is creaturely. I contend that doxology addressed to God is not just for human beings; it is for the blessing of the whole creation. Jews and Christians stand in the middle of our human condition and sing Psalm 103, and something is revealed not only about ourselves but about our environment, our matrix: this world teeming with diverse creatures, weak and strong, that have themselves something to say to us about what it is to be.

The second definition helps us immediately understand that if we are to talk about liturgy and the way it shapes and incorporates our life, we have to talk about its Godwardness, but never in abstraction. The Godwardness in Judaism and Christianity is always and necessarily connected with this rendering of what is profoundly creaturely, recognizing as though for the first time who we are.

A third definition introduces a more specifically and explicitly Christian conception. Suppose we define liturgy as "the ongoing embodied word, work, and prayer of Jesus Christ in and through his body in the world." Here the community of faith and practice emerges. Now we've got something connected with a history of a people gathered and put back into history for a purpose. This definition is Christological. This means that the liturgy belongs to Jesus before it is ours. We join a company—a long company of people who are quite other than we: Paul, Augustine, Teresa of Avila, Dame Julian of Norwich, Francis of Assisi, and all the martyrs. The liturgy of Jesus brings together the dead and the living, the enemy and the friend, the fractured and the whole.

This third definition reminds us that to pray with Jesus means being part of a social body. Christian worship entails being members of a body in time and space and history, a body replete with palpability and tangibility and connection. If we are to join Jesus in his ongoing prayer and work, we must belong to one another. Liturgy as the ongoing, embodied prayer and work of Jesus is always in and through his broken body in the conflicted world, and in his risen humanity before us.

These three definitions I offer you precisely because no single one can comprehend the mystery: We need all three. The connection between liturgy and human life bears directly upon human disability in all three—real humanity in mutual service and life with real divinity.

So then, what is liturgy about? It reveals and practices God's self-giving and our responsive self-giving in this terrifying, beautiful world. But liturgy also rehearses and shapes our doing of the work we're intended to do; to present ourselves, body and soul, to God (Romans 12:1) in service of neighbor. God commands. It invites praise, a life of blessing, in the midst of the mess. Our first vocation is to be gathered and to sing and to speak and to enact, to eat and drink together, to bathe and to be bathed, to be anointed, one way or another, into that slow inexorable dance of redeeming love, haltingly adagio or sometimes presto. Liturgy is about God and human beings encountering each other in the assembly and given life thereby, particularly being given life with the ongoing work of Jesus in the world hidden and yet made palpable and visible, audible, and kinetic by the Holy Spirit. In all those or in one or more of those ways,

23

liturgy functions as a sign that is both critical and generative to the world, both prophetic and priestly.

WHAT ARE THE HUMAN LANGUAGES?

We have already begun to touch on these. The worship of God employs human means of participation: time, space, sound, the visual, movement and gesture, taste and touch. One of the most central *issues* before us is the form and quality of how we are to participate. Among the most significant retrievals of the past thirty years of so-called liturgical reform and renewal is that which was expressed so powerfully in the Constitution on the Sacred Liturgy of Vatican II. In setting out to renew the liturgy, the framers of Vatican II spoke not only about the church but about human life in its depth. In a much-quoted radical assessment in how the laity—the whole people of God—participates in worship, The Constitution on the Sacred Liturgy announces a fundamental desire, "that all the faithful should be led to that full, conscious, active participation in the celebrations, which is demanded by the very nature of the liturgy."[2] The liturgy is the gathering of the community around the book of memory and hope, the waters of baptism, the table of the word and the common meal, whether highly scripted or freely oral.

It is not enough that the clergy preach well, though God knows we need it; or that the services are well-ordered, though sometimes they are distractingly unordered or too well-ordered; or that the presiding ministers do their job well. The real point has to do with how we participate with our finite lives, our bodies connecting the memories of God with the real pain and the real joy, the suffering and the delight, of the human family. The verbal and non-verbal languages must deepen our participation in God's liberating grace and glory. Joseph Gelineau, in a delightful primer called *The Liturgy Today and Tomorrow,* captures this brilliantly. He says, "Only if we come to liturgy without hope and fear, without longings and hunger, will those rites symbolize nothing and remain an indifferent and curious object." He goes on to say, "Moreover, if we are not accustomed to the poetic, the images, the artistic, the musical language or symbolic action amongst our means of expression and communication will find the liturgy like a foreign country whose customs and language are strange to us."[3]

24

We are beginning to discover that to incorporate and include persons who find themselves in disability—who are already deeply engaged in bringing their own life, their own hopes and fears, their own longing and hunger, their own struggles with limits as well as gifts—is to deepen what liturgy is. Those worshipers, when not seen or heard, diminish our liturgy in their absence. The question is: Whose hopes and fears are brought, whose longings and hungers are brought, whose poetry shall sound? *In Heaven There Are No Thunderstorms* is a marvelous book of liturgies from Ursula House in the Netherlands.[4] In the book, descriptions of the liturgies with persons with often severe mental retardation or disability become signs of how liturgy is to be celebrated. The children there open up not only the hungers and longings, delights and fears but the symbols themselves, becoming living reminders of the human face of God. The inclusion of children with mental disability and their hospitality opens up the very nature of what liturgy is: word and sacrament in flesh.

We should say, then, that many languages are involved in participating in liturgy. There is the language of time and temporality. In the liturgical churches cycles of time tell a story over time; it takes time to tell the story of God and the world. But in our efficient and sometimes hectic, fragmented human schedules, when do we sit down and listen? Only by taking time with the telling can we be reminded that time is required to go deep with God into our own temporality, into the language of our own temporal being, our mortality. Who are the people who will teach us that we, the temporarily able-bodied, deceptively think we're immortal? Who will be the signs in church to remind us of the long patience and anguish of God? Unfolding the story of God with us, in Jesus, and the stories of martyrs and holy women and men of faith and courage takes seasons and feasts.

Public worship animates the language of space and spatiality. What spaces do we inhabit? Who dwells in them? How do we encounter the fact that we are always located somewhere and must ever be? How do we configure our worship spaces so that we may, in fact, be palpable, reaching, touching, hearing, speaking? The language of space shapes us in profound ways that we rarely name. What happens when we change things in space? What happens when we create inhospitable spaces? What happens when we finally get to the point where we're asking about how we shall arrange space, not just the spaces as physical places but also the spaces where people have suffered and died and rejoiced? Places where we can struggle to be faithful?

Here is a story about space in an inner-city church I served in New Haven. It was a dying white church in a changing neighborhood; in fact, many of the older congregants were leaving. But the ones who stayed sat scattered in a sanctuary that once held 300, in a little group here, in a little group there. The pastor and I in our great ambitious liturgical renewal said, "Now everyone get down to the front together; we can't worship when we're all scattered about." No one came. It took several Sundays of frustrating, "Please sit down here," and "Come here so we can really pray and really worship." No processions. Finally, one very wise elder woman said, "Now, the problem is that when I come here on Sunday, I'm not coming here alone. I sit over there, but there's Uncle Frank and there's Grandma Birdy and there's my beloved husband and my sister who can't hear well." It had never occurred to us in our haste to rearrange the space and get everyone together, that we were displacing their communion of saints. But the beautiful thing is this: Once she was given time and space to name it, she came and brought the whole family with her. So the next Sunday they were all there. She had finally been able to say what was on everybody's mind. The language of space carried the possibility of the communion of saints.

Next there is the language of what we see, the language of what we hear, the acoustics, the rhythms, the pulse—all of those things are more profoundly formative of our spiritual life than the words we say.

The words we use and the texts we employ in worship are radically dependent on that which is not language: what we see, the silence, what we taste, how we are spatially related, how we move, and above all, who is present. The presence of human faces, how people gesture to one another and touch one another shape us far more profoundly than most of the words we speak. The prayer and proclamation texts are given meaning and point by virtue of all of the nonverbal languages. This is where we can benefit from some new educators from among persons with disabilities. The language of hospitality and the copresence of disabled and able-bodied are truly liberating when found together in our worshiping assemblies. For we need one another to learn these nonverbal, symbolic languages.

HOW DOES LITURGY FORM AND EXPRESS SPIRITUALITY?

Of course it does so in many ways; but for the ways crucial to our work here, think of the liturgy as a school for gratitude. We say the words, and we gesture the words in gratitude and thanksgiving and praise. Suppose that our praise and our thanksgiving and our blessing of God and one another is like the formation of the deep disposition of receiving the world and one another as gift. The world of the ungrateful is very different from the world of those who know gratitude in the face of human complexity. So, liturgy should shape us then in our gratitude—receiving the world and one another as gifts and as variously gifted.

Second, it should shape us in truth-telling. How difficult this is—to speak the truth of lamentation: In chapter 14 Helen Betenbaugh and Marjorie Procter-Smith explore this forcefully. Our churches today lack the ability to lament deeply and profoundly, to confess deeply, and to speak the truth in testimony. We lack the capacity to speak what happens when God gets hold of our lives in some way. So by truth-telling I mean the range of those lamentations, those cries from beneath the altar in the book of Revelation, those cries from a world that marginalizes, oppresses, and despises the very gifts of God that we have to celebrate. But I also mean truthfulness in the inmost being of our lives where secret grief and sorrow and anger abide.

Third, liturgy should form us in the capacity for being hospitable. When liturgy lacks hospitality, it forfeits its right to speak to the world in healing and prophecy. We need that hospitable space and time where the stories can be heard and told and life shared deeply in the singing and in the rites. Without that we are all diminished.

And finally, liturgy is a school for compassion—not pity, not sympathy—but compassion. It is about being companions, breaking bread together signifying that we're willing to weep with those who weep and rejoice with those who rejoice. Such compassion abides in the heart of God. For Christian liturgy is based on the claim that it is God's compassion for us, God's being with us, in passion, in suffering, and in joy, that gives us our clue and that forms us in the ability to be and to receive our life no matter what our circumstance.

Leonard Bernstein's *Mass* contains a startling moment. It is a moment of extreme iconoclasm. After finding himself in the midst of an increasingly chaotic and resistant crowd, that young priest is finally driven to desperation in an attempt to say, "Stop this; stop this; see . . . " At the apex the music comes to this climax; and taking the vessels off of the altar, he smashes them into a million pieces on the floor. That iconoclastic act of breaking open the symbol requires breaking the symbols. And after a stunned silence he sings, "Things get broken." Suddenly, in a flash, before me and this well-dressed concert-going audience, there it was, the central symbol of liturgy in its starkest form. For at the heart of Christian liturgy is a broken symbol. Or rather, unless we break open the symbols by bringing our life to them, taking into account human pathos, they will remain inaccessible.

So the liturgy is not of the idealized world or the projected religious world or the idea or the gospel of success, but the liturgy is of the real, the palpable, the incarnate, at the center of which is the power of a symbol made vulnerable to us in its brokenness.

WHAT HAS DISABILITY TO DO
WITH THE INTEGRITY OF WORSHIP?

The reverberating character of liturgy is found in the freedom from captivity to the unreal, to the projected fantasies; it is to live without the denial of limit and mortality. This is why the presence and gifts of persons with disabilities are crucial. The invitation for all is for all but waits upon our inclusion of those who know and share access to the power of life and its brokenness. There is an ever gracious invitation, the very source of our being, the divine matrix in which all things are sustained, including our temporality and our perishing. God embraces the human bodily form of life so that the significance of Christian liturgy thus lies in its narrative of death and resurrection as the story of human existence: not avoiding, not denying or merely appearing, but rendered palpable, tangible, what it is to be human at full stretch. That is my definition of spirituality: to be human at full stretch before the mystery of God, in mutuality with neighbor. Our culture needs such living reminders of the tension between the *is* of our daily habits and our dullness to the mystery and the *ought* of God's promises.

When congregations are faithful and honest enough to name their discomfort and their delight in the participation of persons with disabilities, they take a first step toward maturity. For a local church that has had little or no history with physical or mental disability, such a transition will bring both discomfort and delight. But the very struggle with discomfort for persons who have no experience with disability is itself a window opening to new dimensions of the grace of God. Even more to the point, the discovery of what particular persons can bring to such a community is often a revelation to the temporarily able-bodied.

A deepening sense of "being church" is thus part of the unexpected side of the work of inclusion. The movement from adopting an "inclusive" attitude on the part of the leadership to the actual life of being a place of "belonging" is itself a maturation, both theological and moral. This, I contend, is part of what it means to be a faithful people of God in the world, to "grow up in every way" into Christ (Ephesians 4:15). Participating in the movement from inclusivity to the spirituality of belonging to one another is an image of the Christian life itself.

If "inclusiveness" is to be more than a slogan, our practice must lead to acknowledgment of common humanity in the image of God and to the discovery of what it means to be "present" to one another. Mere affirmation is not enough; rather, upbuilding one another in love is the point. Loving the other and oneself for the sake of God is a profound capacity that requires entering deeply into our common humanity, particularly into the mystery of limit, into joy in the midst of tribulation, and into discovery of giftedness in difference. To liberate persons to full humanity is a collaboration taking us into the depths of what it means to be human. In a culture that denies limit and glorifies the "perfect" body and mind, this liberation requires churches and synagogues to commit to the risk of discovery.

In one of the earliest Christian traditions, Irenaeus observed that the glory of God is the living human being. I would add, "at full stretch." To live together into the mystery and the suffering and the joy of full humanity is just such a calling. The gift and the task of moving toward authentic socially embodied inclusiveness is a crucial strand in that spirituality. Full participation in liturgy and the ministries of the congregation is more than "having compassion" on persons of disability; it is absolutely central to the revelation of what Christian liturgy is, does, and ought to be in our culture.

What is done in our public worship of God rehearses what we are to be in our life relationships. Issues of justice and power are symbol-

29

ized in worship services, whether we are aware of this or not. The lack of presence of persons of disability in the pews or especially in leadership roles tells us something of the assumptions of everyday life among the assembly. Changing our basic perception requires honest naming of our fears and anxieties. But is not this precisely what good liturgy helps us encounter? Honest struggle in prayer, singing texts that speak to the issues of brokenness as well as giftedness of all of God's children, preaching that names our ambivalences and encourages our patience—all of these are resources within the Christian tradition for transforming our neglect into faithful inclusiveness. At the heart of well-celebrated Christian liturgy is, of course, the prodigal hospitality of God found in the sacraments of baptism and the Lord's Supper. Here, above all, the mutual presence of able-bodied persons and persons with disabilities of whatever form can actually release the power of the sacraments to heal, to strengthen, and to save.

Not every congregation will do heroic or unheard of things to move toward inclusiveness. Sometimes the denominational push toward universal accessibility can actually be counterproductive when a local church feels it cannot possibly do what is asked. But each congregation can start with its own local context. The liturgy itself asks: "Who is here to worship God?" Answering that alone begins the movement toward awareness. What is needed is not policies from above but concreteness from within the life of local congregations. We need not conjure fears and anxieties about "massive changes" when small, specific steps can be taken with persons we know who are already struggling with disability and with aging.

I return to that monastic circle of the healing ritual. Could this be an image of what every congregation could begin to do together? The ancient words of Saint Augustine now take new depth if you think of the definitions of liturgy we have explored, of the notion of how we participate, of what it is to be shaped by such a community and why persons with disabilities are absolutely central to it. Those ancient words of Augustine ring again in our ears: when you stretch out your hand to receive the Eucharist it is your own mystery you receive. Or closer to home, closer to Appalachia, is the paraphrase of Psalm 23 sung to the tune "Resignation," with the words "the Lord's my shepherd" that conclude with the marvelous image: no longer a stranger or a guest, but "like a child at home." So in that rite of anointing at Saint John's, and potentially pregnant in every gathering of two or three in the name of the Shepherd, is offered the reality of being at home with one another in a new way, always in the midst of struggle and uncertainty.

Spirituality is our embodied humanity fully alive before God and neighbor, stretched by story, stretched by touch, stretched by song, stretched by eating and drinking, bathing, anointing. There we shall rejoice with those who rejoice and weep with those who weep, and we shall know the mystery of our own best being. And that is worth everything. It is worth all of our intellectual effort; but more important, it points us toward the spirituality of inclusion that emerges precisely out of the very nature of what Christian liturgy is and ought to be.

---

1. This is the elaboration of a definition that James F. White gave in his *Introduction to Christian Worship*, 2d ed. (Nashville: Abingdon Press, 1990).

2. "Constitution on the Sacred Liturgy," *Sacrosanctum Concilium* in *Documents on the Liturgy, 1963-1979: Conciliar, Papal, and Curial Texts* (Collegeville, Minn.: The Liturgical Press, 1982), 8.

3. Joseph Gelineau, *Liturgy Today and Tomorrow* (New York: Paulist Press, 1978), 98-99.

4. Gijs Okhuijsen and Cees van Opzeeland, *In Heaven There Are No Thunderstorms: Celebrating the Liturgy with Developmentally Disabled People* (Collegeville, Minn.: The Liturgical Press, 1992).

PART I.

INTERPRETING TEXTS

We begin our explorations with three essays on biblical texts framed by a comparative study of healing rituals drawn from ancient and contemporary religious practices. The richness and complexity of images, belief, and attitudes toward disability found in Hebrew Scripture and the New Testament require close scrutiny. Ignorance of the social and cultural contexts of texts bearing upon the relationship of sin to disability and practices of exclusion has contributed to distortions in Jewish and Christian traditions. These essays open windows of interpretation to shed new light on several crucial texts and contexts: the priestly and Levitical codes, Gospel writers' paradigms of healing in relationship to sin, and the striking "paradox of inability" found in Greco-Roman backgrounds reflected in the Gospels and Pauline letters. In Chapter 1, Hector Avalos locates the interpretation of texts in the broader contextual analysis of religious ritual.

While by no means exhaustive of the wider range of issues relevant to contemporary theological reflection on disability, the essays by Sarah J. Melcher (Chapter 2), Colleen Grant (Chapter 3), and Simon Horne (Chapter 4) bring sharp focus to fresh readings of biblical material that have often been used as sources for restrictive theological views of disability. Inherited distortions of disability and impairment within our received tradition are uncovered by all three authors. In each case specific patterns of reinterpretation are proposed, with Horne suggesting how the post-New Testament early church already utilized typological imagination in ways po-

33

tentially useful to us today. Melcher's detailed examination of Leviticus, one of the most problematic text sources, and Grant's rich rereading of Gospel narratives invite us to rethink and to practice a more adequate interpretation of the Bible as we face challenges and new possibilities in theological understanding of human disability.

CHAPTER ONE

DISABILITY AND LITURGY IN ANCIENT AND MODERN RELIGIOUS TRADITIONS

Hector Avalos

Although the importance of liturgy and healing in Christianity has received some recent scholarly attention, most modern Christians are still relatively unaware of the fundamental differences between ancient and modern attitudes toward the integration of health-related rituals in religious life.[1] Indeed, the relationship between religious rituals and disability has a long and complex history. Aside from the value of historical and sociological inquiry, understanding this history helps to explain how modern religious liturgies address the needs of persons with disabilities.

We first must note that if by the term, *liturgy,* we restrict ourselves to the rites of organized religious groups, we would be ignoring a vast amount of ritual activity that occurs in the world. For our purposes, the term *liturgy,* as it pertains to disability and healing, refers to a ritual or a set of rituals intended to reverse, or aid a person with a disability to live with, the condition in question. A disability is a physical or mental feature, real or presumed, which a society identifies as cause for devaluation of a person.[2]

Because of the vast amount of material that we could discuss, it is necessary to set some limits.[3] Rather than a strict chronological narrative, I prefer to integrate a historical discussion with a typological approach, which I have been developing through my work on illness and health care in ancient and modern societies.

On the most general level, three basic types of liturgies may be distinguished in connection with disability and illness: petitionary, therapeutic, and thanksgiving. A liturgy may be said to have a petitionary function if its primary purpose is to petition for healing. The petitionary function may include the request for oracles concerning the prognosis, and not simply the petition for healing itself.

If, in addition to simple petitions, a liturgy is designed to restore the ill, then the liturgy may be said to have a therapeutic function. The liturgy, for example, may integrate the application of *materia medica,* surgery, exorcism, incubation, and the performance of other rituals and procedures that are part of the therapy. A thanksgiving liturgy is intended to thank the deity the patient believes is responsible for the healing. This may be something enjoined by the cult or an optional practice.

It is also useful to focus on various socioreligious aspects of liturgies in order to understand how modern American churches have transformed, or diverged from, their ancient counterparts. In addition to the contrasts between monotheism and polytheism, the starkest contrasts between modern American Christian churches and ancient liturgies may be found in the attitudes toward the temple, icons, animals, drugs, and music.

POLYTHEISTIC VERSUS MONOLATROUS LITURGIES

Most modern Christians would describe themselves as monolatrous in that they worship one deity. Yet, most modern Christians probably do not appreciate the manner in which monolatry has affected their health-related rituals. Indeed, there is a fundamental distinction between polytheistic and monolatrous health care systems. A monolatrous health care system is usually dichotomous, insofar as it bears a set of legitimate and illegitimate options. Legitimate options are those approved by the single deity, while the options associated with other gods are deemed illegitimate. This dichotomy restricts the set of therapeutic options that a patient may choose.

In contrast, polytheistic health care systems generally allow a large variety of alternative divine consultation options for patients. Thus, if one deity does not respond or provide satisfaction, the patient may consult another deity without penalty. At the same time, the large number of gods in a polytheistic system can also result in elaborate rituals. One example may be seen in a ritual against disease (and) what is termed "malaria" by Parpola.[4] In order to perform this ritual, one needs:

a figurine of the daughter of Anu [the primary sky god]
a figurine of Namtar [a minor god of the underworld]
a figurine of Latarak [a little known figure]
a figurine of Death
a substitute figurine made of clay
a substitute figurine made of wax
15 drinking tubes of silver for Gula [goddess of healing]
    and Bēlet-ṣēri [Mistress of the desert]
seven [twigs] of tamarisk
seven twigs of date palm
[seven bot]tles of wine
seven bottles of beer
[seven bottles] of milk
seven bottles of honey

The figurines of the deities, which were probably assembled in the presence of the patient or in some sacred area, represent the supernatural beings that needed to be appeased. The foods were offerings and instruments by which to gain the favor of those deities. Prayers to those deities were probably combined with medical treatments applied to the patient, and the entire ritual might last hours or even be spread over a few days.

For our purposes, the catalog of items needed for the ritual against malaria illustrates that labor-intensive rituals were related, in large part, to the number of supernatural beings that were to be contacted, appeased or repelled. In fact, sometimes the consultant had to spend much of the time in the performance of complicated rituals and in the procurement of paraphernalia for different gods, even if a single illness was the object of the ritual.

The fact that such labor-intensive rituals affected the immediate availability of some health-care consultants is also evident in a letter where the king orders Marduk-šakin-šumi, an *āšipu*, the term for one of the main healing consultants of Mesopotamia, to perform an antiwitchcraft ritual before the twenty-fourth day of the month. The *āšipu* replies, in part, as follows:

We cannot execute it [the ritual] the tablets are (too)
many. How will they copy them [in time]?
However, as to the figurines
which the king has selected,
we shall have them ready within five to six days.[5]

The text again reflects how the complexity of Mesopotamian polytheism resulted in a labor intensive system of rituals that affected the availability of the healers to the king as well as the schedule of rituals. Even with helpers, one type of consultant could not always accomplish the numerous tasks needed in exorcism in the time requested by the king.

In a modern polytheistic religion such as Santería, the variety of gods that could send or cure illness can also result in lengthy and complicated liturgies. Much time can be consumed in preparing the paraphernalia and performing the ritual dances and prayers to each of the possible supernatural senders and healers of disease.[6]

In contrast, a monolatrous system theoretically simplifies the search for the healing deity and thus the liturgy as well. Since only one sender/healer of disease is possible, the liturgy is reduced to appeasing or contacting only one deity. For example, in the biblical story of Elisha and Naaman (II Kings 5:11*b*) the expected ritual for curing "leprosy" is as follows:

> He would surely come out [of his house], and stand and call on the name of the LORD his God, and would wave his hand over the [afflicted] spot, and cure the leprosy.

No long liturgy is expected, and the only deity that has to be consulted is Yahweh. Similarly, the healings by Jesus are quite simple, requiring a short prayer to the one God.

Today, most mainline Christian churches do not have highly complex health-related liturgies.[7] One of the best known liturgies in the Catholic tradition is the sacrament of the Anointing of the Sick. The sacrament was previously better known as Extreme Unction. The new title, Anointing of the Sick, reflects the shift in focus from a policy that virtually restricted official health-related liturgies to the final days of a patient to a policy that recognizes the broader role of health-related liturgy in the life of the patient.

According to Section 1519 of the Catechism of the Catholic Church, the ritual of the Anointing of the Sick, which preferably includes the Eucharist, has the following principal elements:

> The "priests of the Church"—in silence—lay hands on the sick; they pray over them in the faith of the Church. This is the epiclesis proper

to this sacrament; they then anoint them with oil blessed, if possible, by the bishop.[8]

Thus, the official version of the Anointing of the Sick is a relatively simple ritual compared to those in polytheistic religions.

Yet, there are other factors that could neutralize any simplification gained by monolatry, and patients do not necessarily adhere to whatever simplicity there is in official liturgies. Many individuals can fashion their own rituals, as is the case with the *tablero* phenomenon in the Southwest (see below). Repetition of ritual prayers can be lengthy (e.g., rosaries) if patients believe that such repetitions will eventually persuade the deity to heal. If pilgrimages can be considered parts of liturgical programs, then such rituals can last for days even in a monolatrous context. The number of saints that one can petition for healing in popular Catholic traditions can result in lengthy prayers and rituals that may approximate the length of those in Mesopotamia. But in general, the health-related rituals of modern mainstream churches are relatively short.

HOME-CENTERED VERSUS TEMPLE LITURGIES

It is only relatively recently that Western societies have shifted patient care out of the home to some extent, and this shift has affected the place of the sick in the health-related rituals of modern American churches. To understand this change, one must note that health-seeking strategies are usually organized hierarchically. Patients will usually begin with the simplest and most economical treatments at home (e.g., prayer and home remedies) and then move to other more elaborate options if the first ones do not provide satisfactory results.

Home-centered liturgies were very prominent in Mesopotamia. The centrality of home-centered medical care in Mesopotamia is evident in the very title of the diagnostic manual *enūma ana bīt marṣi āšipu illaku* ("When an *āšipu* goes to the home of the sick"), which is also known as *SA.GIG,* ("Diseases of the flesh") and which was in use as early as the eighth century B.C.E.[9] This manual does not mention that the patient should go to the temple for treatment even when the case seems hopeless.

Mesopotamian texts that mention the initial stages of serious illnesses also indicate the importance of home care. For example, it is clear that the ritual against epilepsy (*AN.TA.ŠUB.BA*) was executed at home in the early stages of the illness. One text says: "as soon as something has afflicted him (i.e., the patient), the *āšipu* arises and places a mouse (and) a piece of a thorn bush on the vault of the (patient's) door."[10] Similarly, except for the search for signs, most other extant Mesopotamian prayers and rituals do not mention going to a temple as part of the healing process.

The reason for home-centered liturgies in Mesopotamia is that there was a belief that a disease could not only attack the patient but also the entire household. In fact, sometimes the household was seen as the patient, so it was the logical place to conduct the ritual. One may see such a tradition as reflection of the acknowledgment that illness can affect and disrupt the life of the patient's family. On a social level, such rituals may have served to integrate the entire household and family in the care and recovery of the patient.

Temple-centered liturgies require, of course, a society where the temple is a prominent part of the community. But even here the temple usually is complementary to care at home. The socioreligious attitudes toward *disability* and the definition of *purity* can determine whether a temple will offer petitionary or therapeutic liturgies. Indeed, a temple cannot have a direct petitionary or therapeutic liturgy for patients if their condition is regarded as so impure as to prevent their presence in the temple.

The primary examples of health-related liturgies executed at temples are found at the temples of Asclepius in ancient Mediterranean lands in the late first millennium B.C.E. The temples of Asclepius exhibited all three basic types of healing liturgies (petitionary, therapeutic, and thanksgiving), sometimes integrating them into a cohesive program. The temples of Asclepius did not regard even "lepers" as too impure to enter the temple. In fact, Porphyrius, a Greek author of the third century C.E., notes that at the famous shrine of Asclepius at Epidauros *purity* was defined as purity of thought.[11] That is to say, thinking "holy" thoughts was sufficient to render a person pure. Such a definition of purity seems to emphasize the fact that illness itself was not an impurity that excluded the physically disabled from the temple.

Incubation was a primary therapeutic ritual at Asclepieia. One description of a healing incubation required that the suppliant or his proxy be dressed in white.[12] The patient was assigned a pallet in the

Abaton, the building especially designed for incubation. Some reports say that an attendant would come in at twilight and light the lamps. The suppliant placed an offering on the table, then he retired to his couch. Some depictions of the couch show that it was covered with animal skins.[13] After a prayer by the suppliant and priest, the lamps were extinguished, and the priests departed to their quarters. Some sources (e.g., T. 421) report that, during the night, the priests would dress in the god's attire and visit the suppliant to perform rites. In short, the temples of Asclepius welcomed all types of sick individuals and provided a human support system in the form of priests and fellow patients.

In contrast, the Levitical version of the temple in Israel had a definition of "purity" that regarded those with chronic illnesses as too impure to enter the temple.[14] This, of course, meant that the temple of Yahweh could not offer direct petitionary and therapeutic liturgies for patients. The attitudes of the temple, in turn, can be related to decisions made by states concerning the care of the ill. In the case of the Levitical system, the notions of "purity" may have been an instrument by which the state unburdened itself of chronically ill populations.

However, the Levitical system did permit thanksgiving liturgies at the temple. In fact, in the Levitical system, thanksgiving liturgies were not only permitted but also commanded (cf. Leviticus 7:11-36). Offerings after an illness also may have served as public notice of the readmission of previously ostracized patients to the society (Leviticus 14:1-32).

Thanksgiving liturgies in temples are probably the most common and stable in most cultures. Indeed, it is difficult to find temples that do not offer a place for thanksgiving liturgies. Perhaps the primary reason why thanksgiving liturgies are so stable and widespread is that they have many advantages (e.g., thanksgiving rituals are a source of economic revenue for temples) and yet can eliminate some of the disadvantages (e.g., fear of contagion from the sick) that are significant to some cultures.

Today in the United States health-related liturgies usually begin with petitions and prayers at home. If these do not prove satisfactory, then more organized liturgies may be sought. The patient, if well enough to travel, may go to a church or send a proxy to petition for healing. An official liturgy (e.g. Anointing of the Sick) may also be performed in a hospital, as is often the case in the Catholic tradition when the patient is gravely ill.

The types of liturgies offered by modern churches also depend on the particular attitudes (some of which derive from ancient traditions) toward disability and illness. Thus, some churches consider AIDS patients to be so impure and contagious so as to preclude the development of any direct petitionary or therapeutic rituals in the church.[15] Other churches, however, are developing liturgies for AIDS patients.[16] These ecclesiastical attitudes, in turn, are aligned with larger socioeconomic programs regarding governmental allocations for the care of AIDS patients.

The integration of the temple and hospital may still be seen in the numerous chapels found in hospitals. At first, the presence of chapels in hospitals may seem analogous to the use of Asclepieia (temples of Asclepius) as both hospitals and places of worship. But the integration of chapels and hospitals shows some of the modern ambiguities of combining liturgy and medical science in the care of patients. In modern hospitals the sacred space of the chapel is considered to be subordinate, spatially and philosophically, to the larger medical science domain of the hospital. For many physicians, the chapels in hospitals are there for supplementary comfort, while the real healing is in the domain of the scientist.

In sum, modern American society does not have extensive and complex types of home-centered liturgies akin to those in Mesopotamia and other ancient cultures. In ancient Mesopotamia the sickest of patients would usually be found in the home; in modern American society, the sickest patients are usually found outside of the home (in hospitals or hospices). Whenever complex rituals are performed for the most disabled patients, they often take place in hospitals or outside of the home. In general, modern mainline churches have ceded, even if indirectly, to modern medical science the right to determine the location of the healing rituals for patients.

ICONIC VERSUS ANICONIC LITURGIES

Modern American Protestant churches rarely integrate icons or other types of art into health-related rituals. Yet, the association of various types of icons with therapy is perhaps one of the oldest attested practices in health-related liturgies. Sometimes the only clues left in presumed prehistoric therapeutic liturgies are icons. Judging by the numerous Paleolithic "fertility" figurines found in various places throughout the world, we can only speculate that rituals and healing were integrated from at least the Paleolithic period, the first period of human material culture, which ended somewhere between 20,000 and 15,000 B.C.E. Diane Bolger and other scholars argue that female figurines in Cyprus indicate the possible existence of fertility therapy by the Chalcolithic period (ca. 3800-2500 B.C.E.).[17] Various sites (e.g., Mt. Jouktas, Traostalos) of the second millennium (B.C.E.) in Crete bear figurines of body parts that perhaps were associated with healing cults.

The function of icons can be divided according to the basic type of liturgies in which they are used—petitionary, therapeutic, or thanksgiving. Some of the best examples of petitionary icons are found in Mesopotamia. Figurines of dogs inscribed with petitions for healing have been found at Isin, an ancient site located some 125 miles south of Baghdad, and other places in Mesopotamia. These were often placed in the temples of various healing deities such as Gula or Marduk, or by rivers. A Mesopotamian votive inscription (late second millennium B.C.E.) for Gula, the famed healing goddess, mentions the fashioning of such a dog figurine:

> For the life of Nazi-maruttaš, king of the world, his king, (Ninurta-rēṣušu) did fashion an image(?) of her . . . dog on the bank of the Euphrates, her wide river, in the É-mupada her beloved temple, for his life and the life of the land.[18]

Mesopotamia also bears many examples of therapeutic icons. Often figurines of particular demons and animals, which were considered to bear diseases, were manufactured. Then they were destroyed or cast into a river where they were carried away into the abyss. Thus, the evil was destroyed along with the figurine.

In the Bible, the main example of a therapeutic icon was the bronze serpent manufactured by Moses (Numbers 21:6-9). II Kings 18:4 indicates that, prior to Hezekiah (715-687 B.C.E.), the bronze serpent made by Moses was involved in acceptable therapeutic rituals in the temple of Jerusalem: "for until those days the people of Israel had made offerings to it; it was called Nehushtan."

In more recent times, we find paintings used in therapy. St. Anthony's monastery in France used art in its therapeutic liturgy.[19]

43

Patients, for example, were brought before the famed Isenheim Altar, completed between 1512 and 1515 by Matthias Grünewald (ca. 1475-1528), as part of the therapeutic program of the monastery. Among these panels are some of the most moving depictions of bodily lesions and suffering seen in Western art.

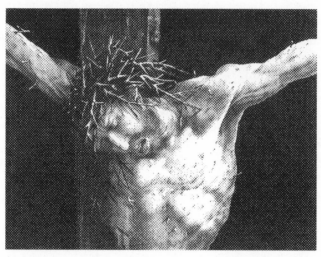

(**Fig. 1**) Originally located at St. Anthony's monastery in Germany, the famed Isenheim Altar contains some of the most dramatic images of bodily lesions on Christ. Patients would reflect upon these paintings as part of a healing program.

Mesopotamia bears some of the oldest examples of thanksgiving icons, the following being one example from the late second millennium B.C.E.

For Gula, mistress of the Egalmah,
Mistress of life, the great physician. . . . ,
Bestower of the breath of life, his mistress,
Ili . . . daya prayed, and she heard his petition.
. . . (this) dog I offered.[20]

The fact that the inscription mentions that the deity "heard" the patient's prayer, establishes the thanksgiving function of the icon in this liturgy.

The most prolific use of thanksgiving icons may be found in ancient Greece in the temples of Asclepius at Athens, Epidauros,

Corinth, and other places. Hundreds of models of breasts, legs, arms, procreative organs, and other body parts may be found in these temples.

One still sees this practice of leaving votives in a number of Catholic shrines. St. Anthony's monastery at Isenheim had models of body parts. Today, at Lourdes and other Catholic healing shrines, patients leave crutches, models of body parts, and other types of votives. The practice of making *tableros* or *retablos* (usually coarse paintings or drawings made on wooden panels by suppliants) among Hispanics in the American Southwest is a continuation of the ancient tradition of leaving votives at shrines. Most of these *tableros,* which often bear inscriptions detailing the reasons for the *retablo*, fulfill a petitionary or thanksgiving function. The following is an example of a *retablo* with a thanksgiving function:

> Venancio Soriano. While at work in Harlingen, Texas, I contracted a grave illness of the left lung that was thought incurable. I offered to visit the Miraculous Little Virgin of San Juan de los Lagos and bring her this retablo as proof of gratitude for her relief.[21]

(**Fig. 2**) An example of paintings, usually called *retablos* or *tableros* that are most common among Mexican Americans in the Southwest. Usually, these paintings are made by patients as petitionary or thanksgiving offerings related to health.

These *retablos* show that the thanksgiving ritual of making the retablo may be viewed as part of a larger liturgical program designed to some extent by the individual patient. The *retablos* also allow

45

patients individual forms of expression within the larger liturgical program.

The practice of leaving models of body parts or other votives has virtually disappeared in most modern Protestant traditions. The use of art or items made by patients in petitionary, therapeutic, or thanksgiving rituals is also rare in Protestant liturgies. This may be due, in part, to the aniconic and anti-magical tendencies of mainline Protestantism.[22] The shift toward a society with higher literacy rates may also have diminished the demand for using art to illustrate religious ideas and texts that most persons could not read prior to the rise of printing and high literacy rates.

ANIMAL INCLUSIVE VERSUS ANIMAL EXCLUSIVE LITURGIES

The absence of animals in modern Christian health-related liturgies marks another major distinction with most ancient liturgies. Indeed, few Christian worshipers today seem aware of the great importance of dogs and other types of animals in liturgies related to illness in the ancient world. Healing rituals that integrate animals may be viewed as theological reflections of the idea that the human-animal world was connected in illness and health. Human disability and illness affected animals and vice versa on more than a biological level.

We may distinguish two modes in which animals were integrated into these ancient rituals: (1) Rituals that required the death of the animal (e.g., sacrifice); and (2) Rituals that did not require the death of the animal. Animal sacrifice, which was quite common in ancient health-related rituals, could be integrated into petitionary, therapeutic, or thanksgiving liturgies. In the cult of Asclepius, for instance, sacrifices often preceded the incubation ritual at Asclepieia, and the most common offering was the cock.[23] In Israel's Levitical temple, animals were integrated only into thanksgiving liturgies since the temple did not have direct petitionary or therapeutic functions for the sick.

In Mesopotamia, there was a very complex use of dogs in healing rituals. Dogs were kept at the temple of Gula at Isin. In fact, her temple was called the "Dog House." One text from the first millennium B.C.E. exemplifies one healing ritual that apparently does not require the death of the animal.

If a man goes to the temple of his god,
and if he touches . . . ?, he is clean (again?);
Likewise, if he touches the dog of Gula, he is clean (again?).[24]

Possible illustration of such rituals may be provided by figurines found in recent excavations at Isin, where there was a prominent temple of Gula.

(**Fig. 3**) Possible depiction of a ritual involving a dog and a patient from Mesopotamia (ca. early first millenium B.C.E.).

In early Christianity we still see some remnants of the use of animals in healing. The story in Mark 5:1-20 of Jesus' transfer of the demons from humans to the swine has roots that reach back to Mesopotamia. But for the most part, Christianity excluded animals from health-related liturgies. The almost total disappearance of animals from health-related liturgies in classical Western Christianity is due to a number of factors. One is that, as is expounded in Hebrews 8-10 and other Christian texts, animal sacrifice was abolished in Christianity and so from any healing rituals that might have required animal sacrifice. The idea that humanity was a special creation and discontinuous with the animal world may have also helped to separate human and animal in health-related liturgies.[25]

The integration of animals in health-care systems, however, has not disappeared. Now the prime health-related utilization of animals is by medical science, not mainstream Christian liturgies. Medical science uses animals for experiments and as ready reserves of antibodies, hormones, and other biomedical materials utilized by human beings. Modern biology has revived and transformed the idea that there is a continuity between the human and animal world, but now such continuity is seen in genetic and biochemical terms instead of metaphysical ones.

DRUG-INCLUSIVE VERSUS DRUG-EXCLUSIVE LITURGIES

Most modern Christian churches would probably deem the use of drugs in healing services to be abnormal or odd. Yet, in most ancient cultures it was normal to integrate all sorts of medicinal plants in healing liturgies. Although the use of medicinal plants probably can be traced to prehistoric times, we find the first records of medicinal plants integrated with liturgy in Mesopotamia. Health care consultants, who were often priests, were experts in both herbal medicine as well as religious liturgy. The same is true in Egypt.[26] Some temples (e.g., the temple of Gula) were repositories for medicinal plants and paraphernalia.

Rituals in the temples of Asclepius were integrated with all sorts of drugs that could be invented extemporaneously or that were already known. Asclepius prescribed, for example, the eating of partridge with frankincense (T. 434). Wine mixed with ashes from the altar was prescribed for a man named Lucas (T. 438).

The elimination of pharmaceuticals from healing services is probably one of the most distinctive developments in the liturgies of modern mainstream Western churches. One of the few remnants of the practice of integrating pharmaceuticals is the use of oil to anoint the sick in some Christian traditions. The practice may originate in the use of oil as a medicinal ointment that could help people rid themselves of disease.[27] Today, anointing is almost totally symbolic in its meaning or is even discouraged by some denominations. Thus, as Marty notes, the United Lutheran Church in America expressed its attitude toward anointing in its 1962 report, "Anointing and Healing": "The use of oil in ministering to the sick would be unwise for our Lutheran congregations today. . . . there is a danger that magical value would be attached to oil."[28] This attitude may have, however, moderated in recent years.

Anointing also has political connotations. Thus, John J. Ziegler has discussed the debate surrounding who can anoint the sick in the Catholic Church.[29] He notes that since the Council of Trent's 4th canon on the anointing of the sick, it has been held as Roman Catholic doctrine that only priests may anoint the sick. But, in the aftermath of the reforms of Vatican II, the shift in focus from Extreme Unction to the Anointing of the Sick has resulted in the reconsideration of the policy that limits to priests the administration of the sacrament.[30]

What is the reason that medicinal substances have virtually disappeared from modern liturgies? Again, the ascendance of modern medicine and pharmacology has resulted in the fission of the role of the medicinal expert and the religious liturgist. Pharmaceuticals are now in the domain of the licensed scientific druggist, and the religious liturgist is generally forbidden from administering pharmaceuticals. Mainline Christian clerics have ceded to modern science any thought of using drugs in therapy. As the aforementioned report of the United Lutheran Church in America indicates, there is also an aversion in mainline Protestant churches to use any means that might appear irrational or "magical."

MUSIC IN ANCIENT AND MODERN LITURGIES

In ancient societies music could form part of any of the three basic types of liturgies we have discussed. Many of the petitionary and thanksgiving prayers in ancient Mesopotamia may have been sung. In the Bible many of the psalms that were involved in thanksgiving rituals were also probably sung (see Isaiah 38:11-20). There is also the famous example of David's use of the "harp" as therapy for Saul's malady in I Samuel 16:16:

Let our lord now command the servants who attend you to look for someone who is skillful in playing the lyre; and when the evil spirit from God is upon you, he will play it, and you will feel better.

Apparently, the therapeutic efficacy was believed to reside in the musical melody itself because the work of the hands, not the voice or singing, seems emphasized. The composition of odes was not an

49

unusual prescription for patients at the temples of Asclepius.[31] According to Pindar, a writer who was active in the fifth century B.C.E., Greek physicians also included singing in their therapeutic repertory.[32] Many Islamic hospitals have kept regular bands of musicians for musicotherapy from at least the Middle Ages.[33]

Music, of course, is a central component in the worship of modern Christian churches. But most modern mainstream churches have eliminated (or devalued) music from any therapeutic liturgies that do exist in such churches.[34] In many ancient liturgies music by itself was considered an effective treatment rather than playing some supplementary role in the liturgy. The reason for the elimination or devaluation of music within health-related liturgies in modern mainstream churches is probably due to the rise of medical science, which usually does not consider music to be an effective treatment for serious illnesses.[35] Here too there are recent signs of retrieval, particularly in music employed in Alzheimer's and hospital contexts.

CONCLUSIONS

The ascendance of modern science and technology has resulted in the transfer of therapeutic rituals from religious institutions to scientific medical institutions. In many ancient and medieval societies priest and healer were often one and the same.[36] Today, the disjunction between religious liturgist and medical healer is quite pronounced in mainline churches. John H. C. Fritz, a conservative Lutheran writer, expresses the division of labor as follows:

> The physician seeks to alleviate and cure the bodily disease, pain, and distress, but the greater, mental and spiritual, agony and distress can be relieved and cured only by words of divine consolation.[37]

A sharp division of body and spirit is reflected in this division of labor. The cleric here has ceded to the scientist the primary responsibility for healing the body.

Indeed, the rise of modern science has affected the types of health-related liturgies offered by religious institutions. Of the three basic types of health-related liturgies, it is the petitionary or thanksgiving liturgies that are the more commonly found in modern mainstream churches. In general, modern temples seldom perform the types of therapeutic liturgies akin to those seen in the temples of Asclepius or Gula. Many modern churches concentrate on helping the sick cope and live with their illness/disability rather than on physical healing per se.[38] Mainstream temples that hold therapeutic liturgies are often seen, by both cleric and physicians, as supplementary and subordinate to hospitals, which are the primary locus of health care outside the home today.[39]

The rise of modern science has affected how health-related liturgies are performed. The location of health-related rituals certainly has been influenced by the rise of medical hospitals. The fact that modern science does not see music as having much therapeutic efficacy may explain why music is seldom used in therapeutic liturgies by churches that have therapeutic liturgies. The fact that drugs are now almost solely in the domain of medical science explains why most modern mainstream religious institutions usually no longer integrate medicinal substances and liturgy.

Despite some recent changes in attitudes toward animals, the stark separation of human beings from nature in traditional Christianity has also led to the elimination of animals from health-related liturgies.[40] Unlike the situation in many ancient societies, modern Americans do not see animals as having any relationship to the health or illness of the person on a metaphysical level. But animal sacrifice has not disappeared in the sense that animals are still dying in experiments, ostensibly in order to save the life of human beings. Thus, animal sacrifice has been appropriated and transformed by medical science.

Therapeutic liturgies remain prominent in what are usually described as nonmainstream churches. Pentecostalism, for example, may be seen as an alternative health-care system. Many of the founders of Pentecostalism in America usually advertised that healing was a principal feature of Pentecostalism.[41] Many converts report that it was the search for healing that first brought them to Pentecostal churches. Pentecostalism tends to flourish in areas where there is little health care or where conventional health care has not brought about satisfactory results. We also see Christian Science, New Age, and other alternative religious groups assuming and reviving some of the therapeutic liturgies that mainstream churches no longer perform.[42]

Some mainline modern churches, however, are attempting to revive all three types of liturgies. Martin Hauser argues that instead

51

of special healing services, healing should be a normal part of church liturgy.[43] A few scientists are also attempting to integrate religious liturgy with medicine, seeing religion not as subordinate but as complementary or even superior to science.[44] Indeed, the extent to which the separation between medical science and religion is inevitable is itself a subject of debate.[45] The extent to which modern mainline churches will revive or redevelop the three basic types of liturgies, which were so interlinked in many ancient societies, remains an interesting and important sociological and historical question.

1. See, for example, Lester Bush, *Health and Medicine Among Latter-Day Saints* (New York: Crossroad, 1993); Martin Marty, *Health and Medicine in the Lutheran Tradition* (New York: Crossroad, 1983); and Robert A. McCormick, *Health and Medicine in the Catholic Tradition: Tradition in Transition* (New York: Crossroad, 1984). For a brief survey of current health-related liturgies, see Gary Brock, "Liturgical Ministry to the Sick: An Overview," *Journal of Pastoral Care* 45:1 (1990): 37-48.

2. On the definition of *disability*, see also Nancy L. Eiesland, *The Disabled God: Toward a Liberatory Theology of Disability* (Nashville: Abingdon Press, 1994), 27, and Claire H. Liachowitz, *Disability as a Social Construct: Legislative Roots* (Philadelphia: University of Pennsylvania Press, 1988), 4-16. I shall not distinguish between a permanent disability and a temporary illness, except when it affects a liturgical approach.

3. Among the abbreviations we shall use are: LAS=S. Papola, *Letters from Assyrian Scholars to the Kings Esarhaddon and Assurbanipal I,II.* (Kevelaer: Neukirchen-Vluyn, 1970, 1983). T.= *Testimonia of Asclepius* as numbered in Emma J. and Ludwig Edelstein, *Asclepius: A Collection and Interpretation of the Testimonies* (Baltimore: Johns Hopkins, 1945).

4. LAS 218, reverse, lines 1-20; Parpola (LAS, II, 212) does not document his diagnosis of the Akkadian phrase, *GIG di'u* as malaria.

5. Parpola (LAS 173; LAS II, 166) has suggested emending his own earlier translation of lines 11-13 to: "Even the preparation of the images which the king saw (yesterday) took us 5-6 days to get ready with." Even if one accepts the new rendition, the argument remains unchanged.

6. On the rituals of Santería, see Migene Gonzalez-Wippler, *The Santería Experience* (Englewood Cliffs, N.J.: Prentice-Hall, 1973) and Joseph M. Murphy, *Santería: An African Religion in America* (Boston: Beacon Press, 1988).

7. I recognize the difficulty in the classification of American denominations. On classifications, see David A. Gay and Christopher G. Ellison, "Religious Subcultures and Political Tolerance: Do Denominations Still Matter?" *Review of Religious Research* 34:4 (1993): 311-332; Dieter T. Hessel, "Mainline Protestantism Sidelined? A Review of Disestablishment Literature," *Christianity and Crisis* 50:13 (1990): 293-98; Margaret M. Poloma, "A Comparison of Christian Science and Mainline Christian Healing Ideologies and Practices," *Review of Religious Research* 32:4 (1991): 337-350; Rodney Stark and Charles Y. Glock; "The 'New Denominationalism,'" *Review of Religious Research* 7:1 (1965): 8-17. I will use the terms "mainstream" and "mainline" to refer to denominations that have a relatively long history in the U.S. and whose members form or have formed a significant part of the ruling establishment of the country. These include the Anglican, Baptist, Catholic, Methodist, and Presbyterian denominations. Non-mainstream traditions here include Christian Science, Pentecostalism, Mormonism, Santería, and New Age groups.

8. "The Ritual of the Anointing of the Sick," *Catechism of the Catholic Church* (Libreria Editrice Vaticana: Citta del Vaticano; English translation: Mahwah, NJ: Paulist Press, 1994), section 1519.

9. The *editio princeps* is that of René Labat, *Traité akkadien de diagnosticos et pronostics médicaux* (Leiden: Brill, 1951).

10. Simo Parpola, *Letters from Assyrian and Babylonian Scholars* (Helsinki: Helsinki University Press, 1993), 238, lines 10-13.

11. *De Abstinentia* II, 19 = T. 318.

12. Aristides, *Oratio*, XLVIII, 31 = T. 486.

13. See U. Hausmann, *Kunst und Heiltum: Untersuchungen zu den griechischen Asklepiosreliefs* (Potsdam: Eduard Tichnote, 1948), 46-48, pl. 1. For a comparative discussion of incubation on animal skins, see Susan Ackerman, "The Deception of Isaac, Jacob's Dream at Bethel, and Incubation on an Animal Skin," *Priesthood and Cult in Ancient Israel*, ed. Gary A. Anderson and Saul M. Olyan (Sheffield: Sheffield Academic Press, 1991), 92-120.

14. As I have argued elsewhere (Hector Avalos, *Illness and Health Care in the Ancient Near East: The Role of the Temple in Greece, Mesopotamia, and Israel* [Atlanta: Scholars Press, 1995]), the Levitical health care system represents only one of many health care ideologies available in ancient Israel. Other Israelite theologies did allow relatively more access to the temple.

15. Ronald J. Sider, "AIDS: An Evangelical Perspective," *Christian Century* 105:1 (1988): 11-14, decries the case of a Florida church which led the fight in 1987 not to admit the well-known Ray brothers (hemophiliacs stricken with AIDS) to public schools. The same church also decided not to admit persons with the AIDS virus into Sunday school. Sider, however, argues that churches ought not desist from preaching about the association of AIDS with God's judgment. See Philip M. Kayal, *Bearing Witness: Gay Men's Health Crisis and the Politics of AIDS* (Boulder: Westview Press, 1993) for further discussion on the effects of homophobia in modern churches.

16. For the development of such liturgies, see Gary L. Chamberlain, "Chronicle: Rituals and Healing in the Crisis of AIDS," *Worship* 63:5 (1989): 463-66; and Shawn Madigan, "Human Stories that Demand Rituals," *Liturgy* 10:3 (1992): 12-19.

17. Diane Bolger, *Erimi-Pamboula: A Chalcolithic Settlement in Cyprus* (Oxford: B.A.R., 1988).

18. Transliteration and translation follow, with some minor editing, E. Sollberger, "Two Kassite Votive Inscriptions," *Journal of the American Oriental Society* 88 (1968): 192-93.

19. Emmie Donadio, "Painting for Patients: Grünewald's Isenheim Altarpiece," *Medical Heritage* 1:6 (Nov/Dec 1985): 448-55; Andree Hayum, *The Isenheim Altarpiece: God's Medicine and the Painter's Vision* (Princeton: Princeton University Press, 1989); and Eugene Monick, *Evil, Sexuality and Disease in Grünewald's Body of Christ* (Dallas: Spring Publications, 1993).

20. For further discussion of this text, see Avalos, *Illness and Health Care*, 216.

21. Jorge Durand and Douglas S. Massey, *Miracles on the Border: Retablos of Mexican Migrants to the United States* (Tucson: University of Arizona, 1995), 160.

22. For example, Marty, *Health and Medicine*, 92, notes that the report on health practices by the United Lutheran Church in America (*Anointing and Healing*, 1962) sees the impact of the Reformation as follows: "The impact of the Reformation spread a great reduction in the role of superstition and magic for the Christian community." On aniconism in Protestantism, see Joseph Gutmann, *No Graven Images: Studies in Art and the Hebrew Bible* (New York: Ktav Publishing House, 1971).

23. Artemidorus, *Onirocritica*, V, 9 = T. 523.

24. *Cuneiform Texts* 39, 38 r 8; See "kalbu" in the *Chicago Assyrian Dictionary* 8:71f.

25. For a history of attitudes towards animals by Christianity and Western philosophy, see Gerald Carson, *Man Beasts and Gods: A History of Cruelty and Kindness to Animals* (New York: Scribners, 1972); and Andrew Linzey, *Christianity and the Rights of Animals* (New York: Crossroad, 1987).

26. Lise Manniche, *The Ancient Egyptian Herbal* (London: British Museum Publications, 1989), 58-59.

27. For some examples of the medicinal use of oil in ancient Mesopotamia, see Avalos, *Illness and Health Care*, 109, 163.

28. Marty, *Health and Medicine*, 94.

29. John J. Ziegler, "Who Can Anoint the Sick?" *Worship* 61:1 (1987): 25-44.

30. On the history of the sacrament of the anointing of the sick, see also Andrew Cushieri, *Anointing the Sick: A Theological and Canonical Study* (Lanham, Md.: University Press of America, 1992).

31. Galenus, *De Sanitate Tuenda* I, 8, 19-21 = T. 413.

32. Pindar, *Pythian Ode* III, 47-53.

33. Fazlur Rahman, "Islam and Health/Medicine: A Historical Perspective," *Healing and Restoring: Health and Medicine in the World's Religious Traditions*, ed. Lawrence Sullivan (New York: Macmillan, 1989), 159-60.

34. On the use of music in healing in some modern churches, see Phyllis J. Warner, "Congre-

gational Hymns: They're Singing My Song," *Brethren Life and Thought* 33:4 (1988): 279-89.
35. Even physicians who advocate alternative approaches to modern medicine, e.g. Andrew Weil, *Spontaneous Healing* (New York: Knopf, 1995) and recommend music as part of a patient's therapeutic program, still see music as supplementary rather than curative in serious illnesses.
36. On priests as healers in Medieval Greek Churches, see Demetrios J. Constantelos, "Physician-Priests in the Medieval Greek Church," *Greek Orthodox Theological Review* 12:2 (1966-67): 141-153.
37. As quoted in Marty, *Health and Medicine*, 76.
38. See Carol Luebering, "Ministries to the Sick and Well," *Liturgy* 2:2 (1982): 55-57.
39. See also Michel Foucault, *The Birth of the Clinic: An Archaeology of Medical Perception,* trans. A.M. Sheridan Smith (New York: Vintage Books, 1975; c.1973) on the effects of hospitals on society; and Philippe Aries, *Images of Man and Death,* trans. Janet Lloyd (Cambridge: Harvard University Press, 1985) on the effect of hospitals on funeral liturgies.
40. On some of these changes, which include concern by churches for a more humane treatment of animals, see Linzey, *Christianity and the Rights of Animals.*
41. See E. Mansell Pattison, "Ideological Support for the Marginal Middle Class: Faith Healing and Glossolalia," in Irving I. Zaretsky and Mark P. Leone, ed., *Religious Movements in Contemporary America* (Princeton, N. J.: Princeton University Press, 1974), 418-55; and Edith L. Blumhofer, *The Assemblies of God: A Chapter in the Story of American Pentecostalism* (Springfield, Mo.: Gospel Publishing House, 1989).
42. Robert Fuller, *Alternative Medicine and American Religious Life* (New York: Oxford, 1989), 136-38.
43. See also Elaine J. Ramshaw, "Liturgy for Healing," *Liturgy* 9:4 (1991): 9-17.
44. See, for example, Larry Dossey, *Healing Words: The Power of Prayer and the Practice of Medicine* (San Francisco: Harper & Row, 1993).
45. See Catherine L. Albanese, *Native Religion in America: From the Algonkian Indians to the New Age* (Chicago: University of Chicago Press, 1990), 121. Albanese thinks that a disjunction between medical science and religious healers is not inevitable even today. She enumerates four possible relationships between cleric and healer: (1) competition and/or hostility; (2) separate but peaceful co-existence; (3) cooperation; and (4) assimilation of roles (e.g., the physician may assume spiritual and clerical functions). See also Albanese, *The Spirituality of the American Transcendentalists* (Macon, Ga.: Mercer University Press, 1988). See Robert Wuthnow, *The Struggle for America's Soul: Evangelicals, Liberals and Secularism* (Grand Rapids, Mich.: Eerdmans, 1989), 142-57, for his observations on the sociology of the relationship between science and the sacred in modern America.

Acknowledgments:

Figure 1: Art Resource, 65 Blecker St., New York, N.Y.

Figure 2: Jorge Durand and Douglas S. Massey, *Miracles on the Border: Retablos of Mexican Migrants to the United States* (Tucson: University of Arizona, 1995), 165.

Figure 3: B. Hrouda, et al., eds., *Isin-Isan Bahriyat I* (Münich: Bayerische Akademie der Wissenschaften, 1981), Tafel 25, IB 29.

CHAPTER TWO

VISUALIZING THE PERFECT CULT: THE PRIESTLY RATIONALE FOR EXCLUSION

Sarah J. Melcher

The literature of Leviticus is rich and intriguing, but access to its mysteries is gained only through patience and through careful scrutiny. Many of its concepts seem exotic to the reader living at the end of the twentieth century. Leviticus seems to create its own universe as it invites the reader to immerse herself in a world beyond her ken. The reader who enters into the recesses of Leviticus and who seeks to ferret out its meanings soon finds herself in a realm where the presence of holiness in the sanctuary is both desirable and dangerous; and the impurities of human beings can encroach upon that presence, even from afar. Purity, then, is an urgent matter in the social world of Leviticus; and earnest priests must "distinguish between the holy and the common, and between the unclean and the clean" (10:10). Within that world and on its terms, the details make sense, and the pieces fit neatly. Outside that world, Leviticus' stipulations seem cryptic and its words incongruous.

The book creating this world of sacrifice and sanctuary, land and ethical conduct, is in the main the product of two schools of priestly writers, those who created the Priestly Torah (the predominant contribution to chapters 1–16) and those who belonged to the Holiness School (who were responsible for most of chapters 17–26). Both schools of writers/compilers were especially concerned with creating an orderly, coherent, and consistent way of life for the community. The common goal shared by both sections of Leviticus is persuasion— to convince the reader to follow the stipulations presented in the verses of the book.

55

Much of the priestly writers' literature is admirable for its content as well as for its skillful construction. In the sacrificial laws, chapters 1–7, provision is made for the poor to bring more modest offerings if they cannot afford the usual animals prescribed. Chapter 19 is thought by some to reflect the highest ethical standards of the Hebrew Bible. These passages exhort the members of the community to respect their fathers and mothers and to leave the corners of the fields for the poor and for the sojourners. The same chapter persuades the individual that "you shall love your neighbor as yourself . . . " (v. 18). Most relevant for this volume, chapter 19 also cautions the community member not to curse the deaf nor to put a stumbling block before the blind (v. 14).

Alongside these passages concerned with ethical behavior are those that charge the descendants of Israel to adhere to standards for sexual behavior or urge the maintenance of bodily purity. Chapters 18 and 20 list in detail forbidden partners for sexual intercourse. Leviticus 12–15 establishes norms for physical purity and discusses rituals required of those who have been affected by impurity. Leviticus 21–22 contains regulations designed for the priests, which set stricter standards for sexual conduct and more exacting requirements for physical purity than those commanded of laypeople.

Generally speaking, one major section of Leviticus envisions a goal of preserving the divine presence in the sanctuary. (Hector Avalos referred to this briefly in chapter 1 [page 41].) The other pictures a life in the land that aspires to holiness like that of YHWH's. Both aims are fulfilled by means that are chiefly physical. Chapter 19 is concerned with the ethical treatment of others, but even the casual reader is struck by the emphasis on an orderly physical world elsewhere in the book. The literary style of the priestly writers seems to reflect this desire for consistent material existence. Mary Douglas, the cultural anthropologist, remarks on the physical inclination of these priestly norms.

> In short the idea of holiness was given an external, physical expression in the wholeness of the body . . . Wholeness is also extended to signify completeness in a social context. . . . Holiness requires that individuals shall conform to the class to which they belong. And holiness requires that different classes of things shall not be confused. To be holy is to be whole, to be one; holiness is unity, integrity, perfection of the individual and of the kind.[1]

Douglas is insightful about these physical standards. Her mistake is to equate those standards with holiness. The writers of the Priestly Torah never refer to a person as holy unless that person has been consecrated to priestly service or to the temporary consecrated status of the Nazirite. In the writings of the Holiness School, members of the community are exhorted "to be holy," but they call no layperson holy. Holiness seems to be a goal that cannot be attained. Nevertheless, as Douglas observes, in Leviticus physical flawlessness appears to be the norm for embodiment. As Leviticus 21:16-24 indicates, to be without blemish is a prerequisite for full priestly status.

STIGMA AS INTERPRETIVE FRAMEWORK

Since physical standards are established in part by devaluing alternatives, this chapter will explore the stigmatizing power of Leviticus 13–14 and Leviticus 21:16-24, the power of the texts to devalue persons based on physical attributes or appearance. Crucial questions asked of these two texts are: Is the rhetorical intention of this passage to devalue certain individuals? What options are available to those who would interpret these passages? How shall people in parish or synagogue apply these texts to the question of who shall participate or officiate in worship? Since stigma is a crucial issue for the passages in this context, the overall aim of this chapter is informed by the social/psychological theory of stigma.

Stigma was established as a pertinent and fruitful pursuit in sociology or social psychology by Erving Goffman's *Stigma: Notes on the Management of Spoiled Identity*.[2] Goffman is the first to define stigma as a socially constructed phenomenon that deeply discredits a human being on the basis of physical attribute, character, or "tribal" affiliation (race, nation, or religion). When a community has constructed a stigma, it has made legitimate a particular kind of response to difference, a response that classifies the person with a stigma as failing to meet the community's standards of normalcy. "On this assumption we exercise varieties of discrimination, through which we effectively, if often unthinkingly, reduce his [sic.] life chances. We construct a stigma-theory, an ideology to explain his inferiority and account for the danger he represents."[3] Societies develop specific terms that describe stigma, terms that are invested with devaluing power—terms like "cripple," "bastard," and "leper." Out of the immediate context, the terms can be used metaphorically to impute negative attributes to other people, sometimes in ways that depart from their original meaning. Around the stigma, additional terms (representing other attributes) tend to cluster, adding on imperfections. The stigmatizing process tends to assign other socially devalued characteristics to the person with stigma. Finally, stigma is usually accompanied by some form of ostracism, either limiting social interaction for the stigmatized or excluding them from the community altogether.

Goffman explains the origin of the term stigma:

> The Greeks, who were apparently strong on visual aids, originated the term stigma to refer to bodily signs designed to expose something unusual and bad about the moral status of the signifier. The signs were cut or burnt into the body and advertised that the bearer was a slave, a criminal, or a traitor—a blemished person, ritually polluted, to be avoided, especially in public places.[4]

Communities do not always construct stigma in such a straightforward manner as that practiced in ancient Greece. In Leviticus 13–14 and 21:16-24, the stigma process is much more subtle. There are differences between the two Leviticus texts as well—the second text is more moderate than the first; the devaluation of status is less severe. But, especially in the case of Leviticus 13–14, there are indications in the passage, and in closely related texts, that the types of dermatological disfigurement or discoloration represented by the Hebrew term, ṣāra' at, are caused by wrongdoing.[5]

The mark of ṣāra'at, according to the texts of the Hebrew Bible, was placed on the person's skin as a punishment for an encroachment against G-d, so ṣāra' at is a sign of moral failure, much as stigma was for the Greeks.

Goffman urges us to consider a "language of relationships" in examining and understanding the concept of stigma.[6] "A language of relationships" applies to Leviticus 13–14 and 21:16-24 in this way: whose "usualness" is confirmed when another's access to community or altar is restricted? In every case of exclusion, someone else's claim to religious or social communion is confirmed.

The issues are subtle in chapter 21, for the priest who has a physical imperfection is not completely excluded from the community or the tent of meeting, but his access to the altar is restricted. He is not declared impure, he need not dress differently, he need not announce his impurity, nor does he need to dwell outside the camp. The priest who has an imperfection is not subjected to all the classic traits of stigma that Goffman outlines. He is not permitted, however, to offer sacrifices; and in that partial sense, he is devalued.

A LITERARY APPROACH

While stigma theory can provide an interpretive framework for comprehending these passages, it is more appropriate to apply a literary method for a close reading. The texts themselves seem to suggest a three-pronged approach. They construct meaning through an arrangement or cluster of signs, with some passages organized around a broader concept, and they attempt to persuade the reader through a skillful use of rhetoric. An organizing principle or concept especially helps to explain 21:16-24, while the arrangement of signs is more useful for interpreting chapter 13.

Umberto Eco's *A Theory of Semiotics* has influenced my treatment of signs in Leviticus.[7] Approaching a definition for sign, Eco prefers instead to describe a sign-function—a correspondence between expression and content. By introducing the sign-function, he dispels the idea of the sign as a fixed and rigid entity, describing, rather, a pliable phenomenon that adapts to the surrounding context of signs. Even within a single text, the sign-function allows for a momentary linking of expression and content, then an uncoupling, and other subsequent correlations later in the same passage.[8]

Eco's clarification of the nature of content is advantageous. Within the correlation, "an expression does not, in principle, designate any object, but on the contrary conveys a cultural content."[9]

So, in the pursuit of meaning or semantics, the object of the quest becomes the content. Content is best defined as a cultural unit, a unit defined by cultural convention, that is, a segment of the semantic field drawn from the cultural background. It is a semantic unit imbedded within a system.

The cultural unit, conveyed by an expression, can be our access to cultural attitudes imbedded within the texts of Leviticus. Eco draws on a definition from cultural anthropologist, David M. Schneider: "A unit in a particular culture is simply anything that is culturally defined and distinguished as an entity. It may be a person, place, thing, feeling, state of affairs, sense of foreboding, fantasy, hallucination,

59

hope or idea."[10] In the same way, ṣāra'at, nega', "affliction" and ṭāmē' "unclean," "impure" are signs whose expression conveys a cultural unit. These units are ultimately derived from the community of the descendants of Israel. But the cultural units imbedded in the texts of Leviticus have been transformed by the compilers. These texts represent the writers' view of communal attitudes and their attempt to shape those attitudes. So the signs of Leviticus are expressions that convey cultural units, as filtered through the perceptions and intentions of these schools of writers.

With this cautionary note in mind, Eco's theory suggests a possible avenue of access to these contents. Two concepts are especially helpful, that of interpretants and the related one of unlimited semiosis. The interpretant is a sign that explains or defines the content of a previous sign. Eco envisions a series of these definitions, providing closer access to the cultural unit. This notion of interpretants reflects the systemic nature of language. A semiotic system defines and explains the content of each sign by means of other signs, "a series of conventions that explain each other."[11] The process is continuous and never-ending, hence unlimited semiosis.

A useful way to access the semantic content of these signs is to look at the series of signs that define that content. Though texts are limited social discourse when compared to the spoken language of a community, still, an appropriate way to discern meaning is through the cluster of signs surrounding a cultural unit, that circumscribe and define that unit.

THE CULTURAL UNITS *NEGA'* AND *ṢARA'AT*

Our first passage, Leviticus 13–14, is a compilation of fascinating texts. There is some evidence of great antiquity; and the preserved ritual is considered to be a step removed from pagan rite, lightly adapted for the priestly system.[12]

Many scholars no longer consider these texts to be about Hansen's disease (known colloquially as "leprosy").[13] Rather than attempting some alternative diagnosis, it is better to accept these texts according to their own representation—as religious-legal discourse pertaining to cultic impurity. Our passages do not suggest a treatment, or make a prognosis. Perhaps the scientific bias of the last few centuries has compelled scholars to impose modern medical categories on cultic texts.[14]

For Leviticus 13–14, two key terms clearly dominate: *nega‘*, "stroke" or "touch," and *ṣāra‘at*. The translation of the Hebrew word *ṣāra‘at* is a disputed topic among biblical scholars. Since its historical linkage with "leprosy" has proven problematic, it is important to find an alternative. This is a difficult task because symptoms of *ṣāra‘at* represent a broad class of skin disfigurements or discolorations (13:2-43). *Ṣāra‘at* appears on fabric or hide (13:47-59) and in the walls of houses (14:33-53). Traditionally, scholars have understood the noun *ṣāra‘at* to derive from the Hebrew root *ṣr‘*. The verbal root has parallels in Arabic, Aramaic, and post-biblical Hebrew, and means "to strike-down." This implies that the noun has a meaning "struck-down" or "disfiguring, degrading disease."[15]

Akkadian parallels suggest a meaning of "struck down" for *ṣāra‘at*. The Akkadian words *saharšubbû* and *ṣennītu* are terms for skin diseases regarded with abhorrence, like *ṣāra‘at*. *Ṣennītu* is etymologically related to *ṣāra‘at*.[16] *Saharšubbû* and *ṣennītu* occur together in several texts; in one case an introductory phrase suggests that they are both incidents of "the punishment of God."[17] Also, as Albert Goetze points out, in at least one incantation against disease, *ṣennītu* (among other maladies) is "said to have descended from heaven."[18] The evidence from Near Eastern parallels implies that *ṣāra‘at* is a special punishment from God, signifying a severe case of divine displeasure.

Turning to another key term, the noun *nega‘*, it seems the most likely meaning is "becoming touched" and/or "becoming struck." According to Jacob Milgrom, the noun *nega‘*, in its origins, probably relates "to attacks from the demonic sphere."[19] As encountered in biblical literature, *nega‘* most often means "stroke." With great frequency, it designates a "stroke" inflicted by someone. God is the usual initiator. Genesis 12:17; Exodus 11:1; II Samuel 7:14; I Kings 8:37, 38; Psalms 39:11; 89:33—all imply that *nega‘* is a form of divine punishment. The arrangement of signs in Leviticus 13–14 illustrates the importance of the concept. The noun *nega‘* appears sixty-one times, most often denoting "the affection" (affliction) itself, several times "the affected person." Since the idea of "stroke" is inherent within the sign itself, as a first level denotation, disease as a result of divine action is emphasized throughout.

Having a *nega'* requires one to go to the priest to be checked, but does not necessarily result in a declaration of impurity. The term seems to describe a range of illnesses—from minor illnesses that do not render a person unclean to those that generate severe impurity. *Nega'* can be seen against its Ancient Near Eastern background as one of many terms describing afflictions ascribed to divine agency. As Hector Avalos puts it, "In Mesopotamia illness was often, if not normally, viewed as ultimately rooted in the will of the gods."[20]

Yet, the Priestly source attributes all divinely sent conditions to one source, the God of Israel. P's view of illness gives the material a distinctive shape embracing a world view that purges the demonic from existence.[21] No rhetorical evidence hints of P taking illness into a new sphere, where disease has only "natural" causes. Nor does the Priestly source make disease a purely secular matter. Instead, P's treatment presupposes diseases dispatched from a divine being. P does not reshape the tradition to the point where disease becomes a random misfortune or accident.[22]

THE VISUAL BASIS FOR EXCLUSION IN THE CASE OF *ṢĀRA'AT*

To explore further the stigmatizing power of the declarations addressed in chapters 13–14, this section discusses the arrangement of signs in the text. According to Eco's theory, the content of a sign can subsequently become the expression that conveys another cultural unit. For instance, while *ṣāra'at* denotes a particular type of "disfiguring, degrading disease," it also connotes "severe impurity" and "isolation." From another vantage point—the expression denotes "content A," while the sign-function as a whole connotes "content B." Eco's theory of unlimited semiosis permits us to consider the second-level contents or connotations a sign conveys as well as the primary denotation accomplished by the original correlation of expression with content.[23] By considering the arrangement of signs in the text and the associations among them, the social concerns underlying the passage become clearer.

Two classes of signs dominate chapter 13; locative signs and signs of examination or appearance. Locative signs denote a spatial location—in the world they create, they indicate a place on the surface of the skin or a location on the body where the symptoms of disease appear. The locative signs include prepositions that locate symptoms to a point on "the skin of the body." They include nouns like "head" and "beard" as sites for other symptoms. Signs of examination or appearance are those whose expression conveys a content with a visual aspect. A frequent example is the sign *wĕrā'â*, "and he will examine," which is used in connection with the priest's role in examining the signs of disease. This verb form and its variants appear forty times in these chapters. This is significant since these verbs appear only forty-eight times in the entire book of Leviticus. Other signs pertain to the appearance of symptoms: the color of the hair or the appearance of depth in a shiny spot.

Together, the locative signs and the signs of examination or appearance create a world where the priest must examine the surface of the skin and symptoms of disease. The priest does not touch or measure; decisions are based on appearance alone. The signs of appearance are so dominant in the text that they infuse the text with visual connotations. Symptoms like "swelling" and "scab" carry a visual connotation, where their appearance becomes a matter of urgency.

There are a few appearances that the priest must declare impure. If the hair of the *nega'* has turned white, and its appearance is deeper than the skin, the priest shall declare it impure. The combination of white hair and raw flesh also results in a declaration of impurity. In the event the *nega'* occurs on the head or in the beard, the combination of an appearance that is deeper than the skin with sparse yellow hair must be declared impure. If a *nega'* lacks these appearances, it is still declared impure if it spreads on the skin. However, if someone develops a reddish white swelling in a bald spot on the crown or temple and its appearance is like *ṣāra'at*, the priest must not fail to declare him impure.

Verses 45-46 of chapter 13 give the consequences of a declaration of cultic impurity. The person afflicted with *ṣāra'at* must tear his or her clothing, mess up the hair, cover the mustache, and cry "Impure, impure." Ironically, the person impure from *ṣāra'at* upon the skin must change appearance to make impure status evident. Crucial for the present discussion, however, is the afflicted person's exclusion from the community. As long as the *nega'* is present on the skin, the person must dwell outside the camp.

A rationale for exclusion may be implied in 13:12-13. In the event that *ṣāra'at* covers all the skin, from head to foot, and all of it has turned white, the individual is declared clean. The text assumes *ṣāra* '*at*, but surprisingly, as long as it covers the entire body (from what the priest can see) and has completely turned white, the priest shall declare him clean! It seems, then, that visual consistency and completeness is a more influential factor than the presence of *ṣāra'at*. Perhaps appearance is the most important consideration here, as the great prominence of signs of appearance would suggest.

ṢĀRA'AT AS DIVINE PUNISHMENT (REVISITED)

Chapter 14 provides clues as to how the Priestly Torah interprets a "stroke" of *ṣāra'at*. One clue arises from Leviticus 14:33-53, about strokes of *ṣāra'at* in houses. Verse 34 states explicitly, "When you enter the land of Canaan, which I am giving to you as a possession and I put a stroke of *ṣāra'at* on a house in the land you possess" (author's translation). YHWH, then, is the source of *ṣāra'at* in houses. The priestly writers, both P and H, construct conceptual analogies between the material or animal spheres and the human domain. The concluding summary (14:54-57) to the long discussion of *ṣāra'at* stresses the similarity of *ṣāra'at* on fabrics, houses, and human beings. The situations of *ṣāra'at* on persons and mold on fabric and in houses have been equated through similar arrangement of signs and by means of this summary statement. If the affliction in houses is attributable to God, one suspects that the same thing is true for human beings.

The sign *ṣāra'at* is invested with the connotation of divine punishment throughout the remainder of its occurrences in the Hebrew Bible. The paradigmatic story of *ṣāra'at* is in Numbers 12, in which Miriam is struck with *ṣāra'at* for speaking against Moses. An important element is the reference to God's anger in v. 9, which helps to establish a motive for divine punishment. Miriam's appearance is an especially crucial matter. Verse 10 states that she is *mĕṣōra'at* (flakey?), "like snow." In Aaron's prayer (v. 12) he pleads, "Let her not be as one dead, whose flesh is half consumed when he comes out of his mother's womb" (author's translation). Jacob Milgrom's theories are supported by this passage: (a) that *ṣāra'at* is a result of divine punishment, (b) *ṣāra'at*'s severe impurity is attributable to its death-like appearance.[24]

Chapter 14 hints at the priestly rationale for excluding the ill or disabled from worship through its requirement of an '*āšām* or "reparation" offering. This offering is an essential element in the ritual to return the person healed of skin disease to full cultic status. While a *ḥaṭṭā't*, or "purification offering," indicates only that a person needs to be restored to a state of cultic purity, an *'āšām*, or "reparation offering," implies that moral wrongdoing, desecration of *sancta,* or an encroachment against the divine presence in the sanctuary, has taken place. This suggests that P regarded a "stroke of *ṣāra'at*" as a punishment inflicted by God.[25]

THE CONCEPT OF *TĀMÎM*, ANIMAL SACRIFICE, AND LEVITICUS 21:16-24

The primary intention of Leviticus 21:16-24 is to prohibit a priest from officiating in the sacrificial cult if he has a physical defect. Though Moses is instructed to speak to Aaron, clearly the passage concerns any direct male descendant of Aaron who is qualified to officiate as priest by virtue of his lineage. The section stipulates that these priests shall be free of defect, a requirement that shall have sway indefinitely, "throughout their generations." Specifically, a priest with a physical imperfection may not approach the altar to present a sacrifice. This is the meaning of the recurring phrase "to have access" in vv. 17, 18, 21, and 23. In addition, in verse 23, the high priest who has a physical defect is prohibited from approaching the curtain that separates the shrine (the portion of the sanctuary containing the table, menorah, and incense altar) and the adytum (the innermost portion of the sanctuary containing the ark). He, too, is forbidden to "have access to the altar" (here, the incense altar within the shrine).[26]

A significant statement is made in verse 22, indicating that the blemished priest may eat "the bread of his God," the priests' allotted portion of the food offerings to YHWH. The statement is meaningful not only because of the leniency it discloses but also because of its implications for ritual status. The priest's physical defect does not render him ritually impure. If he were impure, he would be unable to eat from the holy or most holy portions.

Leviticus 22:1-13 addresses just that concern. If a priest is rendered impure through *ṣāra'at,* a discharge, contact with the dead, and so forth, he may not eat of the holy things until he returns to a pure state. If the priest were made impure by a physical defect, then this situation would be included in the list. If impurity were the governing concern in 21:16-24, that would be indicated by declarations of impurity.

Though a physical defect does not make the priest impure, his physical state does represent a threat to holy places or objects. The "seed of Aaron" who has a physical imperfection is forbidden access to the altar and the curtain, "so that he does not desecrate my holy things" (v. 23, author's translation).

For the writers of the Holiness school, the act described by the verb *yĕhallēl* "he desecrates" or "he profanes" is a very serious violation. It is classified under the general heading of "trespass against sancta," because it represents an encroachment upon the domain of the holy. According to the Holiness writers, acts of *ḥll* are met with the severest of punishments.[27] The desecration of holy things by the blemished priest in 21:23 must be considered a dangerous offense that puts both the trespasser and the sacra at risk.[28]

The concept of *tāmîm,* or physical perfection, is central for understanding the section Leviticus 21:16-24. Though the word *tāmîm* is not mentioned explicitly here, the term does appear in the conceptually analogous passage concerning appropriate animals for sacrifice, (Leviticus 22:17-25; specifically, v. 19).

There are striking conceptual and stylistic similarities between the passages. Leviticus 22:17-25 requires a sacrificial animal to be male and free of defect. So too according to Leviticus 21:16-24, a priest who offers sacrifices upon the altar is assumed to be male (any man from the seed of Aaron, v. 17, [author's paraphrase]), and he must be free of physical defect. Given the Holiness school's propensity for carefully crafted, stylistic arrangement of ideas, the parallels are undoubtedly deliberate.

Verse 18 acts as the introduction to 22:17-25. If a resident of the land offers a sacrifice to fulfil a vow or presents a voluntary offering, the animal, according to verse 19, must be male, *tāmîm,* and a domesticated animal ("of the cattle or the sheep or the goats"). Verse 20 provides an explanation for *tāmîm*—free from any *mûm* (a physical defect). So that there might not be any misunderstanding, verses 22-25 provide several examples of *mûm.* Thus, *tāmîm* is defined negatively, as having no defect. *Mûm* is clarified by means of examples, though one presumes the list is not exhaustive. Verse 22*b* seems to hit on the heart of the matter: Food offerings shall not be obtained from these imperfect animals, for they must not come into contact with the altar, which has been consecrated (Lev. 8:10-11). An animal with a defect must not make contact with sancta, much as a disabled priest must not touch sancta.

EARLY JEWISH INTERPRETATION

Several of the Dead Sea Scroll texts appear to have been influenced by these stigmatizing texts of Leviticus. 4QD[a] associates the appearance of *ṣāra'at* with that of death. A degradation in the condition was described as "the addition of the living part to the dead part" (4-5, 10-11, 11-12). A symptom of scall, its yellow color, becomes an indication of loss of vitality: "for it is like a plant, which has a worm under it, that cuts off its root, and makes its bloom dry up" (7-8).[29] 4QD[g] also identifies *ṣāra'at* with death (5-11).

Several Dead Sea Scrolls passages exclude the person afflicted with *ṣāra'at* or the person with a physical defect from full participation in worship. A halakhic letter, 4QMMT, affords us a glimpse at the Qumran community's concern for issues of purity and cultic participation, and helps to clarify the community's position on these matters over against certain other forms of Judaism. These Qumranic texts tend to intensify the purity standards in the Hebrew Bible and to reinterpret the Bible's stipulations to apply to the community's particular situation. In 4QMMT the spatial boundaries of the "tent of meeting" and the "camp" of Leviticus are reconfigured; "We are of the opinion that the sanctuary is the tent of meeting and that Jerusalem is the camp, and that outside the camp is outside Jerusalem" (Composite text B, lines 29-30).[30] The letter excludes certain persons from the congregation and prohibits them from marrying a congregation member. An Ammonite, a Moabite, a bastard, a person with crushed testicles, one whose male member has been cut off may not enter the sanctuary. Reverence for the sanctuary requires separation from these persons (lines 39-49). 4QMMT maintains that the blind and the deaf are unable to follow cultic practices; the blind cannot see a mixture, the deaf cannot hear the purity regulations. However, like "the seed of Aaron" in Leviticus 21:16-24, these persons may eat the sacred food (49-54). The halakhic letter holds that a person healed of *ṣāra'at* must not enter a house containing sacred food. Though the person has been readmitted into the camp, that person still has residual impurity until sunset of the eighth day, a stricter requirement than that in Leviticus 14:20.

The Temple Scroll prohibits certain persons from entering the temple city (11Q 19 XLV, 7-18). Notably, the Temple Scroll bans the blind person from entering the temple city and provides a rationale, much in keeping with the concepts presented in Leviticus; "so that they shall not defile the city in which I dwell, for I, the Lord, dwell among the sons of Israel forever and ever" (13-14).[31] A person with *ṣāra'at* may not enter the temple city until clean (17-28), dwelling east of the city until that eventuality.

Specific classes of people are excluded from the eschatological community by The Rule of the Congregation (1QS[a]): "the crippled in the legs or hands, the lame, blind, deaf, or mute," anyone with a visible defect, and anyone too old to stand securely (1QS[a] 2:3-9). 1QS[a], like the Temple Scroll, offers a rationale for this exclusion; "for holy angels are in their council." The issue is holiness and the problem of contact between holiness and physical imperfection.[32] Similarly, the War Scroll (1QM VII, 4-5) requires the man who fights in the eschatological battle to be *tāmîm* in both spirit and body. 1QM provides a rationale, "for holy angels are together with their armies" (VII, 6). Angels will fight with men in the final battle, and holiness must not come into contact with physical imperfection. The Habakkuk Pesher, 1QpHab IX, 1-2, reiterates an idea we have encountered before: Diseases of the body are punishment for wrongdoing.

The Mishnah's apparent aim, in its interpretation of Leviticus 13–14, is greater precision in diagnosis, in certification of purity or impurity, and in applying the processes of purification rituals.[33] The Tractate Bekhorot (7:1-7) seeks greater precision in identifying the physical imperfections that disqualify a man from serving in the temple and has an explicit rationale for disqualification. A man whose eyelashes have fallen out and a man whose teeth have been taken out are disqualified "on account of the appearance of the eye" (i.e., because of how they look).

FINAL CONSIDERATIONS

This brief study of two passages in Leviticus makes a few themes very clear. Deviations from the physical norms set by the compilers of the Priestly Torah and the writers of the Holiness school have very serious consequences. Decisions about physical purity/impurity have a strongly visual basis, and deviations from physical norms may be interpreted as signs of God's displeasure. These themes were quite apparent in the biblical texts as well as in the brief glimpse at the history of interpretation.

The tapestry of meanings conveyed by the expressions in Leviticus 13–14 and 21:16-24 have a significant theme in common. According to these passages, within the religious community physical imperfection can result in some form of exclusion. The exclusion can range from restrictions in privileged access to divine communion to complete and potentially permanent exclusion from the residential community.

Given the stigmatizing power of these two Leviticus passages, what can biblical interpretation do to lessen that power without compromising the authority of the scriptural text? Since stigma is socially constructed, surely it can be reconstructed.[34] Although I would not recommend de-sacralizing texts, I do think we can de-sacralize stigma imbedded within them. Feminist interpretation and liberation approaches to Scripture have offered us ways to face the prejudice in texts and to recast their influence. In this instance we are fortunate. Within Leviticus, chapter 19 offers us a different paradigm. Leviticus 19:14 instructs us: "You shall not revile the deaf or put a stumbling block before the blind; you shall fear your God: I am the LORD." Further on, Leviticus 19:18*b* reminds us, "you shall love your neighbor as yourself: I am the LORD." The first verse gives us a different example to follow. It suggests that we should not take advantage of the person who has different physical abilities. One way we can avoid reviling the deaf and putting a stumbling block before the blind is to allow both full access to the altar, to the worshiping community, and to God. One way to love our neighbors is to refuse to devalue them and to resist using Scripture to justify our prejudice.

Leviticus 13–14 and 21:16-24 can serve as examples for us of how we subtly make our own declarations of "uncleanness" or establish physical standards that devalue others. Although we do not require anyone to shout, "Unclean! Unclean!," religious communities lag behind secular organizations in making our meeting places accessible. We don't overtly put stumbling blocks before the blind, but we find subtle yet effective ways to discourage their ordination as ministers, as Al Herzog and Jan Robitscher point out in chapters 7 and 9.

Perhaps we don't openly revile the deaf, but we certainly don't invite them to lead worship. We discourage through our attitudes and through our resistance, failing to see the inherent authority of a call to ministry. By understanding the exclusive strands in a book such as Leviticus, we may still learn what inclusion in the sight of God implies.

1. Mary Douglas, *Purity and Danger: An Analysis of the Concepts of Pollution and Taboo* (London: Ark Paperbacks, 1966), 51-54.
2. Erving Goffman, *Stigma: Notes on the Management of Spoiled Identity* (New York: Simon & Schuster, 1963).
3. Ibid., 5.
4. Ibid., 1.
5. I have left the term *ṣāraʿat* untranslated because of the variety of discolorations or disfigurements of skin and fabric represented by the term in Lev. 13-14. See Hector Avalos, *Illness and Health Care in the Ancient Near East: The Role of the Temple in Greece, Mesopotamia, and Israel* (Atlanta: Scholars Press, 1995), 311-15.
6. Goffman, *Stigma*, 3.
7. Umberto Eco, *A Theory of Semiotics*, Advances in Semiotics (Bloomington: Indiana University Press, 1979).
8. Ibid., 49.
9. Ibid., 61.
10. David M. Schneider, *American Kinship: A Cultural Account* (Chicago: The University of Chicago Press, 1980), 2. Also quoted in Eco, *A Theory*, 67.
11. Eco, *A Theory*, 69.
12. See Jacob Milgrom, *Leviticus 1-16*, The Anchor Bible, vol. 3 (New York: Doubleday, 1991), 833, about its antiquity. Concerning an early date for P, see Milgrom's *The JPS Torah Commentary: Numbers* (Philadelphia: The Jewish Publication Society, 1990), xxxii-xxxv and his *Leviticus 1-16*, 3-35. See also Avi Hurvitz, *A Linguistic Study of the Relationship Between the Priestly Source and the Book of Ezekiel* (Paris: J. Gabalda, 1982).
13. For example, Milgrom, Leviticus 1-16, 816; Klaus Seybold and Ulrich B. Mueller, *Sickness and Healing*, trans. Douglas W. Stott (Nashville: Abingdon, 1981), 68.
14. Diagnosis is evidently impossible; John J. Wilkinson, "Leprosy and Leviticus: The Problem of Description and Identification," *The Scottish Journal of Theology* 30 (1977): 153-69.
15. Theodor Seidl, "*ṣāraʿat*," *Theologisches Wörterbuch zum Alten Testament*, eds. G. Johannes Botterweck and Helmer Ringgren, vol. 7 (Stuttgart: W. Kohlhammer, 1973-77), col. 1127-133.
16. Albert Goetze, "An Incantation Against Disease," *Journal of Cuneiform Studies*, vol. 9 (1955), 8-18 sees the development * *sarraʿatu* * *sarraʿtu* * *sannaʿtu* * *sanneʿtu* * *sennēʿtu/ sennettu* (12). Similarly, the *Chicago Assyrian Dictionary*, 127.
17. CT 40, 1:6-11; CT 38, 30:20-25. Karel Van der Toorn, *Sin and Sanction in Israel and Mesopotamia* (Assen, The Netherlands: Van Gorcum, 1985), 72.
18. Goetze, "Incantation," 13.
19. Milgrom, *Leviticus 1-16*, 776.
20. Avalos, *Illness*, 129.
21. Jacob Milgrom, "Priestly ('P') Source," *Anchor Bible Dictionary*, vol. 5 (New York: Doubleday, 1992), 454-62.
22. Contra the entry *ngʿ* in *Theologisches Wörterbuch zum Alten Testament*, ed. G. Johannes Botterweck and Helmer Ringgren, vol. 6 (Stuttgart: W. Kohlhammer, 1977), col. 219-26. For a discussion compatible to that argued here, see Karl Elliger, *Leviticus* (Tübingen: Mohr, 1966), 180.
23. Eco, *A Theory*, 54-57.
24. Milgrom, *Leviticus*, 816-26.
25. Jacob Milgrom, *Cult and Conscience: The Asham and the Priestly Doctrine of Repentance* (Leiden: Brill, 1976), 80-82.
26. Jacob Milgrom, *Studies in Levitical Terminology* (Berkeley: University of California Press), 40.

27. For examples of these punishments, see Exodus 31:14, Leviticus 20:3, Leviticus 22:9. Exodus 31:14 is newly attributed to the Holiness School; see Israel Knohl, *The Sanctuary of Silence: The Priestly Torah and the Holiness School* (Minneapolis: Fortress Press, 1995), 16.

28. The absence of the death penalty may not be coincidental. See Milgrom, *Studies in Levitical Terminology I*, 41.

29. J. T. Milik, "Fragment d'une source du Psautier, et fragments des Jubilées, du Document de Damas, d'un phylactère dans la grotte 4 de Qumran," *Revue Biblique* 73 (1966): 105.

30. Elisha Qimron and John Strugnell, *Discoveries in the Judaean Desert, X* (Oxford: Clarendon Press, 1994), 48-51.

31. For a similar rationale, see *Discoveries, XLVI*, 11-12.

32. Lawrence H. Schiffman, *The Eschatological Community of the Dead Sea Scrolls* (Atlanta: Scholars Press, 1989), 37-52.

33. For more information about Mishnah's interpretation of Leviticus, see the tractate, *Neg.*

34. Gaylene Becker and Arnold, "Stigma as a Social and Cultural Construct," *The Dilemma of Difference: A Multidisciplinary View of Stigma*, eds. Stephen C. Ainlay, Gaylene Becker, and Lerita M. Coleman (New York: Plenum Press, 1986), 52.

CHAPTER THREE

REINTERPRETING THE HEALING NARRATIVES

Colleen C. Grant

W hen I first began to reflect seriously on the role of persons with disabilities in the life and liturgy of the church, I belonged to a local congregation of one hundred and fifteen members. Among these people, I knew of three families struggling with the effects of mental illness, one woman coping with the debilitating effects of multiple sclerosis, one young man in the midst of completely restructuring his life due to a profound loss of hearing, another man losing his eyesight due to a degenerative disease, two members undergoing treatment for cancer, and one much beloved man who had recently died of complications stemming from diabetes. I suspect that there were also members with other sorts of illness and disabilities of which I had no knowledge. I also suspect that the members of my church were not particularly unusual in their various struggles, but instead represented "one of the basic truths of human existence, namely that such an existence is through and through finite."[1]

This human reality is attested to over and over again in the New Testament. Its pages are filled with characters who suffer from various types of afflictions. In just the first three chapters of the Gospel of Mark, we encounter a man with an unclean spirit (1:23), a leper (1:40), a paralyzed man (2:3), and a man with a withered hand (3:1). In addition to these specific individuals, the narrator tells us in summary form of many others who had various diseases (1:34, 39; 3:10). What all of these characters have in common is the healing word or touch from Jesus. All of them appear in the context of healing narratives.

Given this, one would expect that in our efforts to develop new theological and liturgical understandings around the subject of human disability, the Gospel healing stories would provide helpful guidance. However, the situation is not so clear. In truth, within church communities these stories have often fueled destructive attitudes toward people with disabilities rather than foster visions of inclusion and participation. To understand why this is true, we must consider the nature of the stories and their purpose within the Gospel narratives. To be sure, the healing stories have no singular purpose. The Evangelists placed them in a number of different contexts and shaped them with a number of different emphases in mind. Still, it is possible to make some general observations about the narratives.

THE NATURE AND FUNCTION OF THE GOSPEL HEALING STORIES

Christological Emphasis

First, many of the stories are not primarily about the people healed, but focus instead on the healer, Jesus. In others words, they are Christological stories passed along to describe some reality about who Jesus the Christ was and is. The most basic healing narrative may simply depict Jesus as a healer and worker of miracles. In such stories the details are usually brief, even to the point of summary (for example, Mark 1:31; Mark 1:32-34; Mark 3:7-12; Luke 4:40-41). Information about the person being healed is limited to a description of his or her affliction.

Sometimes, along with highlighting Jesus' ability to heal, these stories emphasize his compassion as well. For instance, in Mark's account of the cleansing of the leper (1:40-45), and Matthew's story of the two blind men on the road outside of Jericho (20:30-34), Jesus is portrayed as one who has been moved to compassion (*splanchnistheis*), a worker of miracles who takes pity on those in need of healing (cf. also Matthew 14:14; Luke 7:13).

A healing narrative may also be told to accent the divine authority of Jesus. When this is the case, the healing account frequently shifts into a story of controversy between Jesus and the Jewish authorities. Sometimes the specific point of controversy is not that Jesus heals but

73

that he heals on the Sabbath. Such is the case with the synoptic account of the man with the withered hand (Mark 3:1-6; Matthew 12:9-14) and Luke's story of the bent-over woman in the synagogue (Luke 13:10-17). In the latter story, the issue is succinctly stated by the leader of the synagogue who indignantly urges the crowd, "There are six days on which work ought to be done; come on those days and be cured, and not on the sabbath day" (Luke 13:14).[2] Here, as in other places, Jesus exercises his authority to reinterpret the Sabbath, in this case describing it as a day on which the woman should be set free from the bondage of her ailment (Luke 13:15-16). In another well-known story the authorities are upset not because Jesus heals on the Sabbath but because he assumes the divine prerogative to forgive sins (Mark 2:2-12).

Emphasis on Faithful Discipleship

There is also another type of healing story found in the Gospels, a type that shifts the focus from Jesus to the individual being healed. Its aim is to communicate something about the nature of discipleship and the necessity of having faith in Jesus. Thus, upon healing blind Bartimaeus, Jesus tells him, "Go, your faith has made you well" (Mark 10:52a). At these words, Bartimaeus regains his sight and assumes the quality of a disciple, that is, he follows Jesus on the way (Mark 10:52b). A similar story from Matthew's Gospel stresses the issue of faith even further, as Jesus asks the two blind men, "Do you believe that I am able to do this?" When the men answer with the words, "Yes, Lord," Jesus responds, "According to your faith let it be done to you" (Matthew 9:28-29). Likewise, Jesus says to the woman suffering from a flow of blood, "Daughter, your faith *sesoken se,*" that is, "has made you well" or "has saved you"(Mark 5:34).

In sum, the nature of most healing stories is such that we either know a lot about Jesus, but very little about the character with the disability, or we know this character only as a paradigm of faithful discipleship. Moreover, both types of healing narratives present particular difficulties when used as lenses for viewing the role of persons with disabilities in the church. In what follows, I will discuss two of these interpretive difficulties, illustrating them through a closer look at particular healing stories.

MODELS OF SIN OR MODELS OF FAITH: PERSONS WITH DISABILITIES AND THE HEALING NARRATIVES

Sin, Sickness, and Disability: The Biblical Connection

Mark 2:1-12 is one of those stories whose primary focus is Christological, though it also features characters who demonstrate superior faith in Jesus. Its structure is that of a healing narrative combined with a story of controversy between Jesus and the scribes. As the narrative begins, Jesus is at home in Capernaum speaking to a crowd that is packed in around him (vv. 1-2). Along come four people determined to bring a paralyzed man to Jesus. Matters become complicated when they cannot get past the crowd to bring the man to Jesus. Being determined, however, they remove part of the roof and lower the man into the room (vv. 3-4). Then comes Jesus' surprising pronouncement. Seeing the faith of his companions, Jesus says to the man, "Son, your sins are forgiven" (v. 5). His words immediately elicit a complaint from the scribes, who are well aware that God alone has the authority to forgive sins (cf. Isa 43:25). From their perspective, Jesus has committed blasphemy (v. 7). Jesus understands that authority is the main point of contention and therefore responds to their questions with a final pronouncement. Verses 10-11 read: "But so that you may know that the Son of Man has authority on earth to forgive sins,—he said to the paralytic—"I say to you, stand up, take your mat and go to your home." The man stands up, walks out, and all are amazed and glorify God (v. 12).

As twentieth-century readers, we may also express amazement not only at the miracle but at these particular words of healing, at the link that Jesus readily makes between sin and disability. Indeed, it is clear from reading contemporary commentaries that most scholars are understandably hesitant to discuss this aspect of the text. For example, Bas van Iersel urges the reader not to "presume too lightly that the symptoms of paralysis are regarded here as due to a moral lapse either of the man in question or of someone else, which would mean that the story suggests a causal connection between sin and sickness, a supposition for which there is no sufficient evidence in the text."[3] Hugh Anderson attempts to generalize Jesus' statement, shifting the blame, as it were, from the individual to humankind as a whole. He states,

75

> It is not that Jesus sees this man as particularly sinful. Nor does he think
> . . . that a man's suffering is proportionate to his sin. . . . The insight is
> that there is indeed a close and age-old connexion between a [per-
> son's] fallen estate and everything that afflicts [that person], with the
> further implication that God's will is for . . . wholeness, or complete-
> ness in every aspect of [a person's] being.[4]

While this statement may reflect sound Christian theology, it is probably not an accurate interpretation of the text. There was, in the first century, a common belief in divine retribution, that is the belief that a person's suffering is proportionate to his or her sin. This view is illustrated in a number of places in Jewish writings. For example, the Wisdom of Solomon teaches that, "one is punished by the very things by which one sins" (11:16). Similarly, in Proverbs 21:13 we read, "If you close your ear to the cry of the poor, you will cry out and not be heard." In other words, one's actions have decided repercussions, and the punishment inevitably fits the crime. It follows from this logic that if one is suffering from some sort of affliction or impairment, it must be the result of a prior action, in biblical language *hamartia*, sin. A clear expression of this view is seen in Psalm 32, in which healing from illness is understood as a sign of God's forgiveness of sin. Whether or not we agree with this perspective, when Jesus equates the forgiveness of sins with physical healing, he reflects this same basic worldview.

The same sort of position is reflected in John 5:2-9. There we read of a man with a long-standing illness who is unable to lower himself into the healing waters of the pool of Bethesda. Jesus sees the man and, upon hearing of his plight, says to him, "Stand up, take your mat and walk." The man does, and all seems well. However, when Jesus next encounters the healed man, he tells him, "See, you have been made well! Do not sin any longer, so that nothing worse happens to you" (5:14). Once more we find that sin is somehow linked to a man's plight and once more, the association is made by Jesus himself. To be sure, in this instance, Jesus does not directly state that sin caused the illness, but his choice of wording, "do not sin any longer" (*meketi hamartane*) implies the connection. Furthermore, there is the omi-nous warning that to continue to sin will result in something worse than thirty-eight years of illness.

Clearly, stories such as these present problems for people with disabilities who seek acceptance and full participation in the life and liturgy of the church. Although the primary aim of these narratives is to convey the Christological claim of Jesus' divine authority on earth, they have also served as proof of the moral imperfection of people with illness or disabilities. Though most people will readily dismiss certain first-century ideas as outdated—the notion of demonic possession, for example—many people hold tenaciously to the notion of illness or disability as punishment for sin. The most recent and obvious example of this is the negative attitude towards those stricken with the AIDS virus. Historically, however, the same moral assessment has applied to other types of illness and impairment.[5]

The Relationship Between Faith and Healing

If we consider the second type of healing story, which emphasizes the faith of the person healed, we are left with a decidedly more positive impression. There is no mention of sin in any of these accounts. Yet even this positive presentation raises questions regarding the participation of persons with disabilities in the Christian community. To hear repeatedly that an individual's faith is the decisive element in his or her being healed implies that those who are not healed must not have enough faith. As Nancy J. Lane has shown, such a notion may be perpetuated in contemporary Christian healing rituals. In her words,

> Healing is expected to change the person who has a disability into one who does not. The burden of healing is placed totally on the person who is disabled, causing further suffering and continued alienation from the Church.[6]

As Nancy Eiesland puts it, "Failure to be healed is often assessed as a personal flaw in the individual, such as unrepentant sin or a selfish desire to remain disabled."[7]

Additionally, the focus on faith and healing in these stories raises the question of just who may be considered a child of God. It is true that at one level the healing stories are stories of inclusion in that Jesus heals and welcomes all sorts of people into God's reign. However, the very fact that they are physically healed by Jesus suggests that physical restoration is a necessary component of their entry into the community. Indeed, in his reflections on disability and the Bible, Donald Senior reports that a friend of his protested the use of Gospel healing stories as stories of inclusion precisely "because those who are sick and disabled seem to gain access to the community only after they are cured. Thus, in effect, disabled people gain access to the community but only on the terms of the able-bodied."[8] Similarly, in reflecting on the healing stories, Frederick C. Tiffany and Sharon H. Ringe ask,

> Why is such a premium placed on able-bodiedness? Why is the "good news" not expressed as a world made accessible to and accepting of persons of all physical, mental, and psychological circumstances, rather than as persons changed to conform to the world's norms?[9]

Even if we decide that such stories should be regarded metaphorically—that in fact all people are in need of healing and restoration to wholeness, and the physically impaired characters who populate the New Testament stories actually represent all of us, we have not removed the problem. The metaphor still demands that we isolate and focus on persons with physical limitations such as blindness, deafness, or paralysis as symbols of brokenness.[10] This, in turn, can become the primary way of viewing people with disabilities.

With all of these difficulties before us, should we abandon hope that the healing stories can provide an interpretive context for a fresh theological understanding of disability? Should we be content to simply claim that the stories are useful insofar as they describe the Christ as a compassionate and inclusive healer? Should we be content to preach this good news to the disabled among us? I contend that although this may offer encouragement to some individuals, it is not enough to move beyond the barriers—both physical and emotional— that have already been constructed within the church. On the other hand, I must also admit that an easy reconciliation between the Gospel healing stories and a vision of full and open participation for persons with disabilities in the life of the church is not readily at hand. I cannot honestly say that these stories, if only interpreted correctly, will be free from the problems I have just described. The problems are real, and the answers are slow in coming.

However, I am also not ready to argue that the stories are devoid of any usefulness to us. Instead, I want to focus on one story that, though certainly not free from hermeneutical problems, nevertheless makes possible an alternative perspective. The remaining half of this chapter will concentrate on a close reading of one healing narrative, John 9, with the hope that it will offer some different ways of thinking about persons with disabilities, the church, and the relationship between the two. In focusing on only this story, I do not mean to suggest that it is the only healing narrative that is useful for a discussion on disabilities and the church. Indeed, I would hope that there are other stories that lend themselves to other ways of reading that would also prove helpful. I offer what follows as only one attempt at reinterpreting the healing narratives.

THE HEALING OF THE MAN BORN BLIND: JOHN 9:1-41

John 9:1-41, commonly known as the "Healing of the Man Born Blind," has been deservedly praised as a narrative in which characterization, irony, and metaphor unite to present a finely crafted drama, rich with Christological significance. Moreover, with respect to our interests, it is often upheld as a story in which Jesus overturns the Jewish understanding of divine retribution. Yet, this is not the point on which I will focus, in large part because the interpretation is misleading. As we will see, whether Jesus meant to refute the idea of divine retribution is by no means clear. My reasons for focusing on the story are grounded in the characterization of the *anthropon tuphlon ek geneteis,* the man blind from birth. Unlike any other healing story, John 9 presents the reader with a well developed character, a personality with whom we can identify. Indeed, despite his anonymity, the man born blind comes alive in this healing narrative in a way that few other characters do. He appears not simply as a broken figure in need of compassion and healing but as a person in his own right. We are able to get to know him as a thoughtful, brave, amusing, but above all, ordinary person.[11] I contend that it is the characterization of the man born blind more than anything else that makes John 9 a particularly useful story for reflecting on human disability and the service of God. It is this aspect of the narrative that I find particularly compelling and that I will pursue in the discussion below.

Scene One: The Healing (vv. 1-7)

As the drama begins, there is immediate indication that the notion of disability as retribution for sin will serve as backdrop. When Jesus and his disciples encounter a man blind from birth, the disciples'

79

opening question to Jesus takes on the issue directly. They ask, "Rabbi, who sinned, this man or his parents, that he was born blind?" (v. 2). The disciples have no doubt that sin lies behind this man's condition; the only question is who precisely is to blame? Their question reveals the belief, also grounded in Hebrew tradition, that a person may be punished for the sins of his or her parents.[12]

Jesus responds to the disciples with the statement, "Neither this man nor his parents sinned; he was born blind so that God's works might be revealed in him" (v. 3). Here is the so-called overturning of the traditional Jewish view of disability. However, as Rudolf Bultmann rightly points out, "what [Jesus] says does not confute the Jewish position nor does it suggest that there is another way of looking at such cases. . . . The saying is concerned only with the particular case in question at the moment."[13] If it is not clear that Jesus overturns the position, it is certain that he changes the focus of the discussion. Whereas the disciples are interested in the past cause of the man's blindness, Jesus speaks of its future purpose.[14] Furthermore, he makes clear that this purpose is no less than revealing the works of God. Jesus' final words to the disciples consist of an exhortation, a warning, and a self-definition, "We must work the works of him who sent me while it is day; night is coming when no one can work. As long as I am in the world, I am the light of the world" (v. 4). The statement both situates the ensuing events within the categories of light and dark and indicates that Jesus is not the only one who must do the work of God. Though the exhortation to "work the works of him who sent me" is directed to the disciples, as we will see, it is the man born blind who carries it out.

Following his pronouncement, Jesus spits on the ground, makes mud, and spreads it on the man's eyes, instructing him to "Go, wash in the pool of Siloam."[15] The man does so, and comes back able to see (v. 7). Note that the blind man has not asked for healing, as did Bartimaeus, for instance (Mark 10:51), nor does Jesus inquire about the man's faith. The healing takes place unconditionally, without any stated expectation either on the part of the one healed or the healer. Second, note that although the blind man "washed and came back able to see," he does not find Jesus waiting for his return.[16] Jesus has left the scene and does not reenter the narrative until twenty-eight verses later. This is the longest absence of Jesus in the entire Gospel and unlike any other healing narrative, it is the events that unfold while he is "off-stage" that are the most significant. What follows Jesus' exit from the narrative are four scenes of interrogation involving at various times the man, his neighbors, the Jewish authorities, and the man's parents. It is in the context of this questioning that the character of the man is more fully developed.

Scene Two: The Neighbors (vv. 8-12)

Upon his return from the pool, the man's presence immediately stirs up controversy between his neighbors and others who had seen him before. The point of conflict is the identity of the man, with some arguing that he is the blind man who used to sit and beg and others suggesting that while he resembles that person, he is actually someone else. As for the man himself, he does not hesitate to announce to the crowd, "I am the man," or more literally, "I am" (*ego eimi*). The controversy and the man's response draw attention to two issues. First, the expression used by the man to identify himself is the same phrase that occurs repeatedly on the lips of Jesus throughout the Gospel. When Jesus says *ego eimi*, I am, it is in the context of divine self-revelation. As O'Day points out, the reader of the Gospel has come to understand the *ego eimi* sayings as bold statements of identity.[17] To be sure, coming from the formerly blind man the phrase is not an indication of divinity, but it does have the quality of bold revelation in the face of a skeptical crowd.

Second, that it is the absence of the man's disability that brings his identity into question suggests that for the people who knew him, "blindness" was his defining characteristic. The man's insistence that he is the same man they once knew points out the fallacy of this thinking. From his perspective, his disability was never his defining characteristic; he knows himself to be the same person, blind or sighted.

His neighbors, however, remain focused on the change that they see in him and ask him, "Then how were your eyes opened?" The man answers matter-of-factly, repeating the earthy details of his healing—the mud spread on his eyes, the command to wash in the pool of Siloam from the man called Jesus, the receiving of his sight (v. 11). But when asked of Jesus' whereabouts he can only reply, "I do not know" (v. 12).

Scene Three: The Pharisees (vv. 13-17)

Following this response, the people bring the man to the Pharisees and the second round of questioning begins. It is only at this point that the narrator informs us that the healing took place on a Sabbath (v. 14). Once more the man is asked to report how he received his sight. Once more he states candidly and succinctly, "He put mud on my eyes, and I washed and I see" (v. 15).[18] The answer spawns a debate between the Pharisees, as some view Jesus' apparent disregard for the Sabbath as evidence that he is not from God, while others argue that a sinner could not perform such signs (v. 16). Thus divided, they look to the man for clarification, "What do you say about him? It was your eyes he opened" (v. 17). The man does not shrink from the question, but again gives his opinion forthrightly, "He is a prophet." As is frequently noted, his response demonstrates further reflection on the person of Jesus. Whereas earlier he referred to Jesus only as "the man," when questioned by the religious authorities, he readily identifies Jesus as a religious figure, a prophet. As in the case of the neighbors, the man's terse statement to the Pharisees ends the conversation and the scene shifts yet again.

Scene Four: The Parents (vv. 18-23)

Now the issue reverts back to the identity of the man, as the religious leaders, here referred to more generally as "the Jews," doubt that the man has ever been blind. To resolve the question, they call the man's parents to interrogate them, asking them, "Is this your son, who you say was born blind? How then does he now see?" (v. 19). From the parents' response, it would appear that whatever boldness the man demonstrates, he did not learn it from them. They confirm that he is indeed their son and that he was born blind, but they will say no more than that. They insist that they do not know how it is that he now sees, nor do they know who opened his eyes (v. 21). However, since the Jews have made no reference to anyone opening his eyes, it would seem that they know more than they are willing to admit.[19] Rather than bring trouble upon themselves, they encourage the authorities to question their son directly, since he is of age. When the narrator informs us that the parents have spoken out of fear of the Jews, we are not surprised. Their timidity stands in contrast to their son's boldness (v. 22).

Scene Five: The Man Born Blind (vv. 24-33)

The authorities do as the parents suggest and once again summon the formerly blind man (v. 24). It is in this round of conversation, as the man confronts his interrogators for the second time that we can see his character truly unfold. The authorities begin by exhorting the man to, "Give glory to God," meaning "Tell us the truth!"[20] Furthermore, they now express their own unified view of the truth about Jesus, stating unequivocally, "We know that this man is a sinner" (v. 24). Once again, the formerly blind man answers his interrogators with bold simplicity, "Whether he is a sinner, I do not know. One thing I do know, that though I was blind, now I see" (v. 25). His statement reflects both his unwillingness to simply accept the view of the religious authorities, and his reliance on his own experience as a measure of truth.

The authorities persist, however, and ask the man a second time to explain how Jesus healed him. The man's reply gives us the opportunity to see that he is a man not only of courage but also intelligence and wit. In one of the more ironic twists in the Gospel, he responds, "I have told you already, and you did not listen. Why do you want to hear it again? You don't also wish to becomes his disciples, do you?" (v. 27).[21] This last question, aside from its incendiary character, is the first indication we have that the man may understand himself to have become a disciple of Jesus. The retort from the authorities accents this fact as they point out, "You are his disciple, but we are disciples of Moses" (v. 28). Their next statement gets to the heart of their problem and to one of the central issues of the Fourth Gospel, the origin of Jesus. They state, "We know that God has spoken to Moses, but as for this man, we do not know where he comes from" (v. 29).[22]

To this, the man makes his longest reply of the chapter. "Here is an astonishing thing!" he exclaims, "You do not know where he comes from, and yet he opened my eyes" (v. 30). For the man, this action is enough to testify to Jesus' divine origin. He demonstrates his logic as he argues with the authorities on their own terms, "We know that God does not listen to sinners, but he does listen to one who worships him and obeys his will" (v. 31), a point his opponents surely cannot dispute. He goes on, "Never since the world began has it been heard that anyone opened the eyes of a person born blind," and the clinching statement, "If this man were not from God, he could do nothing" (v. 33). The success with which the once-blind man makes his point is revealed in the final words and actions of the religious authorities. Unable to refute the logic of his argument, they can only resort to a personal attack, "'You were born entirely in sins, and are you trying to teach us?' And they drove him out" (v. 34).

Scene Six: Jesus Returns (vv. 35-41)

Throughout the narrative, the reader has observed in the man an increased willingness to boldly and cleverly defend Jesus as a prophet, sent from God. For this reason, when Jesus reenters the narrative and asks the man somewhat indirectly, "Do you believe in the Son of Man?" one can readily anticipate what the response will be. Still, this man remains his level-headed and logical self, inquiring first, "And who is he, sir? Tell me, so that I may believe in him" (v. 36). In other words, before granting his devotion, he requests a direct statement of identity. Jesus complies and answers, "You have seen him and the one speaking with you is he" (v. 37). At this, the man offers his confession of faith, also his final words in the Gospel, "Lord, I believe" (v. 38).

Now this man is often described as the quintessential model of a disciple, and he is certainly that. Jesus began by stating that the man was born blind so that God's works might be revealed in him. As the story progresses, we discover that this revelation goes far beyond the healing of his disability. Significantly, the work of God is even more evident in the man's gradually increasing faith and conviction before the opponents of Jesus. Indeed, I would argue that even more than in Jesus' act of healing, the work of God is evident in the man's role as witness to Jesus. In this sense, it is not the man's blindness nor his healing that is essential to the story. Although the healing provides the catalyst for the unfolding events, it does not produce an immediate response in the man. He is not presented merely as a stock character representing faith in Jesus. Neither is he portrayed as a victim deserving of pity (recall that he does not request healing). Rather, the story depicts a real person involved in a deliberative process about a personal experience, a process that is expressed through conversation with the religious authorities. Thus, the story is not so much about what Jesus did as what the man is doing. As he moves through this thoughtful process, readers can readily identify with him as an ordinary, amusing, intelligent man, caught up in a situation that brings out his independence and courage as well.

Finally, we must note that the man's confession does not conclude the story. There is one last exchange between Jesus and the Pharisees. Following the confession of the formerly blind man, Jesus says, "I came into this world for judgment so that those who do not see may see, and those who do see may become blind" (v. 39). Overhearing this statement, the Pharisees ask him, "Surely, we are not blind, are we?" (v. 40). Jesus replies, "If you were blind, you would not have sin. But now that you say, 'We see,' your sin remains" (v. 41). Now most readers readily perceive that this conversation is about spiritual blindness. The Pharisees, insisting on their ability to see spiritual truths, unwilling to admit their blindness to the light of the world, will remain in sin. They stand in contrast to the formerly blind man whose eyes have been opened to the identity of Jesus. The typical sin/sickness metaphor is reversed so that blindness is no longer a symbol for humanity's sinfulness, but instead representative of a state of innocence and openness to revelation.[23]

Yet in spite of this very helpful reversal, there remains a fundamental problem with this interpretation. If we turn too quickly to the notion of spiritual blindness and vision, we may easily forget the fact that the man in this story was quite literally blind. So what happens if we take the closing words of Jesus more literally? How might this inform our understanding about the relationship between persons with disabilities and the church? It may suggest that those who are sighted and who perceive themselves as the "normal" able-bodied members of the church (Surely we are not blind, are we?) may be more in need of healing than the so-called "disabled." In other words, as long as our primary perception of ourselves is as persons who can see, or hear, or walk, or think rationally over against those who cannot do these things, our sin of stereotyping and exclusion remains.

CONCLUSION

In the case of the man born blind, it is not his extraordinary qualities that give him entry to the Christian family—not his disability nor the miraculous healing that he experiences. On the contrary, it is the rather ordinary way that this anonymous character comes to a decision to witness to Jesus—gradually, thoughtfully, and finally, with conviction, "Lord, I believe." Likewise, for persons with disabilities to participate fully in the church should not be regarded as something extraordinary. Most of us, in our finite ways, are quite ordinary members of the body of Christ. We learn from one another what it means to be a child of God.

In closing, another aspect of the John 9 narrative should be mentioned. The early Christians perceived this story to be rich in baptismal imagery—washing in the pool, the discussion of sin, the confession of the once-blind man. Thus, the narrative was frequently depicted in early catacomb art as an illustration of Christian baptism and was used as part of the preparation of catechumens.[24] This tradition is still reflected in our contemporary lectionary, as we read the story on the Fourth Sunday of Lent, Year A.

Upon encountering this text during the Lenten season, the natural inclination would be to gravitate to the notion of sin and cleansing, a central aspect of the baptismal ritual. But there is an alternative way of viewing the baptismal connotations in this narrative, which emphasizes baptism as a rite of initiation into the body of Christ. With this in mind, the formerly blind man becomes something other than a former sinner. He can be viewed as one who has entered into Christian communion and in so doing has "worked the works of God." In other words, we can see him as an ordinary human being, moved to witness to Jesus Christ, in the service of God.

---

1. John Macquarrie, "Theological Reflections on Disability," *in Religion and Disability: Essays in Scripture, Theology and Ethics,* ed. Marilyn E. Bishop (Kansas City: Sheed and Ward, 1995), 30.

2. Translations are from the *New Revised Standard Version* unless otherwise noted.

3. Bas van Iersel, *Reading Mark* (Collegeville, Minn.: The Liturgical Press, 1988), 54-55.

4. Hugh Anderson, *The Gospel of Mark* (Grand Rapids: Eerdmans, 1987), 100. See also Eduard Schweizer, *The Good News According to Mark* (Atlanta: John Knox Press, 1970), 61: "It is not as if this sick man were unusually sinful, but his case makes the universal separation of man from God more conspicuous and illustrates the truth which is proclaimed over and over in the Old Testament, that all suffering is rooted in man's separation from God."

5. Cf. Susan Sontag, *Illness as Metaphor and AIDS and Its Metaphors* (New York: Doubleday, 1990). In her two essays, Sontag traces and compares the metaphors used in speaking of tuberculosis, cancer, and AIDS. Particularly relevant is her discussion of the moralistic and punitive conceptions that pervade this metaphoric language.

6. Nancy J. Lane, "Healing Bodies and Victimization of Persons: Issues of Faith-Healing for Persons with Disabilities," *The Disability Rag Resource* 14 (3): 12, quoted in Nancy L. Eiesland, *The Disabled God: Toward a Liberatory Theology of Disability* (Nashville: Abingdon Press, 1994), 117.

7. *The Disabled God,* 117. Eiesland also makes clear that the ritual of laying on of hands has the potential to be a very meaningful and supportive experience for persons with disabilities.

8. Donald Senior, "Beware of the Canaanite Woman: Disability and the Bible," *Religion and Disability,* 12.

9. Frederick C. Tiffany and Sharon H. Ringe, *Biblical Interpretation: A Roadmap* (Nashville: Abingdon Press, 1996), 183.

10. Using disability as metaphor has a long history in the Bible, particularly in the prophetic tradition. As Steward Govig points out, "Included in prophetic speech are references to conditions of disability: there are 'weak hands' and 'feeble knees,' as well as the blind" (Isaiah

35:3-6; Hebrews 12:12-13). While Govig recognizes that, "lameness and affliction . . . are metaphors for the sins of God's people," he seeks to redeem their use, wondering whether "being on the margins of society and institutional power themselves, such prophets were surrounded with and deeply affected by all the 'cripples' on these boundaries of respectability?*" Strong at the Broken Places: Persons with Disabilities and the Church* (Louisville: Westminster/John Knox Press, 1989), 117-18.

11. My reflections on the "ordinariness" of the man born blind were influenced by Eiesland's narrative accounts of the ordinary lives of two different women with disabilities (cf. *The Disabled God*, 31-48).

12. Cf. Exodus 20:5 and Deuteronomy 5:9.

13. Rudolf Bultmann, *The Gospel of John*, trans. G. R. Beasley-Murray (Philadelphia: Westminster, 1971). Those who would argue otherwise must account for the instances in which Jesus' words are in line with the position. Indeed, great caution should always be exercised before portraying Jesus as one who overturns 'backward' Jewish thinking.

14. Cf. Barnabas Lindars, *The Gospel of John: New Century Bible Commentary* (England: Marshall, Morgan & Scott, 1972; Grand Rapids: Eerdmans, 1995), 342, who points to Luke 13:2 as another instance in which "Jesus deflects the thought from the cause of suffering to its possibilities for God's purpose."

15. The narrator translates the name Siloam as (*apestalmenos*), i.e., 'the one sent.' The Christological connotations are clear, especially given Jesus' reference to the works "of the one who sent me" (*tou pempsantos*) in John 9:4.

16. Gail O'Day, *The Word Disclosed: John's Story and Narrative Preaching* (St. Louis: CBP Press, 1987), 60.

17. O'Day, *Word*, 61.

18. Author's translation.

19. O'Day, *Word*, 65.

20. Cf. Joshua 7:19; I Esdras 9:8; II Esdras 10:11.

21. Author's translation.

22. For the development of this theme in the Fourth Gospel cf. Paul Minear, " 'We Don't Know Where . . . ' John 20:2" *Interpretation* 30 (1976): 125-139.

23. The reversal is lost, however, if we make the assumption that the formerly blind man was also formerly a wretched sinner, along the lines of the popular hymn "Amazing Grace."

24. Raymond Brown, *The Gospel According to John* (New York: Doubleday, 1970), 380-81. According to Brown, " . . . John IX was read on the day of the great scrutiny. . . . When the catechumens passed their examination and were judged worthy of baptism, lessons from the OT concerning cleansing water were read to them. Then came the solemn opening of the Gospel book and the reading of John ix, with the confession of the blind man, 'I do believe, Lord' serving as the climax . . . After this the catechumens recited the creed."

CHAPTER FOUR

"THOSE WHO ARE BLIND SEE": SOME NEW TESTAMENT USES OF IMPAIRMENT, INABILITY, AND PARADOX

Simon Horne

Tell out what you see and hear: those who are blind see, those who are lame walk, and those who are deaf hear. (Matthew 11:4-5)[1]

Impairment and inability in the New Testament are not simply conditions that Jesus eliminates. In the stories of healing in the Christian Scriptures, impairment and inability play a much more important role than does their removal. Impairment and inability are interpretive devices, used by the writers of the New Testament to express themes central to their message. In the ancient world, impairment and inability are frequently understood as paradox—within inability is striking capability. This association is often used to interpret and express both the activity of God in Jesus' life and the response of discipleship.

In exploring this theme of paradox, I focus on two broad areas in the New Testament. First, I follow three characters with impairments who are used in representative ways to embody both the process of coming to discipleship and also particular discipleship qualities taught by Jesus. In the texts of Scripture and the early Church's use of these texts in liturgy, hearers of the word and worshippers are led to identify with these characters who have impairments. These figures are explicitly contrasted with able-bodied characters; paradoxically, the ones who have ability in body, often model inability in faith and discipleship. Second, I explore Paul's uses of inability imagery to interpret the paradoxical activity of God, as epitomized in God's direct statement to Paul, "My power is made complete in inability" (II Corinthians 12:9, author's translation). Paul develops this paradox in terms of the inability of Christ, of Paul's own inabilities, and of inability within the body of Christ.

In the Greco-Roman world, paradox occurring in nature was greatly admired. It was also something to be carefully crafted by artists. Aristotle writes that the greatest effect on the mind, the mind's particular pleasure, was to witness in drama events happening "contrary to expectation, yet necessary from what has gone before." This classic paradox produces in the mind "a marvelous effect."[2] Paradox in this classic form was at the heart of Jesus' life and teaching: what he said and did was both unexpected and within tradition. Wherever he went, he said and did things that people did not expect; yet time and again, Jesus made it clear that what he was saying and doing was in fulfillment of the Law and the prophets. Paradox is used in a general way to emphasize the marvelous works of Jesus: in the previous quotation from Matthew's Gospel, nouns of inability and corresponding verbs of ability are set side by side: "Those who are blind see"; "those who are lame walk"; "those who are deaf hear."[3]

In ancient literature, including the texts of Scripture, paradox is associated with inability in a particular way: *within inability is striking capability.* Across Graeco-Roman texts of many genres, and also in scriptural narrative, this paradox of inability is embodied by people with physical impairments. On the one hand, people with impairments visibly lack a degree of physical ability; on the other, they are endowed with significant and unexpected abilities in other respects, sometimes as a consequence of their impairment. One common use made of this inability paradox by ancient writers is in the blind person who sees. As if to underline the axiom's truth, the authority held in greatest respect in ancient society for his insight into human and divine affairs was a blind person, the epic poet Homer. "Homer was the object of deep reverence in ancient Greece; his writings came to be regarded as a source of general wisdom and were constantly quoted."[4] Such was the belief that physical blindness and enlightened insight went together that the philosopher Democritus made himself blind:

A man worthy of reverence beyond all others and of the highest authority, of his own accord deprived himself of eyesight, because he believed that the thoughts and meditations of his mind in examining nature's laws would be more vivid and exact, if he should free them from the allurements of sight and the distractions offered by the eyes.[5]

A similar association of peculiar insight with people without physical sight is shown by Aristotle, who states as fact that "the blind remember better (than the sighted), being released from having their faculty of memory engaged with objects that are seen."[6] A social commentator of the first century C.E., Dio Chrysostom, writes of blind poets that they had clearly caught from Homer both inspiration and eye disease: "They do not believe it possible to become a poet otherwise."[7] Amongst the great characters of myth, Phineus was the blind seer who guided Jason and the Argonauts.[8] The blind prophet Teiresias saw through the tyrant Oedipus—a paradox that Oedipus ridicules when physically sighted; later, as a person physically blind, Oedipus understood the truth of the paradox: "All the words I utter have sight."[9]

This particular paradox of the insightful blind person is used too by the writers of Scripture. In the example surveyed here, the theme being used to illustrate both coming to discipleship and particular aspects of discipleship is embodied by people with impairments. The first example, treated ably in the previous chapter by Colleen Grant, is found in John 9, the blind man who comes to belief in Jesus (v. 38) while enlightened religious leaders speak their inability to see: "Are we also blind?" (v. 40, author's translation). John uses this blind person who sees in a representative way to exemplify the process of coming to full faith. At first, the blind person sees Jesus as a man (v. 11), then as a prophet (v. 17), later as the one who can identify for him the Son of Man (v. 36); but in his final statement of faith his insight is made complete: "Lord, I believe" (v. 38). Pressing home the blind seer paradox, John continues to refer to the person as blind, even after the healing (v. 17).[10]

In addition, the blind person is used to demonstrate a particular aspect of discipleship: obedience. This theme is reinforced by the repetition of verse 7 in verse 11: the person follows Jesus' instructions precisely, and he does so in the pool called "Sent" (*Siloam*). This hearing and following of the word is a discipleship quality illustrated by Jesus in his teaching, for example in the parable of the two builders (Matthew 7:24-27; Luke 6:46-49): "Everyone who hears these words of mine and acts on them will be like someone wise enough to build a house on a rock" (Matthew 7:24).[11]

A second person with an impairment who embodies discipleship is Bartimaeus (Mark 10:46-52; Luke 18:35-43). From initial inquiry,

Bartimaeus moves to the first unfocused calling out, provoking the hostility of those around him. When personally called by Jesus, he reacts eagerly. And at the moment of direct encounter, he is asked to speak the desire of his heart and receives, committing himself in full discipleship and glorifying God—he "followed Jesus on the way" (Mark 10:52*b*). In addition, Bartimaeus embodies the quality of persistence taught by Jesus in the parables of the friend in the night and the judge and the widow (Luke 11:5-13 and 18:1-8). Bartimaeus's persistence is seen most clearly in his refusal to be put off by the crowd rebuking him. But his persistence also leads Bartimaeus to complete the process of full discipleship. His commitment to follow Jesus on the way is the fulfillment of the quality of persistence that he embodies.

The stories of Bartimaeus and of the blind person in John 9 are generally categorized simply as incidents of healing. Certainly the healing of their impairment is an important theme in both stories, but healing is not the sole or even the predominant theme. Great interest in these characters with impairments is generated by the unusual extent of detail about them and of the reported dialog that they have with Jesus. This interest is then focused toward their representation of the discipleship process and attendant qualities.

Early Church writers also follow this pattern in interpreting the accounts. For example, in his commentary on Matthew's version of the Bartimaeus story, John Chrysostom identifies the representative role of those in the narrative with physical impairments who embody the discipleship quality of persistence, explicitly in contrast to those with physical sight. For this reason, he says of the people with impairments, "Let us then emulate them!"[12] Similarly, in early Christian art the blind person of John 9 is used to represent people about to commit themselves to full discipleship in baptism.[13] Associating paradox and inability, both Bartimaeus and the blind person of John 9 carry out their modeling role explicitly as persons with an impairment. Both are contrasted to people who have sight but who lack the ability to see as the people who are blind can see (Mark 10:48, Luke 18:39, compare John 9:40).

A third character with a physical impairment who demonstrates the process and qualities of discipleship is the apostle Paul, formerly known as Saul. In the story of Saul's conversion in the Acts of the Apostles 9, Saul's physical impairment plays a central role. First, Saul's sudden physical blindness demonstrates that he has encountered the Lord.[14] Second, Saul's physical blindness is contrasted with the dawning of his faith. It is only as a blind person that Saul has the ability to address Jesus as "Lord"(v. 5). Although a zealous Pharisee passionate for God and saturated in God's law, Saul develops trust when he is given a physical impairment: "He could see nothing, so they led him by the hand" (v. 8). This unbidden, enforced experience of trust ignites Saul's process of becoming a disciple: from direct encounter, to partial understanding, to full insight and discipleship (v. 20).

As with the qualities of obedience and persistence embodied by the blind person of John 9 and Bartimaeus, the quality of trust that Saul as a blind person embodies is a characteristic of the discipleship, as taught by Jesus. For example, when foretelling their persecutions, Jesus tells his followers, "You will be brought before rulers and governors. . . . make up your minds not to prepare your defense in advance; for I will give you words and . . . wisdom" (Luke 21:12-15).[15] While Bartimaeus and the blind man in John 9 illustrate paradox in their contrast with the unseeing able-bodied people, Saul embodies paradox in another way. The fact that Saul ever embarks on the process to discipleship is paradoxical, as we see from the reactions of Ananias (Acts 9:13), of the synagogue congregation (Acts 9:21), and the disciples in Jerusalem (Acts 9:26). But Saul has the ability to start this process only when he is given a physical inability; only when he is a person with an impairment can Saul address Jesus as Lord and begin the process toward becoming an apostle—the giving of his physical blindness mirrors the taking away of his faith blindness.

Like the processes embodied both by Bartimaeus and the blind man in John 9, the stages in Saul's coming to discipleship were also put to representative use by the early Church. Each of the elements detailed in the Acts narrative of Saul's conversion are reproduced in early Church liturgies of baptism: being led to the one appointed for the task, fasting beforehand, the laying on of hands, being filled with the Spirit, coming to sight/insight, rising up, the baptism itself, taking food and being strengthened immediately afterwards.[16] The stages of Saul's discipleship are used in early baptismal liturgy representatively for all people coming to baptism.[17]

In his own writings, Paul boasts in his inabilities (II Corinthians 12:5-10). The word he uses here is *astheneiai*—usually, and sometimes inappropriately, translated "weakness." This is a word used both of impairment itself and of people with impairments (e.g., Acts 4:9, Luke 13:11). Paul repeatedly contrasts *astheneiai* with the word *dunamis*, which has as its primary meaning "ability."[18] So in this context of Paul's contrast with *dunamis*, it is appropriate to translate *astheneiai* as "inabilities."

Paul relishes the paradox of inability, using it to interpret his experience of the paradoxical activity of God. In two verses, Paul makes several paradoxical statements about inabilities in which *astheneiai* and *dunamis* are contrasted (II Corinthians 12:9-10). First, God has spoken to him directly, saying, "My power is made complete, (is fulfilled) in inability (*dunamis en astheneia teleitai*)." Second, Paul will boast all the more in his inabilities, "that the power of Christ may rest upon me," and for the sake of Christ, Paul is content with his inabilities, as with other difficulties that result from his discipleship, for "When I lack ability, then I am able."[19]

Paul quotes the message spoken to him without mediation. Seemingly a direct statement from God is required to express such a paradox. How can it be that God's power is made complete in inability? God is the God of supreme ability, to create and to overcome (e.g., Job 41, Psalm 74:14), to save and to destroy (e.g., Matthew 26:53). God's capability is contrasted to the false gods, whose inabilities are ridiculed (e.g., I Kings 18:18-39, Psalm 115:3-7). So how is it that this awesome power of God is made complete in inability?

For Paul, the heart of his message is Christ crucified (I Corinthians 1:23, 2:2; Galatians 6:14). The words themselves are an oxymoron—Christ, the Messiah, the Anointed of God; crucified—dispossessed of all dignity, ability, and life. Paul tells us that this is a paradox too for both Jew and Gentile: the glory of heaven made manifest in the cross, "the most appalling object of antiquity."[20] But we are told at various places in the New Testament that what occurred at that crucifixion was the fulfillment, the making complete of God's power and love in Christ (for example, *tetelestai*, John 19:30).[21] This fulfillment of God's power and love occurred through Christ's inability—first when he laid aside his glory and abilities in being born in human form (II Corinthians 8:9; Philippians 2:6-8) and second in the stripping of his glory and abilities on the cross itself. "He was crucified out of his inability" (*ex astheneias*, II Corinthians 13:4, author's translation). Mark records that on the cross, what Jesus is mocked for is his inability: "He could save others; he is unable to save himself" (Mark 15:31, author's translation). On the cross, Jesus redeemed and saved all people, reconciling humankind with God (Romans 5:10-21; Galatians 3:13); paradoxically, all this Jesus did "out of his inability" (author's translation).

A similar theme is found in the Old Testament, in a passage so rich with this paradox of inability that it is often taken in Christian Scripture to foreshadow Jesus' own passion: the servant song of Isaiah 52:13–53:12 (see for example Matthew 27:12-14, Acts 8:32-33, I Peter 2:23-24). In this Isaiah passage, five words of physical impairment are applied to the Servant.[22] The images constructed with these words of physical impairment are used to accentuate the contrast between what seems to be happening and what in fact is happening. Those observing the Servant believe that his impotence is evidence of being struck by God. In fact, the Servant's inability is willed by God and is highly effective: "We accounted him maimed by God. . . . But by his wounds we are healed" (author's translation)."Yet it was the will of the LORD to crush him. . . . Through him the will of the LORD shall prosper" (Isaiah 53:4-5,10). At the heart of this inability paradox is the image of the lamb's muteness, "like a lamb that is led to the slaughter is silent [mute], so he did not open his mouth" (Isaiah 53:7). The mute lamb is an ambiguous image, and the ambiguity is the fulcrum of the passage. The image signifies both inability (e.g., as muteness does at Psalm 39:9) and also obedience (e.g., Psalm 38:13-15). In the Servant's inability, ambiguously both powerless and obedient, the power of God is paradoxically being fulfilled.

God's power is also fulfilled in the inabilities of Paul himself. It was because of some physical inability that Paul was able first to preach to the people of Galatia (Galatians 4:13). This or some other physical inability, along with Paul's ineloquence or even speech impairment, clearly troubled the Corinthians (II Corinthians 10:10). But these inabilities were the very proof that the wisdom he spoke did not originate in Paul's own ability, "but in the power of God" (I Corinthians 2:1-5). Paul says something similar at II Corinthians 4:7: "We have this treasure in clay jars, so that it may be made clear that this extraordinary power belongs to God and does not come from us." Perhaps consciously, Paul invites a comparison with Moses, whose own speech impairment was evidence that it was God who spoke through him; God chose in Moses someone with such an inability "in order that people might not say that it was his eloquence which convinced Israel"[23] (see Exodus 4:10-11).

Paul not only boasts in his inabilities, he maintains it is evidence "that the power of Christ may rest upon me" (II Corinthians 12:9*b*, author's translation). The word Paul uses here is unique in the New Testament and is very striking, *episkenose.* The image is a tent, *skene,* set up as the place where the power of Christ is present and abides. The allusion is to the tabernacle, the tent of meeting, "the central place of worship . . . the location of revelation . . . the visible sign of Yahweh's presence among the people of Israel."[24] For example, Exodus 40:34 reads: "Then the cloud covered the tent of meeting, and the glory of the LORD filled the tabernacle" (in the Septuagint, here and throughout, *skene* is used of the tent of meeting, the tabernacle). The tabernacle has particular significance in the Leviticus tradition: in that tradition, the tabernacle was regarded as "the only locus of sacrifice."[25] So it is with some irony that the tent of meeting in which the power of Christ comes to be present and abide is located at Paul's inabilities (II Corinthians 12:9). For within this Leviticus tradition in which the tabernacle image is so significant, inabilities excluded a person, specifically a priest, from drawing near to the divine presence to make sacrifice. This includes both literal inabilities, as in the Leviticus impairment passages, exegeted by Sarah Melcher in chapter 2, relating to priests and sacrifices (Leviticus 21:16-23), and also figurative inabilities, as in Hebrews 7:27-28. Paul reverses this Leviticus tradition: Paul states that inabilities are the place where God's power is made complete and that inabilities are the place where Christ's power comes to abide.[26]

Paul's use of the tabernacle image to describe inabilities as the place of Christ's abiding is reminiscent of Isaiah 57:15. Here we see that God abides, God becomes directly present, in the heart that is maimed: "I abide in the high and holy place, also with the one whose spirit is crushed and maimed, to give life to the spirit of the one who is maimed and life to the heart of the one who is crushed" (author's translation). The image of physical impairment is being applied to the heart and spirit. The impaired heart, crushed and maimed, is an image for true repentance—a state that God desires: "The sacrifice acceptable to God is a crushed spirit, a crushed and maimed heart" (Psalm 51:17, author's translation). As with Paul's use of the tabernacle image, this image of the maimed heart in Isaiah and the Psalms, where God's presence abides, reverses the Leviticus tradition that an impaired sacrifice was deemed unacceptable to God and an impaired person unable to draw near to God's presence.

In both these passages of Isaiah and Paul, the place of inability and impairment is the place of divine presence and abiding. Paul says that he boasts in his inabilities so that Christ's power may come to abide and be present; Isaiah says that God comes to abide in the heart that is impaired, to inspire new life.[27] But the similarity in these passages of Isaiah and Paul goes further than the image of God simply abiding. In both, divine power is made complete in inability: in Paul divine power is fulfilled, and clearly so, through Paul's inabilities; in Isaiah the repentant heart, characterized by the image of being maimed, is the vehicle into which divine power breathes new life, new creation.

A third example Paul gives of God's power through inability is within the body of Christ. At I Corinthians 12:12-31, Paul states that all the members of Christ's body are held together in a relationship of mutual concern. He uses the word *merimnosin* (v. 25), "being concerned about, occupied or involved with." Paul emphasizes that this relationship is mutual, regardless of ability or status. It is "the same involvement, one with another" (v. 25). Paul also states that this is how God has arranged, chosen, and intended Christ's body to be (vv. 11, 18, 24, and 28). According to Paul, God's purpose for constructing Christ's body in such a way is quite specific: to prevent the body falling apart (v. 25). Within this purpose of God for the body as a whole, one particular group is singled out by Paul as indispensable (v. 22): those parts of the body who seem to be without ability or respect (vv. 22-24). To these parts God gives extra honor (v. 24), because it is they, not the parts apparently more able and respected, who have the particular role of holding together Christ's body (vv. 22-25).

As someone whose partner is a wheelchair user and as a priest in parish ministry, I find truth in the paradox of inability in a number of ways. One in particular I mention here: people with impairments are widely denied access to full life of the church, but their experience as people living impairment is a requirement for the life of the church to be full. A specific way in which this is revealed is in the understanding of the impairment texts of Scripture. Archaeology and literature from the ancient world show that people with impairments were present and active at all levels of society. They were widely seen and known in the cultures from which the Christian Scriptures emerged.[28] Images of impairment and characters in narrative who have impairments are used in the Old and New Testaments for many purposes and to express many notions. However, in modern Western cultures at least, people with impairments are not present and active at all levels of society, nor are they widely seen and known. Thus those uses and purposes of impairment in Scripture have in many cases become lost to us. The experience of those people who are currently living with impairment will unlock the impairment texts of Scripture, whose riches at present remain largely hidden.

One such key for understanding these impairment texts is the distinction people with impairments make between impairment and disability. I quote the form used by Disabled Peoples International:

> Impairment is the lack of part of or all of a limb, or having a defective limb, organ or mechanism of the body; Disability is the loss or limitation of opportunities that prevents people who have impairments from taking part in the normal life of the community on an equal level with others due to physical and social barriers.[29]

This distinction is useful for people who experience their impairment as not outside God's will, in contrast to their experience of disability. My partner, Mel, is such a person. In a recent conversation, she said, "My impairment is genetic, so when I was made, God included my impairment, and I have no problems with that. What I do have problems with is the fact that society disables me. God did not make me to be someone who is disabled by society." Some parallels to this can be seen in Scripture. God wills impairment; for example, "Then the Lord said to him [Moses], 'Who gives speech to mortals? Who makes them mute or deaf, seeing or blind? Is it not I, the Lord?'" (Exodus 4:11). Compare as well Paul's understanding of the purposeful creation by God of people who seem less able (I Corinthians 12:22-5). However, God abhors the creation of social disability; for example, "You shall not revile the deaf or put a stumbling block before the blind" (Leviticus 19:14); or "Cursed be anyone who misleads a blind person on the road" (Deuteronomy 27:18).[30]

The impairment/disability distinction also opens up an image that Paul uses of God at I Corinthians 1:25: "The inability of God is more able than human ability" (author's translation). Paul does not explain this further, and biblical commentators largely ignore the passage. However, through discussion with people currently living with impairment, this image of God's inability takes on clearer meaning. For people living with impairment, and for their partners and families, dependence is a significant part of life. But living dependently is living in the image of God. For God's power is graciously made limited through human beings' free will. In the giving of this gift to us, God has chosen to be to an extent dependent on us, dependent on human response to the promptings of our consciences. In this dependence on us, God experiences both impairment and disability. The giving of free will to human beings is an impairment of God's ability, which, like human impairment, God chooses, wills, and purposes. But this limiting of God's ability—God's impairment—like human impairment, is wide open to abuse. God is easily disabled, as the person with an impairment is disabled by her partner who refuses to do what she asks or does so grudgingly or with ill temper, so God is disabled by us when we refuse to do what God asks of us or when we do so grudgingly or with ill temper. In Paul's use of the image, God's inability is more able than human ability. God has resources beyond simply using us, who can and do refuse to follow or obey. Even so, our enabling or disabling of God is as delicate as the whisper of our conscience.

In conclusion, I have shown the ways in which impairment, inability, and paradox are used by the writers of the New Testament. In narrative, characters with impairments embody the process of full discipleship and particular qualities, such as obedience, persistence, and trust. Both in Scripture and the liturgy of the early Church people with impairments model this process and these qualities. Paul interprets and expresses the activity of God in Jesus that stimulates this faith and discipleship using inability imagery. For at the heart of Paul's message is the paradox of Christ crucified—God's power made complete in inability. This same paradox of inability illustrates for Paul the activity of God in his own inabilities and the indispensable role of those people who appear less able in holding together as Christ's body. Much of Paul's understanding of the inability paradox is present in passages from the Old Testament: in the effective working of God through the suffering Servant, contrary to all expectation, and in the abiding of God in the maimed heart, into which new life is breathed and new creation brought about. Here, too, in the Jewish tradition, the power of God is paradoxically made complete in inability.

The writers of the New Testament and the compilers of early Church liturgy have laid the foundations of our faith and discipleship.

To these people, impairment and inability are not objects of shame or guilt; they are not parts of life to be got rid of or hidden away or kept at a distance from the presence of God. Quite the opposite: to these people—as they struggle to understand and interpret how God was active in the life of Jesus of Nazareth and how this activity of God in Jesus continues to encounter and be experienced by humankind both personally and corporately—impairments and inability are a paradoxical cornerstone.

---

1. Generally in this chapter, quotations from the Old Testament are in the translation of the *New Revised Standard Version* and those from the New Testament in *The New Testament and Psalms: An Inclusive Version* (New York: Oxford University Press, 1995). Occasionally, to highlight the use of impairment imagery, my own translation is used.
2. Aristotle, *Poetics.* Loeb Classical Library, vol. XXIII, trans. S. Halliwell (London: Heinemann, 1927), 9.1452a
3. The Greek text makes the paradox clearer than many English translations, which in overemphasizing the *ana-* prefix of *anablepousin*, lose the word's meaning of simply seeing—looking up or looking straight, in addition to 'regaining sight.' See H.G. Liddell and R. Scott, *Greek-English Lexicon*, 9th ed., revised, H. S. Jones (Oxford: Oxford University Press, 1968), 99; G. W. H. Lampe, *A Patristic Greek Lexicon* (Oxford: Oxford University Press, 1968), 96; W. Bauer, *Greek-English Lexicon of the New Testament and Other Early Christian Literature*, 2d ed., revised, W. F. Arndt, and F. W. Gingrich (Chicago: University of Chicago Press, 1979), 50-51. Making the paradox clear, the Vulgate versions of this text have simply *Caeci vident*, "Those who are blind see." Both Hebrew and Greek versions of the Isaiah verses to which Matthew alludes (29:18, 35:5, 42:18) also emphasize the paradox clearly.
4. P. Harvey, *The Oxford Companion to Classical Literature* (Oxford: Clarendon Press, 1937), 213. Cf. Jasper Griffin, *Homer* (Oxford: Oxford University Press, 1980), 78. Some examples of allusions to Homer's blindness and insight include "Homeric Hymn to Apollo" Hesiod, *Homeric Hymns, Epic Cycles, Homerica,* trans. H.G. Evelyn-White (London: Heinemann, 1914), 172. Thucydides, *History of the Peloponnesian War,* trans. C.F. Smith (London: Heinemann, 1920), 3.104; Loeb Classical Library *Greek Anthology,* vol. I, trans. W.R. Paton (London: Heinemann, 1916) 2.33; Pindar, *Nemean Odes,* trans. J. E. Sandys (London: Heinemann,1915), 7.23-30.
5. Democritus: *Aulus Gellius, Noctes Atticae,* trans. John. L. Rolfe (London: Heinemann, 1927), 259-61.
6. Aristotle: *Eudemian Ethics,* Loeb Classical Library, vol. XX, trans. H. Rackham (London: Heinemann, 1935), 1248b.
7. Dio Chrysostom: *Discourses,* 36:10f Loeb Classical Library, vol. III, trans. H.L. Crosby (London: Heinemann, 1940).
8. Apollonius Rhodius, *Argonautica,* 2:341-43, 647-49; Loeb Classical Library, trans. R.C. Seaton (London: Heinemann, 1912), 341-43, 647-49.
9. Sophocles, *Oedipus Tyrannos,* 370f e: *Oedipus at Colonnus,* 73f., Loeb Classical Library, vol. I-II, trans. Hugh Lloyd-Jones (London: Heinemann, 1994).
10. Compare too the juxtaposition of words in verse 25: *tuphlos on arti blepo-* literally, "being a blind person I am just now seeing."
11. Compare to Jesus' parable of the two sons, Matthew 21:28-32.
12. John Chrysostom, *Homilies on the Gospel of Matthew,* (Oxford: J. H. Parker, 1854), 58.626.25.
13. On the use of the blind person of John 9 in early Church art, see F.M. Braun, *Jean le théologian* (Paris: Gabalda, 1959), 149-60; Raymond E. Brown, *The Gospel According to John 1-12* (Garden City, N.Y.: Doubleday, 1966), 380-82. Brown also demonstrates current Roman Catholic use of this story in baptismal liturgy. On the use of the story in early Church baptismal liturgy, see also E. Hoskyns and F. N. Davey, *The Fourth Gospel,* 2d ed. (London: Faber and Faber, 1947), 350-5, 363-65.

14. Compare Saul's experience with Isaiah, Daniel, and Micah each of whom had a temporary impairment related to their encounter with God. Isaiah and Daniel are unable to speak until their lips are touched: Isaiah 6:6-7; Daniel 10:15-16 (Daniel elsewhere loses his abilities in general: 8:27, *holeh*). Micah describes inability to speak and deafness as reactions of the nations to the Lord's epiphany: Micah 7:16. Cf. Jacob and Zechariah, who are both given an impairment at their divine encounter (Genesis 32:31, a mobility impairment; Luke 1:21-22, inability to speak).

15. Further examples include Jesus' teaching in the Sermon on the Mount, God "knows that you need all these things. . . . So do not worry" (Matthew 6:25-34, AIV) and the parable of the growing seed, "the seed would sprout and grow, without the farmer's knowing how" (Mark 4:26-29, AIV). Cf. Jesus' prediction to Peter that his unwilling and enforced dependence will be a mark of his discipleship "by which Peter would glorify God" (John 21:18-19, AIV).

16. Cf. Acts 9:9-18 with the texts of the Ante-Nicene Church collected in E. C. Whitaker, *Documents of the Baptismal Liturgy* (London: S.P.C.K., 1960), 1-20.

17. In current liturgies too people being baptised are explicitly led to identify with two of these same people with impairments: the blind Saul, e.g., Roy Kerridge, *The Storm is Passing Over: A Look at Black Churches in Britain* (London: Thames and Hudson, 1996), 76-81, 144-47; and the blind person of John 9, e.g., "Christian Initiation of Adults: Reading and Prayers for Fourth Sunday of Lent," *The Sunday Missal,* rev. ed. (London: Collins, 1984), 186-93.

18. See Liddell & Scott, *Greek-English,* 452. The same contrast is found in the Septuagint, e.g. I Kings 2:5; Job 36:15.

19. Author's translations. Paul's use of a similar paradox with particular reference to II Corinthians 3-4 is discussed in Timothy B. Savage, *Power Through Weakness: Paul's Understanding of the Christian Ministry in 2 Corinthians* (Cambridge: Cambridge University Press, 1996), 162-63; 185-90. In the first part of II Corinthians 12:9, God states to Paul, "My grace is sufficient for you." This phrase is discussed in F. M. Young & D. F. Ford, *Meaning and Truth in 2 Corinthians* (Grand Rapids: Eerdmans, 1987), 67; 103; 128-29; 173-74.

20. Savage, *Power Through Weakness,* 188; 1 Corinthians 1:23ff.

21. This is the same verb as II Corinthians 12:9 "My power is made complete in inability." Cf. Hebrews 2:10, 5:9; 1 John 2:5.

22. Isaiah 52:14, *shahath* (cf. Mal. 1:14); Isaiah 53:4, *makah* (cf. Jer 14:17); Isaiah 53:5, *dakah* (cf. Ps 51:8); Isaiah 53:7, *'ilem* (cf. Isaiah 35:6, Ps. 38:14); Isaiah 53:10, *holeh* (cf. Mal. 1:8).

23. W. G. Plaut, *The Torah: A Modern Commentary,* (New York: Union of American Hebrew Congregations, 1981), 408. Cf. N. M. Sarna, *Exodus,* (Philadelphia: Jewish Publication Society, 1991), 21.

24. Richard Elliott Friedman, s.v. "Tabernacle," *Anchor Bible Dictionary,* vol. 6, ed. David Noel Freedman et al., (New York: Doubleday, 1992), 292. Cf. "The function of the Tabernacle was to create a means by which a continued avenue of communication with God could be maintained . . . a visible, tangible symbol of God's everabiding Presence in their midst," Sarna, *Exodus,* 237.

25. Friedman, "Tabernacle," *Anchor,* 300.

26. In the Tabernacle, God spoke to Moses directly (e.g., Leviticus 1:1). This was Paul's own experience: God spoke to Paul directly in his inabilities—both his blindness and his "thorn in the flesh" (Acts 9:4-5; II Corinthians 12:9). On inability as a place where God abides and speaks directly, see Jean Vanier, *Community and Growth* (London: Darton, Longman and Todd, 1979), 191-93, 199-206, 210-11; *The Broken Body* (London: Darton, Longman and Todd, 1981), 2-3, 60-63, 70-76, 92-94, 99-101, 134-35; Frances Young, *Face to Face,* rev. ed. (Edinburgh: T & T Clark, 1990), 69-93, 143-65, 178-95; Cf. Nancy L. Eiesland, *The Disabled God: Towards a Liberatory Theology of Disability* (Nashville: Abingdon Press, 1994), 89-105, 107-19.

27. As at creation and at the valley of the dry bones: Genesis 2:7; Ezekiel 37:5-6, 10.

28. For example, Richard N. Jones, s.v. "Paleopathology," *Anchor Bible Dictionary,* vol. 5, 67: "Trauma, accidental and afflicted, was one of the most common causes of injury and disability, and is one of the most frequent causes of pathological conditions apparent in ancient skeletal remains . . . A variety of states of disability must have existed anciently owing to many causes." On the uses of characters with impairments in ancient literature, see Lynn Holden, *Forms of Deformity* (Sheffield: Sheffield Academic Press, 1991); on uses of specific impairment imagery in biblical literature, see Craig A. Evans, *To See and Not Perceive* (Sheffield: Sheffield Academic

Press, 1989); on impairment in literature and art of Greco-Roman culture, see Robert Garland, *The Eye of the Beholder* (London: Duckworth, 1995).

29. This form of the definition is given in Vic Finkelstein and Sally French, "Towards a Psychology of Disability," in *Disabling Barriers—Enabling Environments,* John Swain et. al., ed. (London: Sage Publications in assoc. with The Open University Press, 1993), 28; cf. Michael Oliver, *The Politics of Disablement* (Basingstoke: Macmillan, 1990), 2-11.

30. Cf. the prophet's criticism of political leaders at Ezekiel 34:4, where the Hebrew words commonly translated "weak" and "injured" are words used of impairment—*holeh, shabar.*

PART II.

THEOLOGICAL REFLECTION

Having examined in detail some major issues confronting the use of biblical materials in discourse about human disability and impairment, the next three chapters offer instances of explicit theological reasoning. Jürgen Moltmann (Chapter 5) portrays the central theme of Christ's acceptance as the source and model for an approach to persons excluded or marginalized from the churches because of disability. Social liberation of persons with disabilities is indeed revolutionary for those who presume their able-bodiness, for it is grounded in God's radical love and in the claim that every disability is also a gift. Here we see a clear outline of a liberationist view of the calling of religious communities to receive and to learn from persons with disabilities.

Barbara Patterson (Chapter 6) picks up a theme from St. Augustine, rendering a poetically reconceived notion of realized eschatology in liturgical practices. Linking liturgy and a particular reading of incarnation, this essay points beyond the often fearful and implicitly gnostic views held implicitly by many. The heart of her proposal leads to empowering our practice with an eschatological vision of the human body in the image of God, marked indelibly by Christian realism about the body.

Jan Robitscher (Chapter 7) moves from her own personal experiences as a sight-impaired cantor and liturgically trained pastoral theologian to basic issues of space and liturgical adequacy. For her, matters of justice and pastoral concern are intrinsic to the nature of Christian liturgy. Thus, attempts to bypass or to ignore the gifts of persons of disability for liturgy diminish the very act of gathering for Word and Sacrament. She points the way toward a more ample theological perception of liturgical life and the pastoral/ecclesial issues we must face honestly and with integrity born of reflective faith.

CHAPTER FIVE

LIBERATE YOURSELVES BY ACCEPTING ONE ANOTHER

Jürgen Moltmann

Translator's Preface:

This article was originally published in *Diakonie im Horizont des Reiches Gottes* (Neukirchener Verlag, Second edition, 1989). The original introductory paragraphs were particular to that setting and seemed out of place in the context of this book. Also, while some small changes have been made better to reflect idiomatic English, it seemed important in other places to let the more literal translation stand, even if it was not as politically correct in the current North American context. This is particularly true of biblical echos of terms such as the blind, lame, and dumb.
Ulrike R.M. Guthrie

WE HAVE LIMITATIONS AND DIFFICULTIES

I begin with the conviction that there are fundamentally no "persons with disabilities," but rather only "people": people with this or that difficulty on the basis of which the society of the strong and capable declares them to be "disabled" and consequently more or less excludes them from public life. And yet they are people with the same human worth and the same human rights as each and every person. We need to stop focusing only on the problems of the other and stop labeling him or her in terms of a problem by referring to them as "disabled." Instead, we need to begin to discover in the "disabled" person another selfhood and honor her dignity, for she is in fact just like you and me.

Accepting Oneself Publicly

I firmly believe that liberation of oneself comes before mutual liberation. One can only accept another when one has first found oneself. One can only accept another person when one has first freed oneself of everything that oppresses and estranges, everything that makes oneself look small, ugly, and worthless in one's own eyes. To "accept one another" presupposes that we have found our independence, our worth, our self-confidence, and that we therefore act out of a sense of freedom and gift each other with freedom through mutual acceptance. Only she who has found herself can accept other people without oppressing them or becoming a burden to them. Only he who is self-aware can allow himself to be helped by others in times of difficulty without feeling demeaned and humiliated. A person who has a strong sense of self-confidence needs feel no shame about anything. I want to talk about this freedom of the soul before expounding on the commandment of this freedom, the acceptance of other persons.

Love of Self as Measure and Strength of Love of Neighbor

"Love your neighbor as yourself," says the biblical command of humanitarianism. We're used to focusing only on the first part of this phrase: "Love your neighbor." But the second part of the phrase is part and parcel of it; it is in fact the presupposition for the first part: "Love your neighbor as yourself." So one is supposed to love oneself, and one is to love one's neighbor in the manner that one loves oneself. In the love commandment love of self is not forbidden or rejected but rather allowed, encouraged, and quite naturally assumed. Love of self is the measure and strength of love of neighbor. Love of self comes first, love of neighbor second. Love of self is the secret of happiness and freedom in our lives and in our dealings with one another.

To verify this, let's just consider: How can someone who doesn't love himself love his neighbor? How can someone who can't bear herself tolerate her neighbor? Won't someone who despises himself also scorn his fellow humans? Will someone who is full of rage toward himself and his fate not also want to aggressively disrupt his environment? Won't a person who hates herself also hate her neighbor?

Self-hate is the agony of hell, for hate of self is the power of destruction. In contrast, love of self is the power of heaven, which makes every person free and happy. True love of self has absolutely nothing to do with egoism. Egoism is born of the fear of falling short, and it is a battle a person has with herself and with others to make life hell and to destroy all the beauty of life. Egoism is not self-love at all, but rather a type of self-hate. Depression and aggression are closely related. And in the same way egoism and self-hate are merely two sides of the same coin: two aspects of a lost love of self. It is here that the liberation of a person to his full humanity begins: Love yourself, for you are good! Respect yourself, for you are worthy. Be a friend to yourself! I will therefore begin with a discussion of love of self and only then move on to love of neighbor. Before we talk about the integration of persons with disabilities into society and communal life, we want to go in search of our concealed self worth.

THE LIBERATION OF PERSONS WITH DISABILITIES

Oppressed slaves revolted, fought against their masters, and gained their liberation. Exploited workers have organized their solidarity in trade unions and gained their rights. Is there such a thing as a liberation of persons with disabilities?

Becoming Free from Excessive Restraints

There is and must be such a thing as the liberation of persons with disabilities if people are to live together humanely. But first we must take note of a difference: There are burdens that people lay upon other people, and there are burdens with which people are burdened by nature. There are congenital and lifelong disabilities in persons, which can neither be corrected or removed. One has to learn to live with them and to love oneself in the midst of them. But there are also the unjust disabilities created by other people and as a result of the laws of public life of this society of persons without disabilities. No one should just accept this disabling of persons with disabilities. Neither persons with or without disabilities can bear to live with such injustice. Pastor Ulrich Bach rightly distinguishes between being disadvantaged by a disability and being disadvantaged by the rest of society. For a more humane community to emerge from this divided society, we must liberate ourselves from this annoyingly unnecessary disabling of those with disabilities, and we must do it together, those with disabilities and those without.

Free for Necessary Protest

The social liberation of persons with disabilities of course does not come primarily as a result of the good will of those without disabilities but through the efforts of those with disabilities themselves, and only secondarily through those persons without disabilities who are sufficiently liberated and able to listen to persons with disabilities. It is not only that persons with disabilities are allowed to protest against their social disadvantaging and against their spiritual oppression through the advantaging of other people; they in fact must. A person in this position who does not protest gives up on himself. The protest of persons with disabilities against their social disadvantaging is an expression of love, of love of self and love of neighbor.

It is a sign of hope that the voices of those with disabilities in our country, though untrained and scattered, are nonetheless finally becoming too loud to be ignored. The message to "Conform, for you are reliant on other people and dependent on them," has been preached too long to those with disabilities. In order to survive in the world of the hardworking, they had to learn the role of the humble and eternally thankful one. They were often treated like little, underage children. All that remained for them was sadness over their fate and silent self-pity. That route leads only to self-hate. It does not lead to self-confidence.

Faith Encourages Breaking Away

Every person, even the one with disabilities, can do more than she believes herself capable of. Why? Because there are so many things one doesn't believe one can do because one is afraid of defeat. A person who withdraws and retreats into herself out of fear never learns to explore her capabilities. It is only when one opts to step beyond one's limits that one comes to know those limits.

There are people who think everything is impossible. "There's no point" they say from the get-go. "Nothing will come of it," and, "I can't." In doing so they spare themselves conflict, many pains, and also some defeats. Yet they also experience nothing of real life. But there are also those people who believe in the possible: "With God, all things are possible," they pray with great trust. And "All things are possible to him who believes," and in this power they experience their life's possibilities. Of course they also experience disappointments and defeats, but they have the spiritual strength to get back up after each defeat. In beginning to believe, one becomes a person of possibilities. Such a person no longer fits into roles prescribed for him. Persons with disabilities will liberate themselves from the firmly established roles of our society. This is possible because the power of inhumane prejudices is like the power of paper tigers. The fearsome power quickly disappears when even a few persons with disabilities no longer believe in it and break away from it.

Service Must Not Demean

We must admit that it is unfortunately at this point that the fear of those without disabilities toward those with disabilities is particularly great. They want to do everything for them and to make sure that everything is done for those with disabilities so that they lack for nothing. But they don't want to leave them their independence, for they fear they could do something to themselves or others. "Freedom," "self-determination," and "personal responsibility" have become alien words to some persons with disabilities because they are alien to their families and caretakers.

How do persons with disabilities come of age? There is probably nothing in this world that humiliates and robs an adult of his voice more than parents constantly making decisions for him, their nonstop caretaking and leading. Certainly, a person with disabilities needs the help of other persons, and she can also have the inner freedom to welcome it. But even when it is well-intentioned, sympathy can offend. Sympathy can be insulting when it is an expression of fear of letting the foreign suffering get too close to oneself. There is a servant love that enables the other to find his own worth and his own life. But there is also a servant incapacitation that hinders precisely that which it should be liberating and healing.

From Care to Friendship

Wisdom is part of servant love, wisdom to differentiate between responsibility to the needy other and respect for the personal life of the other. Love, responsibility, and caregiving find their limits in the independence of the other person. The responsibility one has assumed for the other must be withdrawn the instant the other comes to himself and his own life comes back to life. Otherwise responsibility can easily become a hidden form of domination. Even Jesus did not come to shackle people to himself through his service or to make himself indispensable. "Your faith has helped you," he would always say when people wanted to thank him for healings. Your own faith! But when leadership is taken back because persons have become mature, because responsibility [for the other] is given up, because the life of the other returns, what remains then? Then caregiving ceases, and friendship begins. Then there is no distinction between the helper and the one who is in need of help. Then those with disabilities and those without gladly live together, genuinely interested in the world of the other.

Liberation from False Ideals

But finally and most important is the liberation of persons with disabilities from despondency and sadness. From whence does this inner burden come? It comes from the prejudices of the strong and the capable that convey to the person with disabilities the laming feeling of being categorized as less worthy. This burden makes him ugly, incapable, and useless in his own eyes. How can one become self-confident and free if one feels scorned? This depends on discovering one's own life and learning to love it. It depends on realizing that this life is my life, this world is my world, this difficulty is my difficulty, and this limitation is my limitation. One needs a great sense of independence and a new orientation in order to learn to love oneself complete with disabilities in a world in which one encounters only scorn and sympathy.

There is no differentiation between the healthy and those with disabilities. For every human life has its limitations, vulnerabilities, and weaknesses. We are born needy, and we die helpless. So in truth there is no such thing as a life without disabilities. It is only the ideals of health of a society of the strong which condemn a part of humanity to being "disabled."

In our society, health means employability and the ability to enjoy oneself. Is it not more than that? No, in reality barely anything beyond

110

that. So, a person who cannot work and is limited in his ability to enjoy himself counts as being sick. I consider this ideal of health deeply inhumane and humiliating to every person. True health is something quite different: true health is the strength to live, the strength to suffer, and the strength to die. Health is not the condition of my organs but rather the strength of my soul to deal with the various conditions of my organs. How do we get this strength of soul, and how can we strengthen it?

I Love Myself Because God Loves Me

We will gain and foster this strength of soul when we begin to love ourselves. Love of self elicits strength of soul, and soul strength gives us the strength to move mountains; and if we can't move them, then it gives us strength not to despair in the face of them. Yet how can a person in the midst of problems come to the point of loving and not despising himself? At this point, I have to get personal. In 1945, in the misery of a dirty barracks in a prison camp, I lost all sense of the hope that had filled my life to that point. I became deathly sad. I became sick. I no longer got up. I did not want to live. But then the miracle happened; through the help of a friend I gained the certainty that there is One who loves you, who believes in you. There is One, who waits for you, for whom you are immeasurably important. Stand up and go meet him! The moment I felt there was One who loved me and who does not abandon me, I crawled out of my forlorn corner and once again began to love myself. My life, even life there behind the barbed wire, once again became important to me. I survived. I overcame my sadness unto death. What did I learn from this? I understood that God loves us, and it is for that reason that we should love our selves. But that is still too general a statement. Instead: God loves every one of us just the way we are, not different, but rather just the way we are; and it is because of this that we can also love that which God loves—our selves. Anyone who after coming to this understanding still despises himself in truth doesn't despise himself but God. I know that orienting one's own sense of life to that of the eternal God sounds simple. I also know how difficult it is in practice to take on this orientation. But it is the only alternative to orienting oneself to a society that rewards the able and represses those with disabilities.

THE LIBERATION OF PERSONS WITH NO DISABILITIES

Disability always has two sides: on the one side is the person who is disabled, on the other, the one who disables. The person with disabilities is robbed of his human rights. That's inhumane. But the one who disables also loses his humanity because he acts in an inhumane way. So it is also those persons without disabilities in our society who need to be liberated. From what do persons without disabilities need to be liberated?

Encounter Liberates from Fear

At this juncture, I will pursue only one relevant point: if they truly wish to become humane people, persons without disabilities must be liberated from their assumption that they are healthy and from their fear of persons with disabilities. Abundant research on the attitude of the general population toward persons with physical and mental disabilities points repeatedly to insecurity and fear:

-90 percent don't know how to act toward those with disabilities

-56 percent don't want to live in the same house as a person with disabilities

-65 percent believe that those with disabilities belong in a nursing care facility

-70 percent say they have feelings of fear when they see persons with disabilities

-72 percent favor abortion if a fetus shows signs of maldevelopment, etc.

The initial reaction toward a person with disabilities is described thus in the research literature:

> The able-bodied person is put off his spiritual balance. The strange sight of a maldeveloped body doesn't fit into the category one has of what another human should look like. The unharmonious appearance that has hurt our aesthetic feelings can lead to reactions of repulsion. . . . The able-bodied person begins to feel quite upset. . . . In the first instance, he doesn't manage to see in the other a person; he sees only the disability and generalizes this to the entire personality.[1]

112

In the interests of fairness one should, I suppose, add that this so-called "initial reaction" is indeed only the first reaction of many people, and that fear and insecurity can very quickly be overcome if practicable ways can be found to facilitate encounter with persons with disabilities. But the fear of encounter only ever disappears in the encounter itself. And so increasing opportunities for such encounters must be sought and arranged.

And yet this fear of being made to feel insecure by the presence of persons with disabilities has produced many defense mechanisms. Some persons with disabilities are treated like lepers. They are banished from the forum of public life; and where they do appear, people flee and depart. Such a defensive attitude can also surface in the nursing homes where those with disabilities are with "those like them" and material care replaces human respect. Some people try to compensate for their feelings of guilt by overdoing the money and time they expend at homes for those with disabilities. Often the desire to be rid of something and buying oneself free are closely related.

But the more persons with disabilities are pushed from public life, the less we know about them. And the less one knows about the lives of those with disabilities, the greater becomes the fear of them. It is this fear that is disabled through encounter and through communal life with persons with disabilities.

Encounter Liberates Our Humaneness

In order to conquer this fear, nothing less than a completely new approach to life is necessary. So long as fear encourages us to strive for the ideals of health, potency, achievement, and beauty, we will continue to develop defense mechanisms toward people who are weak, sick, ugly, and have disabilities. Persons who equate being human with being healthy cannot abide seeing a sick person. Persons who identify being human with power to achieve will despise weak persons. Those who seek out beauty in persons will regard every disability as ugly. But are these values of health, achievement, and beauty actually humane? No, they render humans inhuman, for they force us to suppress and deny our own weaknesses.

Encounter with persons with disabilities justifiably makes insecure these inhuman concepts about humanity. The pride of those who see themselves as able-bodied in terms of health and the euphoria about achievements lead to the repression and disparagement of

113

weaker persons. But how can a person base his feelings of self-worth on his health or his organs' abilities to function without succumbing to the fear of losing them? How can a person see herself as righteous and able to hold it all together only because at the moment she is not disabled, when she knows deep down that it won't stay that way?

This uncertainty, which for many people emanates from persons with disabilities, is a necessary healing uncertainty, for it shows how many people are practicing idolatry and superstition in their lives. We can be free from this madness. Persons with disabilities make apparent the inhumanity of the supposedly not-disabled. They help us on our way toward humaneness. For they force us no longer to base our self-confidence on health and ability, but to seek it in trust in God. It is precisely the unsettled non-disabled persons who must discover true love of self in order to be liberated from their egoism and their fear-filled self-hate. Persons with disabilities alone can help us to do this. Again, it sounds so easy, but in practice it is hard to live out; but it is the only alternative for a society that has built its house on the shifting sands of pride in health and the drive for achievement, in short on the depths of fear.

THE PERSON: IMAGE OF THE LIVING GOD

What is a person? Who is a person in the full sense of the word? Is this or that person really still a human? So some folks ask. They ask because they have a particular picture, an ideal vision of what a person is; and they judge according to this dream image. But in the final analysis who can compare with his own dream image?

Sickness Belongs to the Reality of Being Human

If we are in search of a Christian answer to this question, we need to turn to the Gospels and read. The first thing that strikes us is the fact that people are depicted there as being sick, poor, and in need of help. One only needs to set this alongside the Greek ideal of a person, brimming with health, strength, and benevolence, to realize the difference. In the Gospels, sickness is part of the understanding of what it is like to be a real person. For wherever the Savior appears, the sick come to light. Gathered around Jesus we find the entire wretchedness of humanity: the possessed, the blind, the dumb, the lame, those sick in body and spirit and from all manner of sin. They come out of the dark corners of cities and villages to which they have been banished, out of the wildernesses to which they have been relegated, and into the spotlight where they reveal themselves to Jesus. Thus Jesus sees the internal and external disabilities of the people. Jesus comprehends us, not from our sunny sides where we are strong and capable, but from our shadow sides, where our weaknesses lie.

The Healing Power of Jesus Lies in His Ability to Suffer

Why does Jesus see us like this? Why do the sick come to him? Because in him is revealed a life of contagious healing power. For this reason, time and again it is reported that "he healed the sick," and "he drove out demons." But some sick people who only come into his vicinity or who only touch his robe are also healed. Yet how does Jesus actually help the sick? Is it through magical powers? Sometimes that is what it seems like, but again and again he says: "Your faith has helped you!" "Go! And may it be to you according to your faith," he says to the centurion from Capernaum, and his servant was healed at that very hour. These are not magical healings; they are faith healings. It is for this reason also that one must establish that Jesus did not heal all the sick among the populace, but only a few he encountered. These few healings were a sign of hope to many.

To probe further: By what means did Jesus heal the sick? What form does the healing power of his life take? The answer is quite unexpected. We find it in Matthew 8:16-17:

> That evening they brought to him many who were possessed with demons; and he cast out the spirits with a word, and cured all who were sick. This was to fulfill what had been spoken through the prophet Isaiah, "He took our infirmities and bore our diseases."

So Jesus' power to heal lies in his power to suffer. He heals, not by casting aside and getting rid of the sicknesses, but by taking them on himself. People are not healed by Jesus' supernatural powers, but rather by his wounds. This points us to the way of Christ's passion and to the cross that stood at Golgotha. The entire life of Jesus is basically a single path of passion from Bethlehem to Golgotha; and on this way to suffering and death for the sake of the salvation of the world, Jesus heals the sick, accepts the outcasts, and drives out evil spirits. These

115

are the "signs and wonders" that follow his path. Golgotha is the secret of Jesus' healing power. Many sick people have experienced that before and since his death. But no one has understood more clearly than the prophet Isaiah, to whom Matthew refers, the secret that was revealed in Jesus' life and dying. In chapter 53 he says of the new servant of God:

> He had no form or majesty that we should look at him,
>   nothing in his appearance that we should desire him.
> He was despised and rejected by others;
>   a man of suffering and acquainted with infirmity;
> and as one from whom others hide their faces
>   he was despised, and we held him of no account.
>
> Surely he has borne our infirmities
>   and carried our diseases;
>   . . . and by his bruises we are healed.

"By his bruises we are healed": That is the main thing. It is not through his deity but rather through his humanity, not through his superpowers but through the giving of himself for our pains and our death that Jesus heals. Yet how can his suffering bring healing to those who suffer? How can those who are hopelessly wounded find health in his wounds? It sounds absurd if we think in terms of human ability, but it sounds true and liberating if we look to God.

Healing Through Fellowship with God

"What is not accepted, will also not be healed" reads a theological principle of the early Church. It was a principle for recognizing the true humanity of the Son of God: In Jesus Christ, God himself became Man. He took on complete, real humanity and made it part of his own divine life. The eternal God took on not only the limited and mortal aspects of humanity but also the disabled, sick, weak, helpless, and lifeless aspects of humanity. He took on our disabilities and made them part of his eternal life. He takes on our tears and makes them an expression of his own pain. It is by taking on every sickness and every care and making them his own sufferings and his own cares that God heals all sicknesses and all cares.

God takes on our real life and takes it up into himself—not only our imagined life, not only our phantom life and our inhuman ideals.

God takes on the whole weak human nature and heals it by sharing with it his eternal divine nature.

Healing thus consists in fellowship and in sharing with and being a part in all things. God heals us in that he participates so much in our pains that they become part of his eternal love. The sick and the despairing through all ages have experienced and discovered this again and again. I think here of the crucified Christ on the Isenheim Altar by Matthias Grünewald. Not only is he contorted and disfigured with pain, his whole body is also covered with plague sores. "He carried our infirmities" is what this picture is trying to say. And it said it to thousands suffering from the plague who were brought into this church. They recognized themselves in the man of pain, because he had become one of them. And in looking at this picture they experienced the eternal, unbreakable fellowship with the crucified God. In this fellowship, from which not even the plague could separate them, they experienced many healings.

Every Life Is Divine Life

The incarnation of God, which we recognize in the life, passion, and death of Jesus, is a comfort and salvation for every person. Every person, however disabled she might be, through her life participates in God's life. The Crucified One encompasses every life and makes it his own. We humans who judge according to our ideal images think that the life of one who is blind or dumb or lame or is mentally ill is a reduced life, that is, a life that is less than another. But God loves every human life. So in truth there is no such thing as a reduced or disabled life. In its own way, each life is divine life and must be experienced and respected as such. Somewhere on the Son of Man's way from his impoverished birth to his prayer in Gethsemane and his death on the cross, each of us can find his or her own place or niche where God identifies with him or her and where he or she finds acceptance. That is one aspect of healing through fellowship with God.

But then there is still the experience of the other aspect: "God became human, so that we could become divine." It was with this bold phrase that the early Church described the secret of the healing of humans in communion with Jesus. What is meant here by becoming divine is participating in the abundant life and the indescribable joy of God. God takes on our human lives and makes our weaknesses and disabilities his own in order to share with us his liveliness and his joy.

117

God weeps with us so that we will one day be able to laugh with God. Now for sure this does not break all boundaries nor remove all disabilities. Though there are probably more signs and wonders in every person's life than we realize, this present age of suffering is not yet the age of the future glory. But the certainty that participation in the everlasting life of God will one day wipe every tear from our eyes—for mourning, crying, and pain will be no more (Revelation 21)—is already being experienced here and now in this life. If there were no hope of eternal life, then this present life would also lose its meaning.

We Are All the Honor and Glory of God in This World

What is a human? Who is a human in the full sense of the word? We are now in a position to answer this question. A human—every human—is the image of the living God. Everyone can find him or herself in the crucified Christ, for the crucified Christ reflects himself in each of us, no matter how disabled we might be. The crucified Son of Man is the visible image of the invisible God and in fellowship with him; so are persons with disabilities, all persons with their disabilities.

Whoever is an image of the living God must also be considered beloved of God. And whoever is the image and beloved of God is all the honor and glory of God in this world. Whosoever is God's image and God's glory in this world is good, true, and beautiful; for she is identified with God, the source of all goodness, truth, and beauty. Though according to our human standards we often see "no form or beauty" in other people; though according to our own desires we often see in ourselves "nothing in . . . appearance that we should desire"; yet according to God's standards, others and we ourselves are good and beautiful.

Luther once expressed it this way: "Sinners are beautiful because they are loved. It is not because they are beautiful that they are loved." Human love yearns for beauty and flees ugliness. But God's love makes righteous ones of sinners and beautiful people of the unattractive. It is because we have been the beloved of God since all eternity that we can love ourselves and consider ourselves good and true and also beautiful, and that we can like our appearance. Every one of us is a reflection of God in this world. There are so many people with disabilities, so many sick and disfigured people on whose countenances and in whose visages the beauty of divine grace is reflected.

One only needs to be attentive to it and forget the unnerving beauty standards of glossy magazines. For it is then that one can recognize the radiance of God. Beauty is the transfiguration of life through love. If one has once recognized this, one never forgets it again.

IS EVERY DISABILITY ALSO A GIFT?

The separation of persons with disabilities from those without disabilities is a sign of the sickness of our society in which solidarity and humanness are clearly not yet public learning goals. That is also why the healing of our divided society cannot consist in integrating as well as possible those with disabilities with those who do not consider themselves disabled. No matter how possible it might be even to achieve such an integration (as is being widely discussed today), it would after all not happen according to the standards of those with disabilities but according to the standards of those without disabilities. Persons with disabilities would not be taken seriously with regard to their dignity and their particular world. They would again have to adapt themselves to support the world and values of people who consider themselves to be without disabilities. No: a healing of this divided society must result in changes on both sides.

Discovering the Positive Aspects of Disability

People who consider themselves to be without disabilities must discover the, to them, unfamiliar worlds of persons with disabilities. No longer can they measure disabilities against their own standard of life nor view them as something negative; rather, they must recognize the particular and peculiar life experiences that are found among people with disabilities. By doing so, they will learn something from the life experiences of their disabled fellow humans that otherwise would have remained inaccessible to them. This means that not only must persons with disabilities be integrated into the life-world of those without disabilities, but conversely those without disabilities must likewise be integrated into the world of those with disabilities.

Until now, we so-called "normals" have called a person "disabled" if he or she cannot do this or that. But that is our definition that we have imposed on them. What do we know about what he can do that we can't? Are the negative aspects of a disability in the world of the

119

person affected really only negative and, therefore, senseless? Couldn't we for once try to discover the positive aspects of disability? For example, I believe I have a person with mental disabilities to thank for a new ability to hear the language of the trees in our natural environment.

Being Disabled: A Gift of the Holy Spirit

For this reason, I want to venture a quite provocative and perhaps also annoying thesis: Every disability is also a gift. It is a gift that we do not discover only because we are so focused on what a person is missing, what he has been deprived of. But if we were to free ourselves for a moment from the value standards of our own lives, then we would be able to understand the peculiar worth of the other life and its importance to us. Everyone affected might ask herself: What importance does the person with disabilities have for me and my life? In so doing, she would quickly discover the giftedness of that person with disabilities.

Turning once more to the Bible, we discover the surprising fact that the Apostle Paul enumerates not only strengths and abilities among the gifts and powers of the Holy Spirit (Charismata) but also suffering, setbacks, and sadnesses (II Corinthians 4:7ff.). And when he turns to speak of those people whom God has chosen and called to his Kingdom, he first names the weak, the despised, the foolish, and the children. God establishes his Kingdom with such people in order to judge those who consider themselves strong, noble, and wise (I Corinthians 1:26ff.).

The giftedness of the Holy Spirit also arises within the circumstances in which a person finds himself when the Lord calls him: "Let each of you lead the life that the Lord has assigned, to which God called you" (I Corinthians 7:17). For this reason, being a Jew is a gift of the Spirit as is also being a heathen. Being married and being single are gifts of the Spirit, which arise out of the call into the fellowship of Christ. Consequently, having a disability, whatever form it might take, is also a gift of the Holy Spirit, if through and in the disability one is called to be God's image and glory on earth.

The Service to Society of Those with Disabilities

This positive valuation brings us to Paul's image of the body of Christ. The community of faith is the body of Christ. In this body are many different members: the head and foot, the mouth and ear, and so forth. There are many members working together, but there is one body. Paul does not assume that this body of Christ would be bursting with health. There are weak members and there are feeble members, and God gives the feeble members most honor and glory (I Corinthians 12:23), for God most needs the weak and feeble members for his Kingdom. Why? Surely because the church is the body not only of the risen but also of the crucified Christ. God's resurrection power becomes apparent in the astonishing power of the Holy Spirit. But it is in the pain, setbacks, disabilities, and sufferings of the Holy Spirit that God's ability to suffer becomes apparent. The church as body of Christ is always also the body of the weak, defenseless, crucified Son of Man. The power of the risen Christ always comes hand in hand with fellowship in the sufferings of the crucified One. The circumstances we call disabilities are gifts of the Holy Spirit because they can become a reflection of the suffering Christ.

There is therefore such a thing as service by persons with disabilities to our society. It is this we must discover before we speak of service to those with disabilities. A society is always only as strong as its weakest member. The respect and strengthening shown the weakest members is therefore tantamount to the strengthening of the entire society. Every disability as understood by humans is also a gift as understood by God. A person with disabilities gives others the precious insight into the woundedness and weakness of human life. But a person with disabilities also gives insight into the humanity of his own world. Through persons with disabilities, other people can come to know the real, suffering, living God, who also loves them infinitely.

HEALING COMMUNITY

We cannot get rid of disabilities, but we can overcome the disabling of those with disabilities. We can heal the dis-eased relationship between those with and those without disabilities. This will occur not through solicitous care and helping, but rather through solidarity and living together. Helping and allowing oneself to be helped will then of itself result from living together.

Friendship is the foundation of all mutual help. For friendship links affection with respect. It is only on this basis of mutual recognition and valuation that necessary caregiving and accepted help does not demean or humiliate. Wherever persons with and without disabilities learn to live together, the old roles of the helper and the needy one disintegrate. It is then that both parties learn mutual giving and taking, each with her own gifts, each with her own boundaries.

Awakening the Servant Community

Community can heal our divided society, and it can do so on both sides. It is only in fellowship with one another that both the person with disabilities and the one without can experience a new humanity. So may we, with all our strength, build such communities of persons with and without disabilities!

This is a task for church communities. "Churches without persons with disabilities are disabled churches" says one declaration of the World Council of Churches. The reason lies not only in a lack of church service but also in that we have not yet discovered the Christian community as a servant community. We have not yet been able to discover it as a servant community because we have not yet experienced it as a charismatic community. But the gifts of the Holy Spirit are all readily available to us now.

---

1. Jansen/Schmidt, *Empirische Korrelate zwischen Einstellungen der Umwelt und dem Verhalten körperbehinderter Kinder,* (Cologne, 1968).

CHAPTER SIX

REDEEMED BODIES: FULLNESS OF LIFE

Barbara A. B. Patterson

FULLNESS OF LIFE: QUESTIONS OF EMBODIMENT

In *The Confessions,* Augustine tells the story of his own life as an allegory of human relation to God. He wonders about the tensions he feels between his body's needs, desires, and seductions and his desires for God. These struggles shaped Augustine's discussions about God's partnership in and with our humanity. They helped him discern the human-divine dynamic of the incarnation, how God was also human in Jesus Christ. Grasping this incarnate dynamic was crucial to Augustine for learning how to take on the qualities of Christ in his own flesh and blood. But this learning was difficult. It raised many questions about body and soul. If our bodies are made in the image of God, why do we feel such conflict between our body's desires and our desires for God? Are all bodies good? Who is responsible for the body? What do resurrection and redemption have to do with the body? What difference does redemption make in everyday, embodied life?

Augustine's questions are still our questions. They articulate our own struggles to relate body and soul with God. They also call our attention to serious misunderstandings within Christianity that sustain distorted responses which have damaged the faith and actions of many believers. Some of these misperceptions touch lives very specifically. Others have shaped broader confusions about embodment in relation to gender, ability/disability, exclusion/inclusion, limits, and Christian exemplars. I want to pursue Augustine's key questions about body and soul and the image of God. This pursuit may enable us to discern life-giving responses for our own day and challenge the misperceptions that still distort daily Christian life.

THE BREADTH OF EMBODIMENT IN GOD

Christianity assumes that the whole creation is mysteriously woven as the body of God.[1] Sharing in this mystery, we have common points of ability and disability that connect us to one another and to God. As an able-bodied woman, my struggles with my embodiment are not universal, but they do share general characteristics with others' experiences along the broad spectrum of our embodied stories.[2] We individually recognize some feelings, intuitions, and knowledge that others do not. I have certain physical movements in common with some but not others. These shared and unshared points of embodied expression and experience in no way deny our particularities. But they do help us recognize the breadth of embodiment that is also the breadth of God's body in our world.

Whose Body is Good?

Though we all have problems in and with our bodies, our faith claims that God created our bodies good. This is an important message in the face of the culture's mixed messages about the goodness of the body. For the culture, there are criteria for good bodies. A good body looks a certain way, is associated with a particular class, race, gender, and so forth. In the face of those messages, I turned to the church literally putting my body in the church's body. I put my body deeply in the body of the church through choir, Bible study, youth groups, and participation in service projects. I hoped the church would teach me to embrace my body as a sign of my spiritual worship—my covenant with God (Romans 12:1). I needed support in my struggle against the culture's destructive messages.

But over time, I realized that the church also was sending me mixed messages. Though I was a welcomed and full participant in certain roles, I was not allowed to participate in others. My gender was the problem. I had a female body; and in a certain, limited way that body became a disability for me. It was a problem for ordained ministry, certain kinds of lay authority, and interpretation of Scriptures. My embodied participation was suspect to the church. I was forced to face, as I had faced in the culture of my upbringing, the reality that my best hope was to live in the church as a split body, part good and part suspect.

124

In my case, Christianity's promises of abundant life and good bodies was not a reliable story line. Certain movements, aspects, dimensions of my body were pronounced bad. It should stay numb. I was trained that if I could keep my body numb, I would be protected from its lurking evil, its Eve-like potential for dangerous manipulation, temptation, and destruction.[3] The potential evil of my female body was more obvious than another body-threat I experienced, that of being the child of an addict and living with that crippling abuse. The lessons were, however, transferable. The bodily effects of my addicted family also could be tolerated if I would keep silent about them and numb myself to my feelings and experiences. So, with significant support from the church, I learned to exclude certain aspects of myself that were labeled different, dangerous, sinful, disabling, or not good. I was told that if I could maintain this numbing split, God would save me from my dangerous body. For too many years, I tried.

I worked hard to inculcate in myself a religious strategy for generating numbness. I served others often to the extreme and in detriment to myself. I got busy helping to build the reign of God, and as I did I met others working to overcome their dangerous bodies. For some, body problems were focused on gender or race. For others, the problems were disabilities of limbs, mental functioning, or emotional health. Although our disabilities were different—often significantly so—we shared an experience of being denied recognition and place by the church because our bodies were threatening. Because we did not fit the norms, we were marginalized. Desperately trying to overcome our bad bodies, we prayed that God created all bodies good.

Of course, high costs accompanied our split and numbing life. Becoming of use to others, we became objects to ourselves. Though the church was willing to use our variously threatening bodies in certain venues, it never denied that our bodies remained problematic. So in our different ways, those of us with problematic bodies paid the daily price of struggling to reconcile the acceptance of our bodies in some church places and the rejection of them in others. Church members in wheelchairs were verbally welcomed, but there were no elevators in our buildings. Women were graciously acknowledged for cooking the church suppers, but they could not be members of the church's governing body. In my own parish, I and others I knew lived a split body life learning to believe a lie that God who cherished all

125

bodies could not cherish ours unless they were "fixed," unless they were made no longer a problem.

A Resurrected or Redeemed Body

This theme of "fixing" disabled bodies is an old one in Christianity. Its roots are in the early Church's struggles to make sense of martyred bodies and the power of death. The hope became that in the next life all bodies with problems would be healed and cured.[4] A cured body was defined as a perfect body, one that mirrored the bodies of those with institutional power, in other words, able-bodied men. Jesus' resurrected body became the model. It brought solace and hope to many who lost their family members to death or martyrdom through dismemberment by animals or Roman soldiers.[5] But the long-term consequences in Christianity were that imperfect or troublesome bodies in this world were viewed as partial, marginal, and inadequate. Come the resurrection, they could be "fixed."

Certainly, some Christian attitudes about embodiment provide interesting possibilities for reconceiving disabled bodies as good. One early theological perspective acknowledged Jesus' and others' post-death bodies as "fixed," but it did not assume that a "fixed" body excluded pre-death scars. In fact, those scars were crucial points of recognition in the family of God. For many Christian theologians, the "perfect" resurrection body was not free from scars, diseases, and disabilities. Gregory of Nyssa believed he would recognize his sister Macrina in heaven by her scars. Her earthly embodiment would not be erased. It mattered in the resurrection, and by inference he claimed her disabilities as not only acceptable but also signs of her body's and God's goodness.

Our questions about embodiment have deep roots in our Christian heritage.[6] They demand serious grappling with the long-term distortions that have emerged in the church's attempts to answer basic questions about embodiment and life with God. We must discover in our ancient roots those insights that clarify the destructive forces and life-giving guidance we need. I suggest a first step of clarification. Let us embrace our present embodied life as an expression and experience of redemption.[7] By that I mean, let us embrace our bodies as participants in the contemporary expression of God's liberating body restoring all creation (Luke 4:16-22). Let us accept, as redeemed people in Christ, that we can only speculate what our bodies and souls will be in the resurrection. No one knows that mystery except God.[8] But we can assume that our variously abled bodies through dying and being raised with Christ in baptism are now expressions of God's redemption in the world.

REDEEMED BODIES, GOOD BODIES

Living as redeemed bodies requires serious attention not only to our physical flesh and blood, but also to the ways in which our passions, virtues, and actions are expressed and experienced in our bodies. Augustine believed that participation in redemption required a commitment to the flourishing of all creation. In redemptive life, no anatomies, no systems, no dimensions of creation could be excluded or marginalized. Everything, according to Augustine, was being restored in the beauty of God's image. Redemption certainly had continuity with God's original work of creation, but it also was discontinuous, reshaping anew each day creation's alienation from God toward beauty, justice, and love. This process of change toward good in bodies of various states of embodiment drew from a wealth of dynamic resources and perspectives.[9]

This insight is helpful for reimagining God's creative work in and through all kinds of bodies in our own time and place. It also serves as a corrective to the Neoplatonic strand in other of Augustine's ideas that have been used to reinforce theologies of embodiment that associate creativity with "fixing" the body.[10] Using Augustine's insights about the imaginative restoration of redeemed creation, I want to focus on two views that affect embodiment: all redeemed bodies participating in this restoration are good, and all redeemed bodies retain their particularity and diversity.

Redeemed Bodies as Inclusive Goodness

If we take seriously that God now is restoring the goodness of all creation, then we cannot deny that our present bodies, as they are, are participating in this goodness. Furthermore, redemptive reimaging is occurring at multiple sites, in lots of different bodies, and, yet, each is an expression of the love of the one Creator. Augustine encourages us to see this process as a whole, to see all those different bodies as God does with the "eyes of our hearts." In that way, we

127

recognize that though we are different, we share in the emerging beauty and grace of God's own self.[11] The Hebrew tradition of created, good matter is echoed in this idea of holistic redemption.[12]

As part of this emerging wholeness, our bodies participate in the powerful and flowing renewal of and for us all. Abundant, redemptive life has an expansive quality that recognizes all shared life in God and cherishes it. This holistic view of redemptive embodiment is counter to much of the contemporary emphasis on individual embodiment. It asks us to approach embodied life not only as distinct but also as shared experience, a commonality. Individual experience and growth is part of the web of our common redemptive growth. In this way, we discover incarnate life as inclusive, containing our real and different bodystory with others. No body is marginalized. There is no center to this emerging web except the redeeming God who weaves it as a whole.

In this way, fullness of life as redeemed bodies becomes inclusive community. Explicitly, redeemed embodiment as inclusion means that we can call good overlooked, denied, and unexpected expressions of embodied life. Olympic skiers are able-bodied *and* amputees and paraplegics. Typists use their hands *and* type with their teeth. Dramatists are mentally healthy *and* schizophrenics. Swimming instructors are sighted *and* visually impaired. Celebrations include addicts who no longer celebrate with drugs. Redeemed bodies are inclusive, sharing bodies. There are commonalities emerging much more expansive than the limited imaginations of our too often clouded hearts.

Redeemed Bodies as Particular Goodness

Of course, the more our hearts see the whole of redeemed embodiment, the more we can recognize and appreciate the diversity that shapes it. We recognize dissimilarities in the midst of similarities.[13] Both must be held in high regard not only by our hearts but also by the ways in which we publicly acknowledge and enact solidarity with difference. One summer working as a chaplain in a hospital in Boulder, Colorado, I had an opportunity to learn this balance of solidarity as particularity and commonality.

After work each day, I would swim at the nearby public pool. Slowly I became one of the regular lap swimmers. We had our own section of the pool and most considered us as a group, the "real swimmers."

Early on, I had noticed a swimmer whose stroke seemed perfect. Smooth and high, his arms sped through the water carrying his body forward powerfully. I wanted to have a stroke as good as his. In a certain sense, he embodied the corporate hopes of all of us "real swimmers." How sharply I remember my shock the first time I saw him get out of the water. His left leg was amputated below the knee. Now my vision was being restored. The community of swimmers was reconfigured by the diversity of his body because it expanded our definitions of proper stroke, necessary strength, and techniques for speed. Uniquely one while also inclusively of us, he changed the scorecard of possibilities and opened new venues of hope for us as swimmers and human beings.

My definition of an accomplished swimmer would have to allow for more diversity. My understanding of passion for moving in and with the water was expanded not only for him but for us all. His very particular bodystory of disability reshaped all of our stories, reframing misperceptions of ability/disability and challenging our notions of redeemed embodiment in individual ways as well as communal. I had to meet him. I could not miss the opportunity to learn from his inclusive particularity.

When we began to talk after workouts, we discovered numerous similarities and dissimilarities in our struggles to be good swimmers. We also discovered that we went to the same church. Over that summer, we experienced the breadth of our different and shared stories in the water, in our church, and in our everyday questions and delights. He needed a more accessible place to live as medical complications were changing his mobility. I too was searching for an accessible place trying to be a priest in a church only reluctantly ordaining women. We both were dealing with limited access, but in very different ways, and it was important for us to hold the tension between what we shared and how different we were. We learned together, however, that even our similarities required close attention in the translation. Our conversion toward taking on the qualities of Christ, opening ourselves to God's vision, was multiple and particular in spirit and in flesh. Our fullest experiences of embodied redemption demanded that we honor both.[14]

In that tension, we discovered the goodness of our bodies, how they mattered to us and to God, and how redemption unfolds in very different ways. We realized that our shared life rested on our mutual

129

conviction that Christ redeems by drawing all bodies toward Christ's wealth of resources and experiences in this world. We began to see in, with, and through each other's diversity the living body of Christ at work for us all. In fact, once we gave up trying to be too similar as Christians, we grew more similar as we moved toward Christ from our different directions. Dorotheus describes this process as spokes of a wheel becoming closer to each other as they move toward the hub, Christ.[15]

REDEEMED BODYSTORIES: AMBIGUITIES AND LIMITS

Beginning to understand the expansive and diverse vision of redeemed embodiment, we better recognize how to put that vision into action in our daily lives. We also understand more clearly the stumbling blocks that trip us up and stop us from participating with Christ in inclusive and particular redemption. Two of those stumbling blocks are related to misunderstandings about embodiment that the church has too often supported. They are the stumbling blocks of denying the ambiguities of embodied redeemed life, and denying that we in our bodies have limits.

Redeemed Bodies and Ambiguities

As redeemed bodies, we continually participate in God's unfolding restoration of all creation. We are in some sense always being born again.[16] Though we have vision and hope for a fully resurrected future—whatever that may be—our bodies live now in God's story, which is partial and unfinished. Paul describes this redemptive life. Though we are not embracing an idea of "bodies . . . set free" as a denial of body or preferences for spirit over body

> we are well aware that the whole creation, until this time, has been groaning in labor pains. And not only that: we too, who have the first-fruits of the Spirit, even we are groaning inside ourselves, waiting with eagerness for our bodies to be set free (Romans 8:22-24, NJB).

The writer in Isaiah touches on the same theme: "Behold, I am doing a new thing; now it springs forth, do you not perceive it?" (Isaiah 43:19a, RSV).

Though we do not know exactly what our resurrected body will look like (I Corinthians 15), we do know that we already are participating in the first fruits of redemption in our current bodies. Our redemptive bodies labor with our Mother God in the ambiguities of this birthing, hanging between life, death, and new life. But this redemption promises hope and a vision that what we do in our bodies now will be complete or satisfying later, if not now.

Because God invites us to be partners in this restoration, we are not forced participants in this ambiguous birthing. Yet failing to participate, we diminish the redemptive possibilities of our relationships with our own bodies, with the body of God, and with the bodies of our neighbors. We are faced with choices we did not ask for, do not like, are not prepared for. Often, we have to decide among several seemingly appropriate responses. For example, we are asked to take a medication with significant side effects that also will alleviate our pain and offer happier life. Or we have to choose to stay with our children and survive our partner's beatings because we know better than outsiders how to sustain the maximum number of lives. Or we decide to lobby for legislated funding of one recognized group knowing that monies will be taken from others.

In partnership with God, we are asked to put our bodies on the line for flourishing life; and the choices are ambiguous, whether they be personal, communal, spiritual, or physical. In the freedom of redemptive ambiguity, it is tempting to lose the tensions of inclusive and particular embodiment. The stress of deciding amid ambiguity makes it more difficult to add another layer of ambivalence, that of discerning the balance of our shared and unique visions of embodied life. Sometimes the complexity seems too much to bear. We long for clear rules, definite boundaries, sure criteria for who is in and who is out. But this is a faulty vision of God's flourishing in our world. It negates the importance of keeping the good news of God inclusive and particular. It denies the realities that embodied living with God the creator of new things is ambiguous.

This is Christian practical living, embodying with God the good news that death is not the last word, but flourishing life. But in the mix of death and life—which is our life here—it is at times difficult living, despite the good news. Certainly, there are times of great joy and celebration when the ambiguities bring sure birth and hope. But there also are times of terrifying ambiguity: the sudden onset of

131

diabetes, the loss of a spouse, the decision to change careers, or the determination to quit bingeing. More than we realize, these moments of practical Christian living require body-based choices. They are not moments of abstract piety or disembodied trauma. The body is an important partner in this ambiguous and life-giving process of God's coming reign—a process that moves in and through the deeply embodied emotions of love, rage, pain, fear, joy, abuse, and hope.

Though all of us are embodied, some of us deal much more intensely with the daily ambiguities of life than others. We share in God's body, and yet we are different. That tension of inclusivity and particularity is one we must not lose despite its confusing and often frustrating ambivalence. For example, we must pay careful attention to all the details, practicing redemptive ambiguity that rejects simplistic theologies of conflict as sin or sacrifice. We deny the idea that pain and suffering make one "special" in God's sight because pain is a sign of God's will or a lesson for the sufferer. Such theologies deny the ambiguity of this embodied life. They attempt to do away with those of us living daily with stark ambiguities of disabilities, abuse, and violation. Moreover, these theologies deny the ambiguities of their proponents' own bodies and souls, since no one in this world lives without them.

As Christians living and practicing the reign of God, we see with God's eyes the struggle and potential flourishing of a halting movement resulting from Parkinson's disease. We re-envision this shaking as something quite unique to our brother and sister and also shared in some way through God with our bodies. Together, we are birthing the new vision of embodied flourishing with God. We practice loving one another not *because* of disability, but because all of us live with the ambiguities of our flesh and blood. We are learning about solidarity with the incarnate Christ who did not deny our human ambiguities, but re-envisioned them taking them on in his own flesh for love and justice. Mirroring his solidarity, we embody that continuing response of love and justice for all humankind, real and ambiguous flesh and blood.[17]

Toni Morrison in her novel, *Beloved,* poignantly tells the story of a people embodying hope in the midst of terrifying ambiguity. The characters are technically free from slavery, yet bounty hunters and former owners continue to sweep through their towns and memories. Body scars and disabilities haunt them like ghosts stirring memories of a past without scars and a present that has scars and new life. They celebrate nevertheless, profoundly aware of their freedom and its potential for new possibilities even in the face of their physical, spiritual, and emotional ambiguities.[18]

Baby Suggs, their chosen priest and healer, tells their story this way:

> "Here," she said, "in this here place, we flesh; flesh that weeps, laughs; flesh that dances on bare feet in grass. Love it. Love it hard. Yonder they do not love your flesh. They despise it. They don't love your eyes; they'd just as soon pick em out . . . *You* got to love it. . . . Flesh that needs to be loved . . . love your heart."[19]

In the midst of ambiguities and very real disabilities, Baby Suggs calls her community to live fully, envisioning life through the "eyes of their hearts." Hearing how they are called to love their bodies as they are, scars and freedoms, ambiguities and clarities, encourages us to en-flesh the abundant possibilities open to us if we, with God, turn to our hearts for understanding amid real ambiguities.

Redeemed Bodies and Limits

Along with denying the ambiguities of our embodied lives in Christ, we also often deny the real limits of our bodies. It almost seems unnecessary in one sense to make an issue of limits, but our culture is seriously deluded about how much any body can do and still maintain health and emotional and spiritual flourishing. Many of us with body problems do not accept the limits of our anatomies. In the same way that we deny the diversity of God's restoring creation, we deny the diversity within our own particular bodies. We play games with the truth that certain motions and emotions are too much for us, while others are not. Or we deny that at certain times in our lives, our bodies function differently than at other times. The inability to embrace our limits serves as a warning signal that we may not be able to tolerate another's diversity nor the diversity of the whole creation. More troubling, denying our limits is a way of claiming that we are god.

But if we can learn to accept our limits and live responsibly within them, we will discover that our limitations are problems and gifts. Recognizing that there may be mystery in limits, we can begin to see with God's eyes that we are more a part of the larger body of God and that the whole body together is able. Our limits are real, and they are also not devastating because of the inclusive embodiment we share in Christ. This vision of limits helps us become more attentive to others' capabilities and less resentful of our limits and their capacities because we begin to grasp the web of redemptive capabilities we all share. Embracing our limits helps us discover the best ways of making our energies available to others who have different limits and of offering our need.

The church has become captive to the culture's denials of human limitations. Cultural preferences for images of young, vibrant bodies has had a corrosive effect on the church's images of vitality and power. The "ideal" body, one usually female and emaciated to the point of a radical denial of health, is recognized even in the church as some sort of "perfection." Priests and parishioners need to look "perfect" or "beautiful" in this cultural way in order to draw others to church membership, to send the message that this congregation is "alive" and "with it." (See the implications of this image in Albert Herzog, chapter 9.) The aging, the disabled, the overweight, the mentally ill, the unathletic are not marketable bodies to the culture or to the church. Losing its legacy of all embodied creation as beautiful, the church now contributes with culture to the denial of limits.

These distorted images have had profound effects on women in the church. The emaciated, spent, "perfect" woman has become associated with idolized lifestyles of extreme giving by women. These distortions are bolstered by lying theologies of "perfect" love equating unlimited physical, emotional, and spiritual giving with Christian sacrifice. But this is not redemptive work, nor are these cultural icons redemptive bodies. Redemption is about clear understanding, not about illusions. It is not possible—not even a good idea—for human flesh and blood to give to the point of breakdown. Even Jesus set limits. He rested when he was tired, became angry when he had had enough, left the crowds when he needed time alone.

To flourish in and with our bodies in partnership with Christ, we must correct these misunderstandings about limits. We need to embrace Paul's model of the body as one in which we would honestly assess our gifts, skills, and constraints and offer them as contributing parts of the fully functioning body of Christ (1 Corinthians 12). None of us, I repeat, is the whole body of God. Texts such as Psalms 103, 132 and 139 and stories of Elijah (such as 1 Kings 19:1-18) remind us of that even though human flesh and blood were created in the womb of God. Human bodies are in certain ways susceptible and fragile. Inevitably they die. Our bodies have problems through disease, stress, persecution, and disability. In this world, all bodies—and some more than others—are somewhat confining. It is life-giving to us and others if we can accept the things we cannot change and accept the things we can. Arms and legs can bend, but bones break. Hearts beat with passion, but they also break with despair and suffering. Scripture and certain aspects of our tradition, such as the Egyptian monastics, encourage us to embrace our bodies and learn about limits.

When we offer each other help, we are not judging each other as lacking. We are acknowledging our varied gifts and needs, remaining open to the diversity required for us to co-create with God. Responsibility is enfleshed and, we hope, stirs mutual encouragement and joy, rather than blame or charges of inadequacy. These are hard lessons to learn, and we do not see them modeled enough in the church. But we can begin to model them for each other as individual Christians and begin to reshape the church's expectations. I began to learn this lesson through a Christian friend with whom I work.

She and I are teachers and she called one day to tell me that she could not lecture in my class the following day as she had promised. She suffers from chronic depression, and she realized that she was dangerously near an edge. She knew it would be destructive for her to pretend that she could take on anything else. Even with her lifesaving medication and appreciated therapy, there were times when she still could not cope well. But in God's grace and compassion, she had learned to choose the empowering path of listening to her limits and claiming them publicly. Though teaching a single class seemed a small demand to me, for her that day the added responsibility was overwhelming. In an important way, I also realized that her ability to say no on that day meant that on another day she would again listen to her body and might be able to say yes. I think of Jesus' words in Matthew, "Let your 'yes' be 'yes,' and your 'no,' 'no' (Matthew 5:37, NIV). Though he uttered this advice advocating that his disciples speak simply not using an oath in someone's name for emphasis, we can hear the echoes of our own need to speak plainly about what we can and cannot do.

Initially, of course, I was angry. I wanted to talk her into it because I needed the help, but that would have been a short-term vision. She

135

was living the long-term restoration of our embodied lives in God. She taught me a great lesson about abundant life with limits instead of fantasized capacities. She showed me that on that particular day she could not help, but on another she would if she was able. I could trust her as completely as I trust God. She was not living illusions, but learning to live with her real body and blood. Her responsibility reminded me of the web of God where we learn to help carry other's loads when we can, and when we cannot, to call out for someone else. In her weakness, she trusted the body of Christ and believed that there would be strength enough. Everything was not all up to her.

But perhaps most powerfully for me was the fact that she embodied this good theology. She acted on her assumption quickly and surely. Her decisiveness meant that I had enough time to act and make a different plan. How often Christians cause more pain and anxiety by not saying what is true about our capacities. No wonder the story of God gets bogged down in our repetitive patterns. We are afraid to tell the truth of our limits, and so we lie; and the new possibilities are stymied. But with her, I did learn to step into an unexpected possibility. I found another teacher to teach for me, from a different field. The students found him fascinating because of his discipline's unusual perspective on our topic. Something new had been born because my friend claimed her limits.

Learning to embody redemption as ambiguous and limited enables us to discover new and unexpected ways of participating in the inclusive and particular work of God restoring all things in our world. It is the flesh and blood practice of *metanoia,* the Greek word for turning around, the process of transformation, or conversion. When we stop denying the ambiguities and limits of our embodied lives, we are more able to see how God is changing directions for the birthing of the new thing.[20]

NEW EXEMPLARS: THE GOOD NEWS
OF INCLUSIVE EMBODIED REDEMPTION

Participating in redemption, we will begin to see that some bodies have become preferred over other bodies as symbols of God's restorative power.[21] We recognize traditional expectations of how a redeemed body looks and acts, its capacities and gifts, and how those expectations overshadow other bodystories of new life that do not fit the traditional mold. In truth, all our bodies tell stories of the good news breaking out in our own day and time.[22] If embodied symbols of Christian redemption are to be authentically inclusive, they must contain those other/silenced/hidden exemplars whose bodystories have been excluded. We must correct traditional misunderstandings of what kinds of bodies are appropriate sites for God's redeeming work.[23]

By their exemplary practices, others can encourage us to embody our particular ways of sharing in the restoration of the world. Partially, we imitate their affections and actions, connecting them with our particular skills and gifts. With them, we are drawn into new and often unexpected places, feelings, and action. In so doing, we share the hope of God's solidarity with our work. There are many wonderful exemplars we can look to in the history of the Christian community, but it is equally important to look for them in our own day. We should also be particularly attentive to those from groups traditionally excluded or marginalized.

These individuals are the exemplars of the new thing that God is doing. They are expected and unexpected bodies in expected and unexpected places doing new things. Many of them are in our immediate purview, but have gone unnoticed. Even the more famous or public figures go overlooked because of disability or some other marginalizing label. In Georgia, for example, we have a new United States Senator, Max Cleland. Well-known locally, he is now becoming a national figure deconstructing our images of whose body can witness to the transformative power of God in the world. A triple amputee as a result of the Vietnam war, Max Cleland was considered an improbable political candidate. How could his body create an image of authority and power, key elements for a successful political career? Many believed he could not win a public election with his disability, but he did win—first locally and now statewide.

Moreover, he came to embody hope and courage in the midst of daily ambiguities, gifts, limits, and skills. A practicing Christian, Cleland talks about the sacred power of life and love, which can overcome the kinds of death-dealing destruction he has known. He speaks plainly about what he knows. In doing so, he testifies not only to his particularity but also to his inclusivity in the ongoing redemptive possibilities of this world. He works daily for legislated justice and compassion while his body symbolizes a justice and compassion that we might overlook or deny. Destruction and dismemberment do not have the final say. His example writes a different story about embodied redemption.

Of course, there are many other exemplars who have no public forum. They are the persons touching our own lives who live fully while they manage their diabetes or bipolar disease, deal with sexist and abusive threats, and celebrate victories of reading as a dyslexic or of staying sober. These ordinary stories of redemption remind us that God's body is daily expressing the reimagining of good news of God's solidarity with compassion, grace, and justice. Acknowledging these heretofore hidden exemplars, we discover the possibilities in our own bodies. We understand that our aging joints and forgetful minds are sites of struggle and empowerment. We recognize how profoundly we are affected by an elder, perhaps especially one with some physical, emotional, or mental disability.

Seeing human embodiment through the story of Christ's struggle and liberation as a human body, our conceptions of redemption are broadened.[24] We recognize the dynamic of redemption in unexpected saints who have quietly crossed boundaries of poverty, or not so quietly overturned brutal racism and ethnic hatred. We come to recognize the inclusive nature of transformative hope when we can point to bodies that symbolize and actualize it. We must acknowledge our limited insight so that we may see the unexpected exemplars as readily as the expected.

Of course, embracing unexpected exemplars is problematic for many of us. We resist opening our imaginations to redeemed bodies that are disabled, have problems, and so forth.[25] *Metanoia* now becomes meddling as our exclusive images of redemptive embodiment are stretched beyond narrow privilege and ignorance. Why else does it take us so long to construct access ramps in our churches? Why else do we want those with disturbing smells or different behaviors (not destructive, but different) removed from our worship and communities? Why else do we welcome women's energies into our Christian families, but poorly respond to their requests for inclusive language, alternative rituals, and different forms of governance? Are they not among us as potential saints, teachers for us of redemptive living?

Unless we correct our distortions about the body-symbols and realities of God's salvation, we will deny ourselves and our world many venues of grace and resistance to injustice. We will miss the strong and re-creative lessons read through the handbook of their flesh and blood. Worse yet, we will be trapped in our own isolated interpretations of redeemed bodystories, bored and apathetic Christians living a deadened kind of life with no understanding for the broad inclusivity of God's literal body among us.[26] We must learn to leave behind our distortions and to embrace those who have been labelled as threatening to our misperceived orderings of privilege and power, even religious power.[27]

This expanded vision of exemplars would require serious reconsideration of people living with AIDS as potential spiritual guides. It would urge us to reimagine our relationship with non-Christians, remembering that they too are embodied as part of God's creation now being redeemed. Looking for the new thing God is birthing in them might mean, for example, that we would put our bodies on the line in solidarity with their bodies though our explicit faith traditions are different. New exemplars would call us to reconsider our relationships to those who suffer daily torture and oppression, mental illness, and disability. If we do not offer them our full attention, we will not be able to develop the discernment we need for finding God's path in the midst of all bodies' potentials for evil and good. We will be fooled as were those who crucified Christ.

Here again, I am aided in my own understanding by a personal experience. I was part of an unusual funeral last year. My friend had been diagnosed with a virulent form of leukemia. He courageously underwent several courses of chemotherapy with some good results. After his first rounds of treatments, he went home and grew stronger. We had a celebration at his house hoping that the remission would be long-lasting. He looked strong and sure, and we took these as signs of good life. But the cancer returned, and the next round of treatments was not as successful. Too shortly thereafter, he died.

At the funeral, we were clergy and laypeople from many traditions—Christian, Hindu, and Tibetan Buddhist. We came because we loved this man. Though he had died a relative unknown, except in academic circles, he had done more for interfaith dialogue and understanding in Atlanta than anyone of his day. His vitality had touched us all. Even at his funeral remembering those last images of his worn and fragile body, we still saw him as a strong and compassionate friend. His disabled flesh was very able, and we wanted to honor his request that his funeral be an interfaith celebration of life. But none of us could quite imagine how it would work to have a funeral beginning with the chanting of the Wisdom Sutra by Tibetan monks, continuing in the Episcopal tradition, and ending with a Hindu blessing. None of us could imagine what we would learn during that funeral. It had eluded us, as had a certain dimension of him and his vision for interfaith dialogue. We had heard his words. Now we were living them in our bodies, and that made all the difference.

We realized that day a new understanding of the web of God's redemption in our own community. He had embodied and lived out this understanding for many years knowing, worshipping, and working with peoples of all faiths. As we gathered to remember him, we saw and heard each other—often for the first time. Moreover, we realized a small portion of his larger vision about the redemptive work of God. We could share our devotion to the holy. We could be together in our diversity. We did realize that he had been a modern exemplar for us, and we had not understood that before. Having been forced by his wishes to open ourselves to the unexpected, we understood redeemed embodiment as never before. How silently he had been teaching us that all along.

REDEEMED BODIES: THE GOOD NEWS

As redeemed bodies, we daily are exploring with God transformative possibilities of life here and now. Particularly and inclusively, we participate in the re-imaging of all creation through our bodies' ambiguities, differences, limits, and joys.[28] We learn to discern who we truly are as God's own body, discovering aspects of our Christian story that have been denied, marginalized, and/or oppressed. But claiming these misperceptions and correcting them, we can begin reimagining with God a flourishing embodied life of unexpected freedom and serious choice. We can learn from one another changing, becoming *metanoia* for each other and with God in our own bodies. Without patronizing pity or passivity toward ourselves or others, we write with our bodies a redemption that we do not as yet fully know, partial and emerging as the dawn on Easter morning when Jesus asked Mary if she recognized him. Looking more carefully, she did.

---

1. See Sallie McFague, *The Body of God: An Ecological Theology* (Minneapolis: Fortress Press, 1993). She describes ways redemptive flourishing becomes real in all flesh and blood as well as earth

and sky. McFague's ecological theology reminds us to consider the full body of God when we think about embodiment in Christian affections and practices. Her bibliography is an excellent resource for additional contributions in this area.

2. Martha Nussbaum, *Love's Knowledge* (Oxford: Oxford University Press, 1990), 62, 70-82, relates Aristotle's ideas of practical reason and ethical decision making as embedded in concrete particulars and more universal values. She discusses human desires and needs of the body as an example of this interweaving of particulars and universals.

3. In her book, *Dancing on My Grave* (Garden City, N.Y.: Doubleday, 1986 with Greg Lawrence), Gelsey Kirkland poignantly describes the need to numb her feelings about the effects of expectations placed on her as a famous dancer from the New York City Ballet. She describes how this numbing affected her senses of self, body, relationship, and purpose.

4. Augustine in *The City of God*, trans. Henry Bettenson (Middlesex: Penguin Books, Ltd., 1984), Book XXII.15, 12-20 makes this claim. These texts became foundational for Christian understandings of resurrection and the body. They continue to influence the contemporary church and certain aspects of Western culture's assumptions about the body.

5. Caroline Walker Bynum, *The Resurrection of the Body in Western Christianity* (New York: Columbia University Press, 1995), offers a remarkable survey of the early Church's struggle to define Christian concepts of the body after death. Continuity of body, understood as actual physical flesh, was crucial. Individual configurations of matter were considered unchanged and undisrupted despite violent body damage on earth. For the early Church, influenced by Augustine, Gregory of Nyssa, and others, the believer's body was perfectly reassembled in resurrection. But that perfection was differently defined by various theologians. For example, in the face of his sister Macrina's violent death, Gregory could not tolerate the idea of being unable to recognize her at the resurrection. Therefore, he developed a theology of the resurrection in which Macrina's body would be identically restored having continuity with her earthly body, including scars from her life, 99, 111-112. Other theologians did not think resurrection bodies would have scars. Peter Brown, *The Body and Society: Men, Women, and Sexual Renunciation in Early Christianity* (New York: Columbia University Press, 1988), 6-7, examines how Greco-Roman constructions of continuity through family, especially the proper bearing and raising of children, reinforced these theological themes of continuity in matter now and in the afterlife.

6. Bynum, *The Resurrection of the Body*, xix, describes how similar are some of our questions about embodiment and Christian life to those of the early church. Bynum also remarks on contemporary culture's obsession with embodiment as identity and survival though these obsessions reflect much less the spiritual concerns about death and life after death than those of the early Church. The early Church also found Jesus' resurrection to be an important source of hope for facing the daily struggles of their present lives as Brown discusses in *The Body and Society*, 381. In fact, Brown also points out in his book, *Augustine of Hippo* (Berkeley: University of California Press, 1967), 314, that Augustine and many of the early Church fathers emphasized resurrection as a liberatory experience, which drew believers in hope toward Christ's redeemed future.

7. I am deeply grateful to Roberta Bondi for her insights about the relevance of redemption rather than resurrection as the focus of our present Christian lives. This is an especially important differentiation when asking contemporary questions about disability and faith. Her books, *To Love As God Loves* (Philadelphia: Fortress Press, 1987) and *In Ordinary Time: Healing the Wounds of the Heart* (Nashville: Abingdon Press, 1996), provide excellent insights into themes of redemption as related to daily Christian practice.

8. Augustine, *The City of God*, Book XXII.19, 24, 30. Dale Martin, *The Corinthian Body* (New Haven: Yale University Press, 1995), describes connections between Platonic and early Church conceptions of the body-soul relation. He relates these connections to particular issues regarding resurrection and the body, which faced the Pauline church in Corinth. Body and soul are interwoven concepts, though for the Platonists in general, the body was "perhaps . . . of a less or a lighter or different stuff," 7-9.

9. See Augustine's descriptions of the role of creativity and imagination in God's relationship with creation and humankind in *The City of God*, Book XXII.24.

10. Philosophical influences on Augustine and the early Church fathers placed the body not only in the context of a kind of foil for the perfect harmony of the soul but also as an ordering site and sign for the stabilization of the city and culture. These assumptions about the body

forced some theological notions of matter into similar and rather narrow categories. For certain prevalent schools of philosophy and theology, therefore, the body became identified with potential derangement of order and resultant chaos. This tension soon was translated as God's punishment for sin associated with the body. For additional insight see Peter Brown, *Augustine of Hippo*, 328, and Augustine, *The City of God* XXII.22.1. The construction of body as potentially "deranging" or "disordering" also heightened concerns over body imperfections and dysfunctions. The open multiplicity inherent in God's diachronic redemption of the world was lost. Without the restitution of the full spectrum of embodiment as a crucial partner in redemption, our contemporary body stories will continue to be captive to destructive categories that ignore certain central aspects of the Christian tradition.

11. See Brown, *Augustine of Hippo*, 417.

12. John A. T. Robinson, *The Body: A Study in Pauline Theology* (Bristol, Ind.: Wyndham Hall Press, 1988) discusses the Hebrew conception of the whole as parts. In the Hebrew mind, the body and any of its component parts and the whole were never placed in opposition. In fact, "there is no word for the whole in Hebrew. Almost any part can be used to represent the whole, and the powers and functions of the personality are regarded as exercised through a great variety of organs, indifferently physical and psychical," 13.

13. Simone Weil, *Waiting for God*, trans. Emma Craufurd (New York: Harper & Row, Publishers, 1951), 204-7, describes how difficult it is for human beings to tolerate difference. Her descriptions of the need for autonomy and difference in communities of friendship resonate with all of us.

14. McFague, *The Body of God*.

15. Quoted in Bondi, *To Love*, 25.

16. This concept of being born again was important to Jesus' understanding of abundant life. See John 3:1-16.

17. Jürgen Moltmann, *The Church in the Power of the Spirit* (New York: Harper & Row, 1977), 112. The thematic of a suffering God, who lives our ambiguities and disabilities with us in redemptive partnership and transformative hope, is especially evident in the works of contemporary liberation theologians. See especially, Dorothy Soelle, *The Suffering God* (Philadelphia: Fortress Press, 1995); Gustavo Gutiérrez, *We Drink From Our Own Wells* (New York: Orbis Press, 1984); Sharon Welch, *Communities of Resistance and Solidarity: A Feminist Theology of Liberation* (Maryknoll, N.Y.: Marynoll Press, 1985).

18. There are many individuals and groups in today's world whose embodied lives are ambiguous, including Holocaust survivors; Vietnam veterans; Tibetan Buddhists; those raped, tortured, beaten; those living with disabilities; and others.

19. Toni Morrison, *Beloved* (New York: Penguin Books, 1988), 89.

20. Just as an interesting side note, even contemporary models of management realize the importance of being able to change directions, to learn new things. In his highly successful book on management Peter Senge, *The Fifth Discipline: The Art & Practice Of The Learning Organization* (New York: Doubleday, 1994), 11-16, uses "metanoia" as a key concept for a learning organization participating in the contemporary economic markets. Without the capacity for metanoia, organizations and individuals cannot creatively shift and learn in response to the needs of contemporary work and life.

21. Nancy L. Eiesland, *The Disabled God: Toward a Liberatory Theology of Disability* (Nashville: Abingdon Press, 1994) describes how Christian symbols are shaped by embodied experiences of believers and others. Using the phenomenological model of symbolism developed by Paul Ricoeur as a starting point, she constructs an inclusive process whereby "the Christian tradition [can] recognize the lived experience of persons with disabilities" as a source of Christian symbolism along with the experiences of able-bodied persons. In this way "people with disabilities [can] . . . acknowledge the symbols of the Christian tradition, not as over against [them], but as a part of [their] hidden history," 23.

Eiesland is making the point that Christianity has confounded its symbol-making process to the real lives of disabled persons, hiding their embodied experiences from the "normal" body practices that shape Christian narratives and signs. Likewise, feminist theorists such as Audre Lorde and Jane Gallop write about a similar erasure or silencing of women's bodies and voices in symbol-making processes of culture and religion. The feminist image of women telling their stories to each other has developed as a way of bringing forth more diverse and unexpected experiences thus reshaping symbols to better reflect the diversity and ambiguity of human experience.

22. Moltmann, *The Church*, 98.

23. Melanie May, *A Body Knows: A Theopoetics of Death and Resurrection* (New York: The Continuum Publishing Company, 1995) is a wonderful body narrative that offers an expanded anatomy of redeemed life as well as the tools for calling to speech and listening. Her contemporary theology of transformative practices contrasts in some ways to those in traditional Christianity because she includes unexpected sites of Christian redemption such as lesbians, interreligious friendships, and so forth.

24. For additional thoughts on this topic see Robinson, *The Body*, 74; and Eiesland, *Disabled God*, 99-100.

25. In his book, *The Problem of Pain* (New York: MacMillan Publishing Co, Inc., 1962), C. S. Lewis writes about the difficulties of opening our imaginations to God as real flesh and blood. He uses the analogy of a child's game of hide and seek. The day we recognize that there truly is a holy presence available to and with our lives is the day that we realize we never meant spiritual quest to come to this, to a genuine encounter with the living God. We did not mean for our imagined body of God incarnate in and with us to become active.

26. See Robinson, *The Body*, 51, 61, and Eiesland, *Disabled God*, 107. See also John Cobb, *Christ in a Pluralistic Age* (Philadelphia: The Westminster Press, 1975) in which he provides a helpful contemporary theological paradigm for expanding traditional Christologies and lifestyles in response to a multifaith world.

27. Sociologists, anthropologists, and cultural analysts are exploring ways in which bodies define normative and liminal boundaries of society, religion, culture, and politics. Two books relevant to this chapter are Bryan S. Turner, *The Body and Society* (New York: Basil Blackwell, 1984), and Mary Douglas, *Purity and Danger: An Analysis of Concepts of Pollution and Taboo* (New York: Hammondsworth, 1970). Feminist theorists also have been especially concerned with the oppressive ways in which women's bodies have served as cultural and religious boundary-setters. Many of these analyses have been influenced by the works of Luce Irigaray, *Elemental Passions*, trans. Joanne Collie and Judith Still (New York: Routledge, 1992) and *Speculum of the Other Woman*, trans. Gillian C. Gill (Ithaca, N.Y.: Cornell University Press, 1985 [1974]); Helene Cixous and Catherine Clement, *The Newly Born Woman*, trans. Betsy Wing (Minneapolis: University of Minnesota Press, 1988). Other helpful works include, Jane Gallop, *Thinking Through the Body* (New York: Columbia University Press, 1988), and Elizabeth Grosz, *Volatile Bodies: Toward A Corporeal Feminism* (Bloomington: Indiana University Press, 1994).

28. Wendy Farley, *Eros for The Other: Retaining Truth in a Pluralistic World* (University Park, Penn.: The Pennsylvania State University Press, 1996) describes the radical importance of inclusion for the practice of Christian love. Her final chapter, "The Practice of Truth," 185-200, outlines guidelines for the pursuit of truth as eros for the other in a pluralistic context.

CHAPTER SEVEN

THROUGH GLASSES DARKLY: DISCOVERING A LITURGICAL PLACE

Jan B. Robitscher[1]

Whether or not we are ever labeled as being "disabled," all of us enter this world with limitations and possibilities, dreams and desires, and a longing for a place in the human community. Because these are never perfectly fulfilled in this life, we all see "through glasses darkly." Those who live with disabilities, however, and who have been brought to the community of faith by baptism have these same desires, but magnified. The words of the baptismal service rightly emphasize incorporation into the body of Christ. My childhood experience was that the church could be a refuge from mistreatment or rejection at school or in society. I sang in the choir, participated in Sunday school, and attended my congregation with my parents. But when rejection comes from the church, as I have experienced in a long quest for ordination, it is keenly felt—and I see the church "through glasses darkly." But it is not only those with visual or other disabilities who see "through glasses darkly." Those who are considered part of the able-bodied community also see "through glasses darkly" when they view persons with disabilities without a vision of their potential place in the household and service of God.

This chapter will explore three dimensions of "discovering a liturgical place": finding a physical, architectural place to worship; finding a place within the worshiping community; and finding a place in which to exercise the various charisms of liturgical leadership. That place could be one of faithful attendance and participation (at whatever level) in the liturgy. Or it might be one of more active participation: reading, serving at the altar, serving Communion, singing (or signing) in the choir; or seeking counseling or other programs and

144

ministries in which to participate. Or, if God should call, it might mean placing oneself before the church for ordination or other forms of church leadership. So "finding a liturgical place" is a multifaceted experience that is central if the body of Christ is truly to be complete. I will focus particularly on churches within the liturgical tradition of my own experience as an Episcopalian. But the theological principles apply to many Christian churches.

FINDING A PLACE FOR WORSHIP

Before we can begin to discover how persons with disabilities can go about "finding a liturgical place," we must first deal with finding a place in which to be liturgical people. For too long, churches have been inaccessible to persons with disabilities, the message (whether conscious or not) being that only the unblemished may approach the altar. With new building codes and a new awareness, many churches are trying to renovate for accessibility; but sometimes this results in the mixed messages that all may enter but only some can come to Communion or that all may worship but only some can obtain pastoral counseling. That space is important to a worshiping community is not a new concept. Since its beginnings, architecture has influenced Christian worship, and setting aside for a moment the issue of architectural barriers, I believe there are things we can learn from our ancestors in the faith, particularly the Celts and the builders of medieval cathedrals.

The Celts, who lived in sparsely populated lands with a harsh climate and hard existence, built mainly small churches attached to monastic communities and small villages. The sites for these small churches were carefully chosen as much for their natural resources as for the holy qualities of a particular place.[2] Once chosen, the site was enclosed by a wall, which served both for protection and to mark the place of the saint's bones to which the monastery was dedicated.[3] The other important feature of these holy places was their function as a "place of resurrection"—a place where a saint died and, therefore, a good place to die, be buried and, protected by the saint, to rise again at the last day. Churches were small, usually of wood, and only later took on the larger medieval stone structure. These were intimate places, built to preserve what little heat there was, where worshipers

145

(both lay and monastic) gathered and the Eucharist was celebrated at a free-standing altar, the priest facing toward the liturgical east.

Contrast with these intimate liturgical spaces the great medieval cathedrals. Here, the worshiper entered the other world—an earthly representation of heaven. Dwarfed by the soaring architecture and dazzled by light filtered through stained glass, worship was an experience not of intimacy with people (community), but was rather directed heavenward (toward God). Different values and functions directed this architecture. The emphasis was on the spectacle value of liturgy and the aesthetics of architecture, art, and music. Of this architecture John Dillenberger writes:

> Whereas the earlier Romanesque churches . . . were examples of the focusing of light on particular points, the Gothic achievement was the diffusion of light throughout the building. Gothic architecture and the philosophy surrounding it is a way of thinking similar to the Eastern conception of the icon. It is also a way of thinking that sees God in and through material images, which in fact does not see a spiritual world apart from its embodiment. It is totally incarnational.[4]

Such a statement might surprise some Protestants, especially those of an iconoclastic bent. What happens in architecture and sacrament is the embodiment of the presence of God and is a reflection of the fact that all presence is mediated. The idea that architecture is incarnational, that we can see, touch, and feel Christ through it, is vital, but not in any way limiting, to our ability to worship. It should thus make us pause to realize how barriers in architecture shut people out of this experience of incarnation. There is no one perfect architecture for worship. Some peoples and cultures were drawn to intimate spaces and some to vaulted edifices. This happened for practical as well as religious and aesthetic reasons. I believe centuries later we have not changed much; some are drawn to larger or smaller spaces for worship. What is important today is that, whatever the size, our worship spaces be places of access and welcome. To illustrate this, I want to relate accounts of several Episcopal churches with varying degrees of access, and also to consider the space in which this chapter was first presented, Cannon Chapel at Emory University.

Grace Cathedral has recently completed a restoration to its original master plan. The first thing one sees approaching from California Street is the Grand Staircase—some 30 steps that lead to the beautiful bronze doors of the main entrance. Although I know that there are other approaches to the church proper as well as to the Cathedral and diocesan offices (for example, by elevator from the garage, or through the Cathedral Gift Shop entrance), no signs currently indicate where these alternative means of access can be found. Such access is definitively not through the front door. Our diocesan Commission on Access (which includes an architect) tried to work with the Cathedral to get a ramp alongside those steps and some on-street disability parking, but in a diocese that prides itself on its inclusivity, we were unsuccessful.

My own parish home, St. Mark's in Berkeley, is a bit more accessible. There is wheelchair access to the church through a side door near the front. From there, it is quite easy to go through the church to the patio and the newer of our parish halls (the other one is up a flight of stairs), which has bathrooms that are technically accessible, though the doors are very hard to open. The parish offices are accessible through another entrance that now has an on-street disability parking space. The one thing that is not accessible—at least to someone in a wheelchair—is the altar, separated by several steps from the congregation. This is not so much a barrier to receiving Communion, as it is brought to those who cannot come to the rail. But the message about who may aspire to liturgical leadership is, however unconscious, unmistakable.

Now this is not to say that we should flatten every church regardless of the aesthetic or historic character of the place! Nor will all the ramps in the world guarantee that people with certain physical disabilities will come or that they will readily be incorporated into the community. It is to say that, for a long time, the message has been, "Welcome—*unless* you are a minority or gay or homeless or disabled . . ."

About three years ago, Christ Church in Portola Valley, California, did a major renovation. When members of the Episcopal diocese's Commission on Accessibility were invited to come to see the work in progress, one of the clergy made a surprising statement:

> When we started this project, we were not thinking in terms of total access. Then one day it hit us that we could make the whole place accessible—even the altar—and we could finally say architecturally what we meant by being inclusive.

The church is now entirely accessible, with an altar that is ramped at the corners. In doing their renovation, they had stumbled into the realization that the body of Christ is not complete unless everyone can be present and participate fully. The space and its configuration speak hospitality. A good example of this in a smaller church in the Atlanta area might be the Church of the Epiphany on Ponce de Leon Avenue, where the entrance is accessible, and the altar space is also ramped.

So we turn to Cannon Chapel, designed by architect Paul Rudolph (whose father was in the first class at Candler) and built in 1980 under the new codes of accessibility. It is a gathering place for a seminary community and a place where the wider community of faithful people can gather as well. This chapel has its fans and detractors.[5] But I believe it has several wonderful qualities: access by elevator, a wide entrance, the high, barrel-vaulted ceiling with its clerestory windows, which draw the eye upward, away from self and toward the light. Intimacy is achieved partially through flexible floor seating and bleacher seating, which regrettably has no access by elevator.

The places I have described are all fairly large, and a similar survey could be done of smaller, more intimate spaces. What is important is to realize that architecture and attitude are bound up together. Spatial configuration and hospitality are intimately related. Henri Nouwen wrote about this some twenty years ago though he might not have known how far-reaching would be the effects of his words:

> So we can see that creating space is not easy in our occupied and preoccupied society. And still, if we expect any salvation, redemption, healing and new life, the first thing we need is an open receptive place where something can happen to us. Hospitality, therefore, is such an important attitude.[6]

The hospitality expressed in the architecture of sacred space is really a sacrament (outward sign) of the hospitality of the people who worship there. By making churches accessible to persons with disabilities, we open ourselves to their life stories and medical problems, but we also open ourselves to acknowledge their unique gifts and contributions to the community and to church leadership. These gifts could be as simple as a gift of presence, pointing us beyond our own mortality to the hope of eternal life. Or they could be as complex as art for the sanctuary, a hymn signed for the deaf, or Communion distributed in a different way so that all can come to the Banquet Table. And the words of the prophet Isaiah will be fulfilled:

> Every valley shall be lifted up,
>   and every mountain and hill made low;
> the uneven ground shall become level,
>   and the rough places a plain.
> Then the glory of the LORD shall be revealed,
>   and all people shall see it together,
>   for the mouth of the LORD has spoken.
> (Isaiah 40:4-5)

FINDING A PLACE IN COMMUNITY

Everyone wants a sense of belonging. But persons with disabilities are often isolated and alone in spite of the overwhelming truth that baptism is into the body of Christ. Brett Webb-Mitchell speaks of "the betrayal of people with disabilities" by the very church they love so much.[7] This betrayal can be obvious, as in the barriers of architecture, or more subtle, in being made to feel different and therefore not welcome. As much as the architecture, it is our worship patterns that will bring to light our most authentic "community self"—for good or ill—and will also show us the way to become more inclusive of persons with disabilities. Much has been written about making worship itself more accessible.[8] Many churches have gone beyond outside ramps to examine the sign value of gestures and the tactile as well as visual impact of objects used in worship. Some have installed audio loops, made their service leaflets more readable, trained their ushers, or provided interpreters if deaf persons are present. But to the extent that all are not welcome and some remain at the edge of community, we still see "through glasses darkly."

Returning to the idea that all presence—whether human or divine—is mediated, we realize that disabled persons must mediate this presence as they are. What prevents this mediation is the opposite of incarnation—the spiritualization of presence—of which the Letter to James speaks so movingly. The homeless are not housed and clothed by wishing them well (James 2:14-17), and persons with disabilities are not incorporated into the community of worship by wishing they were whole. Only through conscious efforts at hospitality can we accept others as they are and then begin the process of helping them

149

to find their place in community. In this the churches have much to learn from persons of disability.[9]

Even when churches want (or are required) to renovate for access and make conscious efforts to create an attitude of hospitality and to make the liturgy accessible, an unnerving attitude often exists. It can be summed up in the words of that famous line from *Field of Dreams,* "If you build it, they will come." "They" might be injured by an accident (like Christopher Reeve), have Down syndrome, be living with AIDS, or be among the increasing elderly population. As one person put it, "The very people who built our churches now are unable to come to worship in them!" "They" will enter "our" community, "our" space. "They" will mediate the presence of God and of community in a different way. What then? How will they be welcomed? How will they participate in worship? How can Sunday school materials be adapted? What if they want counseling? This fear can become paralyzing. How can we break down the barriers between us and them so that we realize that all of us have disabilities, whether visible or not? How can we face our own mortality knowing that at any moment we could become disabled?

Often these fears are quite irrational. I once heard a story that a man with his guide dog was refused entrance to a church because they were afraid the dog might have fleas! Unless there is an attitude of genuine hospitality, those who do come will not stay. Consider the following stories:

> A choir director once asked me how to integrate a deaf person into the choir. I asked, "Does this person really belong in the choir or is there some other ministry? If so, could this person be a librarian, or could a "signing choir" be established? How about using hand bells, where timing more than hearing is most important."

These questions are practical, pastoral and theological.

Then there was the story in the *Braille Monitor*[10] about a blind couple (Missouri Synod Lutheran) who was new to a parish. "We can't ask them to help. What could they do? They're blind!" was the first remark they overheard. Finally, after years of working at becoming involved, they volunteered to host the coffee hour after church and "forgot" to ask for help! It took some doing, but it proved to be the start of their integration into many activities in that church community. Here is servanthood—bringing their gifts to serve others. This attitude, of course, is the heart of liturgical participation: the giving and receiving of gifts, divine and human.

Finally, there is a vignette from Bonnie Poitras Tucker, Professor of Law at Arizona State University, who is profoundly deaf (and, she says, not particularly religious):

> "Let us pray" the chaplain says. And every head in the audience bows; every eye in the audience closes. Except mine. I bow my head at half mast and keep my eyes wide open. Else how would I know when the prayer is over and it's time to look up again?[11]

All of these stories point us toward a vision of the church as a place where the kingdom of God can break in upon our lives in a tangible way. But this vision might also help us broaden our definitions of disability. For when we invite and accommodate persons with disabilities so that they become vital and contributing members of the community, then we are living out the parable of the great banquet of Luke 14 where Jesus teaches that God is free to invite any and all—and especially the poor and disabled—to the feast:

> Who do the people who are poor and those who are disabled symbolically represent in this story? All of us. Those who are disabled also represent us. They represent all of us who come before God to sit at a table of love and life with one another and share in a meal, with all our wounds and sense of brokenness, with all our limitations and knowledge of our inadequacies, with all our sins well known already by God we come to share in the banquet presented before us.[12]

If a parish does grow beyond its fears and begins to welcome persons with disabilities, then at some point these persons may begin to present charisms for liturgical participation such as reading, singing, signing, or serving. When this happens, sometimes practical problems must be solved. In order to serve at the altar of my home parish (which I do on a regular basis), I had to devise a space consisting of a carpet remnant and a "tie-down" (a short cable with a leash hook at each end) so that my guide dog would have a place to sleep during church. It works beautifully, and no one has ever complained. Most of these problems have simple and rational solutions. What is harder is to allow time and education to assimilate the sign value of this participation, to cultivate the attitude of welcome among

151

the whole congregation, and to accept the kind of risk that will lead to discoveries of hidden talents and gifts waiting to be offered.

This risk involves the realization, which Paul stated so well (Galatians 6:17), that in this world we are called to see Christ crucified, and to recognize the marks of Christ's suffering in our own infirmities. The presence of persons with disabilities will also bring us living examples of the power of God shown in great weakness (II Corinthians 1). The consolations that we receive in our affliction enable us to console others. This awareness of redemptive suffering will do much to break down the barriers of "us" and "them" and will enable a mutual ministry of, with, and to persons of disability.

If the church is really a place of mutuality, then it is not only the existing community that must accept persons with disabilities as they are. Persons with disabilities must also accept the community as it is while at the same time challenging it to grow and change. We must make our needs known so they can be accommodated. Responsibility must be held by everyone if the community is to function properly. Paul writes in several places that the body of Christ has many members and that each is necessary to the working of all the others (Romans 12, I Corinthians 12). A reflection on this and a warning can be found in an essay from the collection *Like Trees, Walking:*

> If Paul has anything to say to us it is that our church of talking heads had better find the rest of its body parts, and find them quickly. If your church acts just like a society that sends people with physical, mental or emotional impairments to the sidelines, then it is acting more like the body politic than the body of Christ.[13]

But there are also stories of hope, as in this account of a liturgical experience, this time at a retreat:

> Each morning and evening we [Frances Young and her family, including her profoundly disabled son, Arthur] gathered in the oldest place of Christian worship still in use, St. Peter's, Bradwell, an Anglo-Saxon chapel . . . Members of the community bumped Arthur's chair across the fields. . . . As usual, Arthur could not be kept quiet. So one evening the person leading prayers created silence through the music of the Othana Psalms (one might use the music of Taizé or familiar hymns or praise choruses) and Arthur suddenly seemed to be the Christ among us.[14]

FINDING A PLACE OF LITURGICAL LEADERSHIP

Consider your own call, brothers and sisters: not many of you were wise by human standards, not many were powerful, not many were of noble birth. But God chose what is foolish in the world to shame the wise; God chose what is weak in the world to shame the strong; God chose what is low and despised in the world, things that are not, to reduce to nothing things that are, so that no one might boast in the presence of God (I Corinthians 1:26-29).

These words, written by Paul about vocation, would surely cause concern if they appeared on a modern-day application for ordination. If it is difficult for persons with disabilities to gain physical and social access to the church, it is nearly impossible, if such persons should feel called by God, to gain access to that process which leads to ordination for liturgical leadership. This process, across denominations, has become very adversarial as churches try to cope with too many applicants for too few jobs. Even so, the record is not good for persons from minority groups, and most especially persons with disabilities, who seek to follow the call of God. In this there is still much seeing "through glasses darkly." Before exploring the historical reasons for this barrier, it might be well to examine some more recent history regarding the ordination of persons with disabilities. (See also Herzog, chapter 9.)

Nancy Eiesland documents this barrier as it happened in the American Lutheran Church:

The General Convention of the ALC wholeheartedly embraced the concerns of persons with disabilities [in its 1980 statement] and encouraged systemic change. Yet just five years after the unanimous ratification of this resolution, the council of the ALC announced at its 1986 General Convention that people with "significant" physical or mental handicaps would be barred from ordained ministry.[15]

The Episcopal Church has not been much better. It is ironic that the church now celebrates the lives of Thomas Gallaudet, priest, educator, and leader in ministry to the deaf and Henry Winter Syle, first deaf priest ordained in 1876 over the objections of many who felt his deafness was an impediment to ordination.[16] There is also the example of Samuel Isaac Joseph Shereschewsky, Bishop of Shanghai in the early part of this century. A Jewish convert who became an

153

Episcopal bishop, he was paralyzed and yet completed his translation of the Bible into Wenli, typing some 2,000 pages with the middle finger of his "partially crippled hand."[17] Otherwise, few references to persons with disabilities are noted by the denomination. It would take another hundred years before the headline would read: FIRST WOMAN DEAF PRIEST ORDAINED IN PHILADELPHIA.

The most recent edition of the *Constitution and Canons of the Episcopal Church* contains the statement:

> No one shall be denied rights, status, or equal access to an equal place in the life, worship and governance of the Church because of race, color, ethnic origin, national origin, marital status, sex, sexual orientation, disabilities or age, except as otherwise specified by the Canons.[18]

How this mandate is to be carried out—or not—is left to each diocese, with wide variations in interpretation.

My own story of "discovering a liturgical place" clearly intersects with this chapter. It is not a heroic, overcoming, success story—at least not yet. For the past fifteen years I have been in and out of the ordination process in two different dioceses. I first felt called while in college. Two problems existed. The first was that the Episcopal Church had just voted to allow women to be ordained to the priesthood. The second problem was that I am partially sighted from birth; while I had heard of the church accommodating persons who became disabled after they were ordained, I had not heard of anyone with a disability entering successfully into the ordination process. In addition, I was considered too young at a time when the Episcopal Church was looking for older, "second-career" candidates. I had no idea of the power of symbol as I began to take on roles of liturgical leadership: acolyte, cantor, intercessor, and lay eucharistic minister. Although assuming various leadership roles felt—and still feels—really good to me, I did not realize how frightening I was to people who had never seen a person with a disability in such positions before. God was being mediated to them in a new way—or perhaps in an old, New Testament way. Not the perfect "priest=Jesus" model, but "the Disabled God" of which Nancy Eiesland writes so eloquently. Those lines of Paul about "strength in weakness" were being made visible. Hearing Scripture is one thing, seeing it is quite another!

From the time I first made public my desire for ordination, I heard such comments as:

"You *can't* be a priest because you can't drive."
"You will *never* be a good counselor because you have shifty eyes."
"You'll *never* be the rector of a parish."
"Wouldn't you really rather be a deacon?"
"I only ordain people who are strong enough to 'play in the traffic.'"

Over time, I heard them repeated often enough that I found it hard not to believe them. In spite of Paul's encouraging words about vocation, I began to doubt my ability to fulfill the call. When asked why I wanted to be ordained and what I would do if I were approved, I wasn't sure what to say. I no longer had a satisfactory answer. If I said that I felt called to be a "normal" parish priest, I was accused of being "delusional." If I spoke of a part-time ministry, then I did not have a definite ministry and therefore did not want to be ordained badly enough. It became hard to envision what a satisfactory answer would be when the parameters are all negative. The emphasis was on what, in the observations of others, I can't do, rather than the possibilities of what I can do or could do under the right set of circumstances. Again, the words of Paul come to mind, and I wonder what would happen if anyone were to answer these questions with his honesty:

> When I came to you, brothers and sisters, I did not come proclaiming the mystery of God to you in lofty words or wisdom. For I decided to know nothing among you except Jesus Christ, and him crucified. And I came to you in weakness and in fear and in much trembling. My speech and my proclamation were not with plausible words of wisdom, but with a demonstration of the Spirit and of power, so that your faith might rest not on human wisdom but on the power of God (I Corinthians 2:1-5).

There are many reasons why the ordination process is inaccessible to persons with disabilities. Some are historical, while others are more recent. Almost from the beginning, the church adopted the Levitical mandate that priests were to be "without blemish" (Leviticus 21:16ff.) and tied it to the Christo-monastic "priest=Jesus" model. Such a model implies that the priest equals Jesus in glory—physically perfect. It was not long before canon laws were established to ensure that, at a human level, this would be the case. Priests not only had to be male, they had to have "all their members"—"be physically perfect."[19]

But other parts of the biblical record showed concern for persons of disability, especially in parts of the Levitical code (see Leviticus 13 14), the story of Mephibosheth (II Samuel 9), and in the life and ministry of Jesus to the marginalized (see especially the parable of the great banquet in Luke 14). The concern is shown perhaps most of all in the writings of Paul, who, as his words quoted above attest, was brutally honest about his own disabilities, about his place as an apostle, and about God's ability to call the most unlikely people to ministry.

The canons prohibiting the ordination of persons with disabilities were only changed by the liturgical denominations in the early 1970s. In changing them the churches, perhaps unknowingly, produced a change of major theological significance about how the incarnation is related to human imperfection as well as to leadership in ministry. There is, however, a large gap between the possibility of ordaining persons who are disabled and its fullest implementation.

Other reasons for the denial of ordination are more recent in origin. Persons with disabilities are still often viewed as "less than" others; and therefore when such persons claim a vocation, they are rarely taken seriously. Even the health form, required of all in the ordination process, is based on an insurance form. It measures "risk factors" and, until very recently, concluded with a question that read something like, "Is there a deformity or mannerism which might be distracting to others?" The way the question now reads is not much better: "On the basis of your examination, is the candidate free from any medical condition or other impediment that would make him/her unsuitable for the tasks of ordained ministry?"[20] There is nothing about how this person copes with his/her disability or what obstacles, physical or otherwise, he/she has had to overcome. So the disabled continue to be viewed "through glasses darkly"; as an insurance risk! This view only reinforces the notion that those who are helpers must never need help. We seem to have lost the concept of the "Wounded Healer," which Henri Nouwen brought to our consciousness in his book of that name.[21]

Another barrier is society's definition of leadership. One day while teaching a class at the Episcopal School for Deacons, we did an exercise in which students were asked to name qualities they thought would make a person a good leader. Leading the list were:

tall
works very hard (workaholic)
pretty/handsome
high energy level
physically strong
smiles a lot

Not until the end of the class did students realize that they had excluded most persons with disabilities in their qualities of leadership—that we were back to Leviticus 21 and the "priest without blemish." Though not always conscious, parish committees and others involved in the ordination and job calling processes often base their decisions on looks, energy level, and style of dress. Two recently released reports, "Recruiting for Leadership in Ministry: Challenges and Hopes,"[22] which was issued by the Episcopal Church, and a similar ecumenical report, discussed recruitment of younger persons, women, and other minorities at some length, but neither report mentions persons with disabilities.

The life history of the person seeking ordination and how that is interpreted by psychological testing in the process to ordination is also an important issue. Many persons with disabilities experience much hurt in childhood from teasing and misunderstanding, and even in adulthood may experience emotional and sexual abuse. When the inevitable "fall-out" shows up on the psychological tests used to evaluate those seeking ordination, they often may be amplified because these tests were not designed for or normed to populations of disabled persons. Couple that with psychologists who are not knowledgeable about—or are prejudiced against—persons with disabilities, and you have a recipe for disaster and most certainly for exclusion. This accumulation of negativity sometimes makes persons with disabilities pursue ordination all the harder and feel more hurt when things do not go well.[23] There must also be appropriate help and room for celebrating healing, growth, and maturity as a person grows into a vocation that is much larger than oneself.

Another issue is physical access to the ordination process itself. While access to seminaries is improving, it will take a long time for places designed for able-bodied men just out of college (for centuries the only ones who could be ordained) to become adapted both in architecture and attitude for persons with disabilities. The Church

157

Divinity School of the Pacific was rebuilt in the 1960s for able-bodied men just out of college. It is now only marginally accessible. Yet a Committee on Accessibility now works within the school structures to effect changes in architecture and attitude. This committee is modeled upon our diocesan Commission on Accessibility Awareness, which works with parishes to promote physical access and acceptance of as well as education about persons with disabilities.

Further up the organizational ladder is the bishop (or other ecclesiastical authority) whose office may or may not be accessible in architecture or attitude. The attitudes of persons in these positions of authority is all important. Consider the conversation with a member of the Commission on Ministry (COM) at the end of a long day of interviews:

COM: Do you know who [The Rev.] Nancy Chaffee is?
Jan: Yes. She was one of the first persons with a disability to be ordained to the priesthood. I believe she has cerebral palsy.
COM: Well, I hope you don't become like Nancy Chaffee.
Jan: Why?
COM: Because she is a "one issue" person.

Little wonder I have not made much progress toward ordination! Recently I learned that application of this "one issue person" attitude is not limited to me, but pervades the diocese. The reason is quite simple: parish and diocesan committees fail to look beyond their last rector/pastor as a model of what a priest should be—and even then there is little or no consensus. They are also very undereducated about the options for various types of ministry such as the vocational diaconate, priesthood, religious life, or lay ministry. These are all different vocations with different requirements of temperament, charism, and skill. For example, my parish committee assumed that because I am on the faculty of the diocesan School for Deacons, I was surely called to be a deacon, whether or not I really felt so called. At some point there must be agreement between the one seeking ordination and those in authority as to what the vocation really is and reasonable support for that decision. Taking the necessary time and prayer to discern this will prevent committees from shuffling a person who is disabled into a ministry such as the diaconate simply because, in someone's opinion, he or she might not make it as a priest.

Integrating a pastor who is disabled into a congregation can present some other special challenges. The same fears that surface about welcoming persons with disabilities into parish communities are magnified if the person being welcomed is now in a leadership position.[24] Such persons are often viewed as flawed or may be seen (rightly or not) as "using" their disability for their own gain. If the pastor denies or tries to hide his or her disability, other problems might emerge. As with the other problems we have discussed, these too are able to be solved with education, patience, and persevering love. Here the "icon" of the disabled pastor points not to perfection, but to Jesus' suffering and to the hope encompassed in his resurrection.

We come finally to some serious questions—ones that are rarely asked in the current ordination processes and that encompass not only persons with disabilities but the very nature of the ordination process itself:[25]

(1) Can the person do the work of the ordained ministry?

(2) Is our definition of lay ministry/diaconate/priesthood/episcopate too narrow?

(3) Are there reasonable limits (such as maturity or the ability to function in a job) that could help objectively to define a person as being ordainable? Conversely, could movement in the process to ordination be predicated upon evidence of growth rather than time limits?

(4) Can we redefine normal, especially in terms of psychological testing, better to include persons of disability?

(5) Are there ways of making the ordination process more accessible, both in architecture and attitude, and are there ways of mediating these concerns so they are not interpreted as challenges to authority or as demands?

(6) Are there ways of educating all who are involved in these processes about persons with disabilities, especially regarding what they offer the church and what cultural barriers must be overcome to help people envision a person who is disabled as a liturgical leader?

(7) Finally, what would happen if the church decided to tackle the employment problem either by invoking the historical principle of ordaining persons to a place or by developing a theology of the Spirit wherein persons who fulfilled the appropriate requirements

would be ordained from an abundance of gifts rather than from a scarcity of resources, in which case jobs would be developed beyond traditional parish/hospital ministry?

Recently, I interviewed with a bishop on the East Coast. The conversation was remarkable in several ways. First, he surprised me by saying that he was going to ordain a partially sighted woman that very weekend! So the issues surrounding such an ordination had already been faced by the bishop and the Commission on Ministry. In our conversation the focus was on what I have to offer the diocese. We had candid discussions about the practicality of moving across the country, finding a suitable parish for the final discernment of the call, church politics, the lack of jobs, and even the process of maturing through all the rejections. But the tone of the interview was hopeful—something I have never before experienced. How it will all end I do not know, but I commend it to the hands of God.

Finding a place of liturgical leadership, then, involves finding a place and community from which leadership charisms can be called. But it also involves a willingness to be vulnerable, to allow God's strength to show through our weakness. As a disabled person in community, and particularly in leadership, one must often be willing to become an icon through which people can view not only the disability of incarnation (God becoming human) but the promise of resurrection (humanity taking on divinity) and eternal life. The icon may be expressed bodily, through one's own person, or may be seen through other gifts such as art, music, preaching, or spirituality. One's disability becomes a sacrament—an outward sign of the presence of God. This is perhaps best expressed through some words that Phillips Brooks, perhaps the greatest preacher of the nineteenth century (as well as the author of "O Little Town of Bethlehem"), wrote about self-offering. While he was probably not thinking primarily of ordination, the words seem appropriate:

> Dare to think of your humanity as something so divinely precious that it is worthy of being offered to God. Count it a privilege to make that offering as complete as possible, keeping nothing back. And then go out to the pleasures and duties of your life having been born anew into His divinity . . . as He was born into our humanity.[26]

CONCLUSION

When I was a child and received my first large print Bible, I remember poring over it, finding all the familiar passages I had heard in the Presbyterian Church and discovering many other wonderful and challenging stories, Psalms, and teachings. At some point I found I Corinthians 13. About the love part, I was not certain, as my experience at school—and even on occasion at church—had been mostly of rejection. But there was a verse toward the end of the chapter that intrigued me greatly.

My large print King James Version Bible read: "For now we see through a glass, darkly; but then face to face." In my child's mind, there was only one way this could make sense: "For now we see *through glasses darkly*'; but then face to face."

"Through glasses darkly" is the way I perceive the world, both physically and spiritually. From this vantage point, I have tried to discover a place in the world, the church, and, specifically, in the church's liturgical life. Seeing "through glasses darkly" has helped me to discover that the way we see now is not how we shall see, either physically or spiritually. An eschatological dimension points beyond this life.

The Hebrew view about personhood was (and is) that we are a unity of body and spirit, that our present flesh supports our spiritual life. The unity of body and spirit is an important concept. We now know how much this unity impacts our health, and it keeps us from spiritualizing physical problems. So we claim with the Psalmist that we are "fearfully and wonderfully made . . . " (Psalm 139) and that creation itself is good. And just as we mediate presence as we are, so God's presence is mediated to us as we are, in the flesh, the word made flesh, Jesus Christ.

Unfortunately, the dominant theology of the historical church took the opposite position that we have a good soul trapped in a bad body. I do not find either the Hebrew or the Early Christian theses to be sufficient in the formation of a theology that encompasses the reality of disability, with all of the darkness of living in a fallen world fraught with human prejudice and sin, and the claim that creation is good. Acknowledging the reality of Christ's redeeming work and of the Holy Spirit's presence in the community of the church is all essential to finding "a liturgical place." Neither of these theologies call us beyond ourselves to allow God to infuse in us the gifts of faith, hope, and love, which enable us to become who we are—the body of Christ.

"Finding a liturgical place" is not simply a matter of the past and present but also of the future. Without this Christian future dimension, we are simply good people doing good works. English theologian Frances Young's compelling work, *Face to Face: A Narrative Essay in the Theology of Suffering*, writes of the tension of the "already and not yet" very clearly:

> Humanity is flawed not perfect. . . . The dark side of hope is disappointment. Is there then no hope? What is appropriate Christian hope? In the New Testament the present reality is subject to corruption and decay, but the future "Kingdom of God" is anticipated in Jesus, and the new creation is begun in Christ. The dark side of hope is the pain and judgment involved in the world's giving birth to God's new creation.[27]

Young developed this theology as she reared her profoundly disabled son and discovered a vocation to ministry in the Methodist Church in the process. Her theological vision encompasses the creative tension of "already and not yet." She holds present realities against future ones and speaks of being bold enough to look at the "dark side" of love, humanity, God, hope—even discipleship and vocation—in order to come through this "dark night" into God's marvelous, dazzling light, with faith, hope, and love intact.

For Christians there is also a future dimension. In the burial liturgy we say: "For to your faithful people, O Lord, life is changed, not ended; and when our mortal body lies in death, there is prepared for us a dwelling place eternal in the heavens."[28] God will give our spirit a new body, one more appropriate for the glorious universe we will inhabit. Like Jesus after his resurrection, we will be recognizable to each other and to God—our wounds will still be visible. But, also like the risen Jesus, we will be unencumbered by them. We will finally be able to see them—and God—not "through glasses darkly," but "face to face." Perhaps we will testify to the gifts we enabled the church to receive. Words from the Revelation to John also come to mind:

> Then I saw a new heaven and a new earth; for the first heaven and the first earth had passed away, and the sea was no more. And I saw the holy city, the new Jerusalem, coming down out of heaven from God.

... and I heard a loud voice from the throne saying,
See, the home of God is among mortals.
He will dwell with them as their God;
they will be his peoples,
and God himself will be with them;
he will wipe every tear from their eyes.
Death will be no more,
mourning and crying and pain will be no more,
for the first things have passed away.
(Revelation 21:1-4)

No longer hindered by barriers of architecture or attitude, we will be free to discover that our liturgical place is to offer our praise, worship, thanks, and love to God who has created, known, and loved us from the beginning and who will lead us into eternal life. Perhaps Reinhold Niebuhr expressed this best when he prayed,

O God, who has made us the creatures of time so that every tomorrow is an unknown country and every decision a venture of faith, grant us, frail children of the day, who are blind to the future, to move toward it with a sure confidence in your love, from which neither life nor death can separate us.[29]

1. Thanks be to God and to all who helped bring this chapter to birth, especially my family for giving me life, love, and support; to Prof. Don Saliers who invited me to this project; Prof. Louis Weil for first encouraging me to write on these issues; the Revs. Rick McCall, Jane Menton, Scott Sinclair, and Tina Pippin for contributing ideas, editorial comments, and spiritual support; Diana Peters and the CDSP Committee on Access and Carol Kent and the Commission on Accessibility Awareness of the Diocese of California for keeping me aware of disabilities beyond my own; and to Robbin Mills and the Law Library of Emory University for the use of their computers during the Christmas semester break. Finally, special thanks to my guide dog, Doll, for her love, patience, and for all the lessons in "dogmatic" theology during this long writing process and during the conference, which was her last work before retirement.
2. Lisa M. Bitel, *Isle of the Saints: Monastic Settlements and Christian Community in Early Ireland* (Ithaca: Cornell University Press, 1990), 17.
3. Ibid., 58.
4. John Dillenberger, *A Theology of Artistic Sensibilities: The Visual Arts and the Church* (New York: Crossroad, 1986), 42-43.
5. For another point of view, see John Dillenberger's review, *A Theology*, 204.
6. Henri Nouwen, *Reaching Out: The Three Movements of the Spiritual Life* (Garden City, N.Y.: Doubleday, 1975).
7. Brett Webb-Mitchell, *Unexpected Guests at God's Banquet: Welcoming People with Disabilities into the Church* (New York: Crossroad, 1994), 1.
8. See especially National Organization on Disability, *That All May Worship: An Interfaith Handbook to Assist Congregations in Welcoming People with Disabilities* (Washington: National Organization on Disability, 1991).
9. Regarding the vocation of the sick, elderly (and by extension, the disabled) to the Christian community, see James L. Empereur, S.J., *Prophetic Anointing: God's Call to the Sick, the Elderly and the Dying* (Wilmington: Michael Glazier Inc. 1982).

10. "The Blind Church Member: What Conversation is Unlikely to Reveal," *The Braille Monitor* (February, 1995): 100-2.

11. Bonnie Poitras Tucker, *The Feel of Silence* (Philadelphia: Temple University Press, 1995), 89.

12. Brett Webb-Mitchell, *Unexpected Guests,* 89.

13. Gerald F. Moede, ed., *Like Trees Walking: Biblical Reflections on Healing* (Princeton, N.J.: Consultation on Church Union, 1988), 33.

14. Frances Young, *Face to Face: A Narrative Essay in the Theology of Suffering* (Edinburgh: T&T Clark, 1990), 137.

15. Nancy L. Eiesland, *The Disabled God: Toward a Liberatory Theology of Disability* (Nashville: Abingdon Press, 1994), 75-76.

16. Episcopal Church, *Lesser Feasts and Fasts—1994* (New York: Church Hymnal Corp, 1995), 338.

17. Ibid., 389.

18. Episcopal Church, *Constitution and Canons of the Protestant Episcopal Church* (S.1.:s.n., 1994), Title 1: Canon 17. Sec.5, 49.

19. See Walter Wink, "Holy and Without Blemish Before God: Disability and Normalcy," *Auburn News* 1:1 (Spring 1993).

20. Health Form, Church Pension Fund.

21. Henri Nouwen, *The Wounded Healer: Ministry in Contemporary Society* (Garden City, N.Y.: Doubleday, 1972).

22. Kent D. Fairfield, "Recruiting for Leadership in Ministry: Challenges and Hopes," *The Committee of the Board for Theological Education* (New York: The Episcopal Center, December 1, 1993).

23. See also Julie A. Wortman, "Barriers to Ordination," *The Witness* (April, 1992).

24. See the excellent article, G. Lloyd Rediger "Handicapped!" *Church Management: The Clergy Journal* (1982).

25. For more questions to help with vocational discernment and a more humane approach, I recommend the book *Listening Hearts* by Susan G. Farnham, Joseph P. Gill, R. Taylor McLean, and Susan M. Ward (Harrisburg: Morehouse Publishing, 1991).

26. Phillips Brooks, "Christmas Day," *Phillips Brooks Sermons in 10 Volumes* (New York: Dutton, 1881-1911).

27. Frances Young, *Face to Face,* 207, 209-15.

28. Episcopal Church, "Preface, Commemoration of the Dead," *The Book of Common Prayer* (New York: Church Hymnal Corp, 1979), 382.

29. Quoted in a sermon by Dr. Glenn R. Bucher, President, Graduate Theological Union. Used with permission.

PART III.

INTERPRETING CULTURE

I n order to understand the cultural interpretations of disability, we must probe the values, ideas, and images permeating the webs of meaning that inform people's lives. These resources that people draw on in making sense of their own and other lives are, implicitly if not explicitly, saturated with religious and moral interpretations. They address the deepest human concerns and give purpose to ordinary lives. The chapters in this section explore how disability is interpreted in story, work, and organizational life.

In Chapter 8, Adele McCollum investigates the cultural meanings of disability as revealed in folk sayings and stories. She notes how the significance attached to disability shapes how people feel, believe, and act, and underscores changes in how social groups incorporate people with disabilities. According to Albert Herzog (Chapter 9), clergy with disabilities often must negotiate between self-assessment of their abilities and those of their denomination's leaders and local religious bodies as they do the work of the ministry. Fulfilling their calling often challenges traditional norms about how ministry is done, offering the church theological and practical insights gleaned from their experiences. Negotiating divergent views about disability has not always been a smooth process, Nancy Eiesland (Chapter 10) reports. She tracks the changes in the meaning of disability among rights activists and organizations affiliated with them, noting the growing rift between activist groups and denomination-sponsored groups and programs.

CHAPTER EIGHT

TRADITION, FOLKLORE, AND DISABILITY: A HERITAGE OF INCLUSION

Adele B. McCollum

According to some analysts we are currently in a period when liturgy—"the work of the people"—is frequently disconnected from the lives of ordinary folks.[1] Richard Neuhaus, president of the Institute on Religion and Public Life, notes a perceived crisis in that believers in the United States feel they are being dominated by a secular elite and an educated clergy that has aligned itself with this elite.[2] Neuhaus further contends that the religious power now lies with the theory-laden views of the elite, dislodged from its rightful home in the life and spirit of the people. He is not the only one to say so.

This cleavage between religious professionals and ordinary believers is certainly not unique to contemporary American society. During the chaos of the Warring States Period in China, the rulers had lost touch with the people.[3] As a moral leader, Confucius sought answers by recalling a tradition borne of a more harmonious time. From this tradition he hoped to glean ideas that would restore harmony and bring the warring factions together. Confucius opposed legalism based on top-down control and turned instead to the ordinary lives of village people. Arguing that the beginning of human and international relations lay in the hearts and minds of the people, he directed his attention to the traditional folkways and the renovation of individual families and neighborhood. He consulted the ancient texts and sought to restore tradition to the people. He reasoned that if every social interaction were elevated to the level of ritual, behaviors of neglect, abuse, and maltreatment of others would soon become obsolete. When respect and care for others were enacted, the society and subsequently the world would become humane and responsive.

Such a truncated description of Confucian ethical thought serves as a pointer to the practicality of addressing alienation in society and the necessity of respecting the lived reality of the ordinary folk. Engaging this model can provide insight into the current situation in the United States. Discrimination, isolation, marginalization, and hostility, while not aimed at land boundaries, are instead directed toward identity groups, representing difference. If we examine the established folkways of American tradition, do we find, as did Confucius, a more harmonious time that can be replicated? If so, can the tradition borne of this time function to integrate all people regardless of differences? Can Confucius's goal, the harmonious order of society, be ours, and can his ideas be useful now?

This goal of seeking a time of inclusion and acceptance of difference is particularly vital for people with disabilities. In this chapter, folklore is mined for references revealing beliefs and attitudes toward people with disabilities both physical and cognitive. These folktales may also assist us by providing clues about how people with disabilities have been and may continue to be included and assimilated in folk societies, and perhaps in a larger society aware of its folk roots.

LORE AS DATA

Folklore is one source from the past through which we can listen to the words of the people as values are shaped and attitudes validated. Folk sayings and stories incorporate or embody local community maxims in such a way that we incorporate them unconsciously. "By the word 'folk-lore' a folklorist means myths, legends, folktales, proverbs, riddles, jokes, folk verses, folk beliefs, superstitions, customs, folk drama, folk song, folk music, folk dance, ballads, folk cults, folk gods. . . . Folklore—urban or otherwise—is oral, traditional, usually anonymous and varying."[4] Folklore is "how we live day to day, the habits and customs we acquire from watching our parents and those around us," according to Steven Swann Jones. It is "the very stuff of which we . . . are made."[5] Keith Cunningham contends that "Informal conversational narratives are quality data; individuals traditionalize material in this form because it is an effective communicative device particularly suited to expressing ideas and values. . . . The fact that an individual presents material in this culturally accepted legend form and style means it has a special status and embodies traditional ideas and values."[6] Beneath tales, stories, games, and conversations lie traditional ideas and values that have escaped the consideration of many scholarly disciplines.

Only recently have these folk and popular cultures and narratives finally become the focus of new studies in religion and disability studies, and serious attention is being given to their languages both oral and written. Feminist and critical theorists have contributed to this acceptance of folk culture by arguing that one ought to study horizontally rather than vertically, meaning that studying one's own culture is more likely to do justice to those studied and lend integrity to the work.[7] The inclusion of folklore in the database of acceptable canon broadens the access of all people to the traditional although hidden values of their own cultures.

In this chapter I focus on the folklore of predominantly white middle classes in North America—my own lore. Among white, educated members of the middle class, folk culture, or so-called old wives' tales, is held in disdain. In fact among scholars and cultural critics, a distinctly middle-class folk culture often goes unnoticed and unacknowledged. However, folk life is a major culture bearer of values and attitudes and is called upon especially to indoctrinate children with values concerning other racial, class, gender, or ability groups.

As with many of us, while growing up I was instructed to avoid deceptive tales. My head was filled with rituals of etiquette and manners, proper children's games, "good" books, "worthy" poems, and rules for public behavior. Those stories, songs, and games that supported the approved values were identified as true while those that did not were called "tall tales" or superstitions. The message, of course, was that these stories' content is so potent that children can be permanently influenced for good or evil if exposed to them. Furthermore, believing the wrong stories threatened banishment from good society as a misfit. The lore accomplished its desired effect: I appreciated that common culture was serious business and absorbed the view that real wisdom lies in stories, rhymes, and lore. Though overt attempts to censor or sanitize lore were rare, I learned quickly and surely that indecorous and inappropriate tales were to be interpreted in such a way as to disregard them or recognize their negative

169

judgments and avoid replicating them. That emphasis, not only on the content of the tale but on the value of interpretation, became part of a life-long methodology, a hermeneutic of story and popular culture.

DISABILITY AND FOLKLORE

Folk culture exposes values and attitudes toward disability and people with disabilities. In traditional folklore there are few direct references to people with disabilities; and when mention is made, it is accompanied by warnings against laughing, ridiculing, or considering one's self more highly than the other. This admonition is generated by the firm understanding that a person expressing ridicule is at risk of becoming disabled. Yet in one contemporary form of lore—the urban legend—references to disability, disaster, and violence are much more direct and often fall into the area of sick jokes and ridicule. A change has happened in ordinary life; it shows up in the folklore.

A major distinction between the traditional inclusive attitudes of folklore and the modern urban cruelty of exclusion lies in a change of attitude toward the idea of place, of being a part of a place, rather than being dislocated. Increasingly, the ideas of neighborhood, community, and shared value systems are nostalgic memories. Consciousness of playing a part in a communal project, of being "at home" somewhere, has diminished, and with it the subtle folkloric acknowledgments that everyone, however abled, has a part to play in that place. Communal interdependence that promoted an inclusion of difference has been supplanted by mob individualism. This oxymoronic condition warrants that within the home or identity group conformity is required, while the alien group or individual is subject to relentless distancing that results in marginalization or ostracism.

Folklore reveals that there was once a time when people were included in whatever way they could manage. Because much traditional folklore was generated from times and cultures where no individual was dispensable and every talent was needed for survival, it provides models of inclusion. We will examine some of those models. How have values changed to reflect shifting social and ethical standards? Are there sufficient positive attitudes found in folklore that, if applied, could enhance social attitudes toward disability? Is it

170

possible to identify those that are negative and reconstruct them for our lives?

Since the cumulative imagination of the folk culture develops at the level of lived reality, it informs the construction of social practice, communicates areas of innovation, and provides insights into the channels by which graciousness and inclusion are spontaneously generated and practiced. In folklore physical performance and intuitive thought are allied in such a way that life stories are told without the alienation of mind/body dualisms. This alliance of body and mind is spontaneous in folklore, and yields the possibility of constructing and reshaping social practice and attitudes toward disability inclusion. Our past is borne by our folk culture just as surely as it is by the Great Books. An advantage of folklore for recovering past attitudes is that it is less filtered, less purified, less edited by cultural authority than is theoretical knowledge. It is therefore less tainted by the separation of mind and body so ubiquitous in scholarly discourse. This positions folklore as an ideal mainspring for recovering attitudes toward disability and people with disabilities that might be useful for the present.

People with disabilities are reminded at every turn that life begins in embodiment. Let us then begin not with the life of the mind, with faith, with intellectual curiosity, or with the excitement of ideas. Let us yield to the preeminence of the immediately present body and build meaning through the physical, mundane, profane, secular, daily world of survival. Often those of us with disabilities are expected to represent motivation, transcendence, and inspiration and to think about "our blessings." Allegedly, virtue can come from enduring suffering and ridicule.

But the reality of life with a disability means having to think about the things that others take for granted. It means planning differently, including more time and less distance in each excursion. Obstacles, exertion, energy levels all need to be calculated in advance. For some it is a daily reminder of mortality. Many things other folks do spontaneously have to be done deliberately. If tradition can be found in folklore, let us attend to the world of the "folk" in the world in which most of us were reared and in which we still reside. Let us get down to earth and begin with life as usually lived in the physical body, making no inflated claims about meaning and existence beyond this life, and let us do it by using folklore as a way into meaning.

FOLKLORIC THEMES RELATED TO DISABILITY

The preeminent first source for all folkloric research remains the Stith Thompson Motif Index.[8] It is, however, merely the initial place of inquiry for category and taxonomy. An exhaustive international scholarly search locates few references for lame, blind, cripple, monster, idiot, moron, handicap, disease, illness, and disabled. This fruitless search does not indicate that there are few people with disabilities in the lore, but rather that disability is not recognized as a separate category or motif in folk lore. The absence of a separate category for disability points not to denial but to incorporation. Disability is pervasive and taken for granted; it need not be separated and labeled.

This prevalence can be seen in the following themes or motifs. Some recur more frequently than others. All are oft repeated and are found in connection with tales, games, or rhymes that explicitly include people with disabilities. In each case I have attempted to present examples from both traditional lore and from modern urban legend in order to demonstrate changes in attitudes over time toward people with disabilities.

Innocence

Tales of innocence are particularly American and are employed to justify personal effort in the face of all odds. The innocence found in American folktales usually is a tale of overcoming adversity. "American innocence in its most familiar guise maintains that in the abyss of every failure lies the prospect of spectacular success."[9] There is little in American lore that emphasizes Job-like qualities of patient perseverance. When such appears, it is usually referred to as the "Motif of Punishment for Breaking Tabus."[10] Rather than blaming, most of these tales glorify the innocent victim who overcomes. This is, after all, the American legacy of hoping always and heading West to attain that which is hoped for.

Similar to innocence stories and often attached to them are those of folk church healing services. In these, the sick person is healed by laying on hands and prayer on the part of the community. However, the healing occurs only insofar as the petitioner is sin-free (innocent) and has sufficient faith. In both types of story communal participation is necessary to the story. Not only must the affected character be innocent, but she must also display a certain stoicism. Complaining negates innocence. Those who suffer intensely, not in passive acceptance, but with "spunk" are the admired characters.

An unambiguous instance of innocence, blessedness, and the requisite of communal participation occurs in the cult of disability associated with popular Catholicism. In his essay, "Mildred, is it fun to be a cripple?," Robert Orsi reviews the devotional Catholic ideas about the justifications for disability. Disability was merited, provided by God as prime opportunity for spiritual growth, or it is a way of vicarious suffering, enabling one to gain Christlike stature. The conviction emphasized is that the "innocent victim" must become the concern of the community. Orsi writes:

> At a time when several American industries were dedicated to the desperate work of helping people avoid or deny pain, which was increasingly understood as an obstacle to performance, achievement, and consumption in a culture that has treated physical distress and difference as sources of embarrassment and shame as well as signs of personal failure, the Catholic ethos posed . . . a powerful alternative. Catholics offered a storehouse for what everyone else was disposing of; the notion of sickness as a source of spiritual energy for the whole church recast the uselessness and isolation of sickness into participation and belonging. . . . The Catholic Union of the Sick in America assigned the physically distressed a privileged place in the spiritual economy and offered them a way to reconnect themselves to the world around them literally *through*, not despite, their illnesses.[11]

Literature renders additional examples of the importance of communal participation to suffering people and to the surrounding community. Lee Sturma compares Flannery O'Connor and Simone Weil and argues that O'Connor participated in a "community of believers" and so "knew what to do with her suffering" and was not predisposed as was Weil to seek additional pain and martyrdom.[12] That is to say, participation in a community of faith is important not only to the person with a disability but to the receptive community itself. So long as the sufferer is innocent, the community can find redemption in caring.

Gray Henry indicates the "enormous blessing" that illness and disability hold in her tradition of Islam. She writes of her paralyzed friends who were "always placed along the sidelines . . . " and, when she contracted Guillain-Barre Syndrome, says she began to view herself as a "dwarf or hunchback." Her conclusion is "that what is exemplary in these people [*sic*] was not what they did, but what they were," and so she decided that "the best thing I could do for others was to sanctify my soul . . . " She continues, " I no longer patiently tolerated [my illness]—I loved it, I flowed with it . . . I saw how blessed I was to have been given . . . something as total as paralysis."[13]

Both Weil and Henry pursued their suffering alone, contributing little and remaining on the sidelines of collegial life. They are models of the marginalization of people with disability and clearly neither they nor their communities benefit from their isolation. Contrarily, the folk tradition indicates that inclusion of people with disabilities in communal activity benefits everyone concerned.

Occupation

Occupational injury tales include many familiar characters such as Captain Hook or Peg Leg Pete who are big and brave and in truth are often favorably abled as a result of their prosthetic devices. These tales are found in abundance in the lore of the East Coast fishing trade and, of course, in literature in the character of Ahab. There are additional lumbering tales of injury from the great Northwest. However, reports from such places as Bluefield, West Virginia, and Scranton, Pennsylvania, have produced little in the way of stories of healing, joking, or advantage about mine accidents or black lung disease. Interviews with Pennsylvania mine women yielded only the fear that women in the mines were a cause of disasters. All cited specific anecdotal material to support this.

Related but in a collateral category are heroic civil servants, police and firefighters who are maimed or injured in the line of duty. These heroes with disabilities are raised up for public adoration because they are not supposed to be vulnerable in the first place. They are, after all, the protectors of the rest of the people. The near canonization of the "holy family" of Officer Steven MacDonald in New York demonstrates this folk belief at work.[14] Such stories are a modern version of the good shepherd boy who is injured defending his flock. Thus, the stories of the bad boy who cried wolf and the corrupt police officers ignite the ire of the populace and stand in stark distinction to folk virtue.

Related, but in a different type-field are the innumerable war stories in which every injury is the result of a heroic act.

Deception

Very popular are tales of self-injury by deception such as the person who is tricked into sticking his hand into a hollow tree and getting stung by bees or the person who is deceived into believing that there are sheep at the bottom of the river and sustains a disabling injury while satisfying his greed for the sheep. And there are tales of the deceiver who falls into his own trap and is injured. The recent fascination with the urban Sting operation is akin to this and is often met with the popular response: "Well, you brought it on yourself, silly." This is a combination of blaming the victim and asserting justice at the same time. Blaming the victim allows people to distance themselves from the event; they, of course, wouldn't be so gullible. These stories are intended to impart the idea that whether you are stupid or at fault, justice will prevail. This provides comfort to an anxious society and assures believers that all is right with the world. All one need do is avoid fault or stupidity and one can avoid disabling consequences.

Curses

Motifs of the curse include blindness, the hand that drops off, insanity, deformity of offspring, and other physical malformations. In colonial/Puritan New England women identified as witches or heretics gave birth to "monster" children. In fact, in the case of a birth deformity the woman could be subsequently accused and banished. One minister went so far as to perform a home-style autopsy on one of the infants;[15] he was so convinced that the mother was a witch that he believed the infant's body would yield the evidence.

Urban lore, most of which dates from nineteenth-century industrialization to the present, includes most prominently the socially cursed blind or crippled beggar, the opposite of the athletic hero who overcomes. Urban folklore is filled with techniques for seeming to make one's limbs disappear or appear deformed by folding, dressing, and positioning. The profession of begging frequently depends upon creating an appearance or impression of disability. Attitudes toward the beggar vary by time period and region of the country. Sometimes the beggar is pitiable, sometimes regarded as a psychopomp in disguise. But more recently in the urban setting the beggar is seen as the despised freeloader, victimizer rather than victim.

Healing

Another theme in folklore has been that of folk healers and healing. The literary structure of folklore organization has made it difficult to deal with what folklorists call "believed traditions." Therefore, this is best addressed elsewhere.

SPECIFIC EXAMPLES OF MOTIFS

I have surveyed approximately 4,000 folk tales, hundreds of children's games and rhymes, and as many sick jokes and ridiculous riddles as I could tolerate. On a steady diet of folklore one could become either very discouraged by the text or encouraged by the subtext. The evident surface messages indicate attitudes and actions that many people with disabilities find offensive. But the underlying messages characteristically bespeak toleration, empathy, and a modest inclusiveness.

While traditional lore is ambivalent toward disability the urban legend is more unsettling. Such stories clearly embody increasing brutality unmitigated by the humanistic values or sense of community of former times. The ambivalence and double message of tradition have been exchanged for unrelieved callousness.[16] The most glaring factor in the difference between the tolerance of traditional folklore and the contempt of contemporary urban lore is the loss of a sense of inclusive community where one belongs and feels safe.[17]

Having briefly surveyed motifs let me cite some specific references to disability in folklore. The following examples are drawn from all regions of the country to demonstrate their universality and pervasive influence. The names change, the language varies, but the structure is the same. Folkloric superstition to the contrary notwithstanding, I have listed thirteen paradigms and elaborated a few.

• *The blind character* with insight, not outsight; the folk version of Tiresius.

176

• *The Wise Fool:* Both the blind but insightful character and the wise fool hold special knowledge of the ways of human nature. They see through things.

• The king, woodcutter, or farmer with *the honest but retarded son.* This exhibits the association of innocence with disability.

• *Teasing rhymes:* Usually about children who are too fat, too skinny, bow-legged, timid (fraidy cats), or cross-eyed. Examples of such rhymes are:

Fatty, Fatty, two by four
Hanging on the kitchen door, (or "can't fit through the kitchen door")
When the door began to shake
Fatty had a bellyache.

Skinny, Skinny run for your life,
Here comes Fatty with the butcher knife.

Debbie bum beddie,
De-I-go feddie,
Tee-legged, toe-legged
Bow-legged Debbie

I found few children's rhymes teasing people with truly disabling conditions other than the bowlegged ones that presumably refer to rickets although the disease was unidentified at the time the rhyme originated. In other words, there are limits to the teasing. If a person were really in a precarious position nothing could be said.

• Moron jokes are primarily related to *mental disability,* but sometimes correlate mental and physical conditions by implying that the mental disability leads to a physical disability. For example, Why did the moron cut his arm off? Because he wanted to take shorthand.[18]

• *The not quite human character:* hunchbacks, dwarfs, mermaids/men, trolls, all are depicted as having particular understanding of nature. These disfigured characters fall into the category of the psychopomp who knows the natural world so well he can show the path through the woods, the source of eternal life, or the perils along the way to the goal. This differs from the categories of the blind character, the wise fool, and the retarded son because this character has insight into the natural world rather than extraordinary understanding of human nature.

- *The universal stick-fast motif* whether the tarbaby, the golden goose, or the hare at the well found in Ewe culture.[19] Why include this within disability studies? Because the person becomes disabled in terms of the dominant culture by having an extra appendage, by being slowed down, or by being unable to pursue daily activities because he is stuck fast to some problem. Anyone suffering from Obsessive Compulsive Disorder or tied to a supportive device will understand why it is included here. This condition often develops as a result of deception. Urban versions of "stick-fast" include the kissing couple with braces that get stuck and the sexually stuck couple. Both of these indicate punishment for illicit behaviors but without the empathy displayed in the traditional stories.

- *Clever people with physical disabilities who improvise,* such as found in "The Cat with the Wooden Paw."[20] In Thebes, Illinois, the local blacksmith named Jack (This is one of several "Jack" stories) had a cat who was a very good mouser and kept the shop free of rats and mice. But one day that cat got a forepaw cut off and began to get thin and sickly because he wasn't getting enough to eat. So the blacksmith fixed him up a wooden paw and the cat began to grow sleek and healthy again. One night Jack decided to see what went on at night. After dark the cat got down by the mouse hole and waited. When a mouse stuck his head out, the cat seized it with his good paw and knocked it on the head with the wooden paw. The cat piled up eighteen mice that night alone.

This is the story of the innovator, the American build-a-better-mouse-trap legend although the character is regarded as doubly clever because he overcomes a disability. Of course people intended to express admiration for this character and to display envy over the cleverness. Often the result was quite different. The person with a disability who was not so innovative or clever came to feel unworthy or deficient.

- *The Disabled Change Agent.* Tiny Tim is perhaps the best known example. This passively accepting creature has the ability to soften the heart of the mean-spirited, which usually results in the transformation of the offender and the distribution of grace and goodness through-out the world.[21]

- *The Weak Sister.* Typical of this motif are Clara in *Heidi* and Beth in *Little Women.* Most recently the film and play, *The Secret Garden,* has highlighted one of the few such stories that features a boy in this category. Predominantly, the characters are girls who are sickly and need a special friend to stay with them, take them to the seaside, or otherwise brighten their days. Almost all are either rich or gifted with a special virtue of patience or kindness. They are admired for enduring without complaining. Also they are pitiable but generate a certain jealousy in others because of their "giftedness" or specialness. This type of tale presents a foil to show that health is better than money. Frequently if they retain their patience and blessedness, they experience miraculous recovery proving that virtue is its own reward.

• *Family disability* with one person who doesn't have it and is regarded as special. The "Twist or Wry Mouth Family" is such a tale. This is a remarkable style because the person who is different is the one in the family who does not have what society clearly regards as a disability or malformation. All the members of the Twist Mouth Family had their mouths twisted out of shape, save one son. That son was sent to college and on the first day he came home for vacation the family sat up late hearing stories of what he had learned. Finally, it was time for all to retire and the mother said, "Father, will you blow out the light?" "Yes, I will." he replied. But his mouth was twisted so he blew this way (narrator demonstrates). Then the father says the same to the mother, and she tries but she blows this way because her mouth is twisted (narrator demonstrates). Then Mary, the daughter is asked, and she tries but she blows this way (narrator demonstrates.) The other son tries with the same result. Finally John (Jack) the college student is asked, and he blows the light like this (narrator blows straight) and it goes out. The father said, "What a blessed thing to have larnin'!"[22]

• *Sick jokes.* These are in addition to Moron jokes and are a distinct part of modern urban culture. The harshest of these used to be "Halitosis is better than no breath at all." The cruelty of these is exhibited in the exploding cat in the microwave, lawyer jokes related to road kill, and so on.

• Finally, there are those *stories that end with a very direct moralistic phrase:* "Mr. Alligator and Mr. Fox" is an example. It is a familiar type and resembles Aesop's fables. I will not here explicate the blatant racist implications. Mr. Fox's children would go too close to Mr. Alligator, and he'd open his big mouth and eat them. Then poor Mr. Fox would come around looking very sad, and Mr. Alligator would ask him what the trouble was. Mr. Fox would say, "O, I have trouble,

Mr. Alligator." And Mr. Alligator would laugh and say, "What trouble? I don't know what trouble is." So one day Mr. Fox set fire to the broom sage all around the marsh, and Mr. Alligator found he could not get out. He cried, "Oh, Mr. Fox, come help me out. I never knowed what trouble was till the marsh caught fire." But Mr. Fox sat off to one side and laughed while Mr. Alligator found out what trouble was. Moral: "Some people laugh at the misfortunes of others. It is not until they have trouble of their own that they realize what it is."[23]

This was the sort of story employed to indoctrinate children with ideas of how to treat people kindly.

A LOOK BACKWARD

In reviewing my own childhood, it seemed evident to me that no one supposed we could actually isolate or exclude people with disabilities. The existence of difference in ability was a given, seemingly distributed among all people. After all, Uncle Ran and Aunt May both had hearing trumpets; Aunt Bertha couldn't get out of the chair without two men to pull her up; Nanny walked with a cane and was forever falling down, especially during the blackouts; Cousin Richard came home from the war without one foot; and lots of friends had polio. Billy was pigeon-toed; I had casts on my feet for "pronation." Each one of us participated in the family, school, church, and neighborhood. Billy couldn't walk on stilts; I couldn't run bases very fast; Pete couldn't pitch because of his glasses. Beverly was too scared to jump off the garage roof onto a blanket. It seemed as if everybody had something they couldn't do, and we all got used to it and accepted it.

The evident differences between acceptance and marginalization appear to be the amount of daily contact, local association, side-by-side participation, and the absence of "otherizing" by labeling. This assertion is supported by Keith Cunningham in " 'He Gits Around Pretty Good Once He Gits on a Horse': Traditional Views of Disability-Rehabilitation in Paradise." This fascinating survey draws on interviews from the Library of Congress American Folklife Center's Paradise Valley Folklife Project.[24]

A single example will suffice to demonstrate the way in which some of the technical language of medical disability studies discriminates by exceptionalizing.

A buckaroo tells the story of an unusual accident in which a small plane crashes into a pickup truck in which his foreman was riding. The buckaroo says, "He's crippled, but he gits around pretty good. He's not fast, you know; he can't do much walkin'. If he gits on a horse, once he gits on, he's all right."

Cunningham reports that "over 96 percent of the 629 conversational narratives on the Paradise Valley field tapes deal with conditions that would be considered disabilities in mainstream, contemporary culture."[25] The tapes cite examples of hearing impairment, mental illness, horseback injuries, senility, ESL difficulties of immigrants, and numerous losses of digits while "taking dallies,"[26] as well as the pervasive disabilities in the general population from strokes, birth trauma, and other injuries. Yet, none of these is labeled or regarded as extraordinary.

The tapes also describe in some detail "various kinds of what would be considered in mainstream culture, rehabilitation activities including hospital and outpatient treatment, use of various types of braces and physical therapy programs." While the reported incidents seem to match the American statistical base for disability and rehabilitation, none of this is referred to in these folk accounts as either disability or rehabilitation.

A number of anthropologists cite the high tolerance for "deviance" in folk communities. The man who was hit by the airplane "gits around pretty good." He is neither "disabled" nor a "person with a disability." People get seized up or "stove up." It is an expected everyday occurrence. Cunningham's conclusion is that in such societies, as long as people can take some care of themselves and not cause a great deal of trouble for others, the community will tolerate occasional outbursts of rage, accidents, signs of aging, residual effects of disease, and even disabling alcoholic binges.

This acceptance of disability is sometimes identified by an intellectual elite as "having a positive attitude toward the stigmatized." In the lives of the folk it's "just the way people are" or as someone said to me, "Yup, he's kinda different."

Schneider and Anderson in their 1980 study of attitudes of acceptance of disability identify a number of characteristics of accepting and nonaccepting communities.[27] They cite the following as negative factors in acceptance of the stigma attached to disability: (1) a less industrialized culture; (2) strong prejudice against racial or ethnic difference; (3) personality disturbance in the observer; (4) the sex of the judge (males showed higher negativity) (5) occupations with high emphasis on physical ability.

The Paradise Valley statistics would appear to be high on these supposedly negative characteristics but nevertheless had a high rate of acceptance of disability as a normal part of community life. Why? Schneider and Anderson claim that the single most important factor in acceptance is contact. The more direct contact there is with people with disabilities, the more positive is the attitude. In folk cultures based on stable neighborhoods or groups, inclusion of people with disabilities has been more usual than in the present urban areas of the United States. Field experience supports the conclusion that the more face-to-face contact and the better a person knows people with disabilities, the higher the level of acceptance and inclusion.

PRACTICAL APPLICATION

What can we learn by examining the changes that occur in the move—could it be called the decline—from traditional folklore to urban legend?

Traditional folklore, exhibiting as it does attitudes of acceptance and ideas of inclusion, is grounded in stable culture that tends to generate daily contact with the same people. Modern urban culture, on the other hand, is mobile, transient, and offers a shield of anonymity in which the person seen today is gone tomorrow. In traditional folklore, we see evidence that daily contact creates a certain amount of acceptance. Over time, folks get used to one another's differences. A measure of positive "taking for granted" develops that seems to promote first acceptance and then full inclusion. In other words, "being there" and "showing up" clearly influence social recognition of people with disabilities. Brief or momentary contact, the sort forged by modern urbanization, allows little time or space for the daily interaction that makes difference familiar. Urban anonymity, individualism, exclusionary gangs or cliques can all be predicted to reduce inclusion of difference.

Situations that produce the most ordinary contact can be predicted to produce the highest level of acceptance. It is at this point that the socializing capabilities of religion and religious bodies can be engaged. That is to say, amidst the maelstrom of urban disjunction a major function of religion can be creating communities of daily contact in which people who are not alike simply live and work together. One activity that has been undertaken by religious denominations is the creation of retirement or continuing care facilities. While much of this work is laudable, it also creates communities of isolation confining the aged and those more likely to be disabled in set apart circumstances. Periodic visits from preschool centers and scout groups do not provide ordinary, everyday experience but emphasize the otherness of difference.

Labeling, which is rampant in the medicalization of disability, is another form of "otherizing" that inhibits affirmation. Religious bodies seem predisposed to promote this otherizing by adopting attitudes that proclaim, "*We* must include *them.*" This assertion is simply another type of labeling. Religious institutions that elevate people with disabilities as models of transcendence or courage serve to denormalize these same people. For example, special education, which pulls children out of the group, militates against acceptance. In preschool and educational programs housed in religious institutions, there is the opportunity to create multigenerational teaching, inclusive classrooms, and everyday contact.

Keith Cunningham indicates yet another factor pertinent to religion and values. He notes the paucity of stories in Paradise Valley dealing with disability and the supermundane. Almost *no* stories from Paradise Valley address religious or supernatural belief. This deemphasis on the supermundane is matched by what he calls a rationalist view that people should be judged by what they can do rather than by what they cannot do. In Paradise Valley a person who gets around pretty good once he gets on a horse, is, all in all, getting along pretty well. Cunningham is prepared to argue that this attention to the commonplace rather than to the transcendent encourages attitudes of acceptance toward people with disabilities.[28]

Self-examination on the part of religious bodies is in order. Often the first message of religious institutions has been one of transcendence rather than one of teaching at-homeness in the physical, bodily world. My research suggests consideration that the Kingdom may not be of this world; but if there is one, it is probably available *through* this world and not without it. One way of giving attention to the moral status of the body might be consciously to create the "kingdom on earth." The locus of moral conviction and moral activity needs to be shifted "down" from the vertical to the horizontal plane, from the elite to the commonplace, from the transcendent to the incarnational. Developing village attitudes in the midst of urban isolation means creating horizontal, seamless webs. Insofar as people with disabilities are part of the local landscape they *are* part of the web. "Reaching out to them to include *them*" isn't sufficient. The fly caught in the spider web is included, but victimized.

Instead of pulling others into already existing institutions and programs, one way to replicate village life and daily contacts is to live in concrete contact groups. Shared housing, group homes, ungraded classrooms, granny houses, multigenerational housing, extended home living, communal kitchens, shopping cooperatives are some of the ways religious groups can promote daily contact. This is a true social liturgy. I am not advocating a utopian kingdom on earth but suggesting that incarnational religion can be manifested by a degree of realistic engagement with the world as it is. It means reducing individualism, privacy, and private ownership. It means reaching across the back fence before reaching for the stars. And it means forgetting that there is a "them." Folks would understand the West African proverb that goes, "I am because we are; We are because I am; I am We."

---

1. An etymological study of "liturgy" clarifies the historical shifts that have taken place in our usage of the term. The root is the Greek *leitourgia*, meaning any public service or work. Its root is *lei* relating to *laos* or *leos*, meaning "of the people," and from which comes *laity*. The term is related to another term, *lewd*, the earliest meaning of which was vile or ignorant as in the folk, or "not of the clergy." Liturgy thus understood emphasizes public service that derives from the people or the folk. Given its root, separating liturgy from the populace means neglecting its fundamental meaning. Eric Partridge, *Origins* (New York: Macmillan, 1966), 361.

2. "Religious Fundamentalism," *Soul of a Nation: Religion in America, Films for the Humanities and Sciences* (Princeton, N.J., 1995) (video recording). Sr. Producer: Michael W. Doyle. Producers: Christopher Salvador and Doug Thomas. 29 minutes.

3. From the eighth to the third centuries B.C.E., China saw the steady deterioration of the Chou dynasty until, at the time of Confucius, rival principalities were in unending war against one another. Atrocities of war reached a peak in the century following Confucius. Huston Smith has often compared the period to that of Palestine during the Judges. See Huston Smith, *The Religions of Man* (New York: Harper & Row, 1965), 165-6.

4. Brunvand, Jan Harold, *The Choking Doberman and Other "New" Urban Legends* (New York: W. W. Norton: 1984), ix-x.

5. Steven Swann Jones, *Folklore and Literature in the United States* (New York, 1984), 40.

6. Keith Cunningham, " 'He Gits Around Pretty Good Once He Gits on a Horse': Traditional Views of Disability-Rehabilitation in Paradise," *Western Folklore* 48 (January, 1998): 59.

7. Sandra Harding, ed., *Feminism and Methodology*, (Bloomington: Indiana University Press, 1987), 1-14.

8. Stith Thompson, *Motif-Index of Folk-Literature*, 6 vols. (Bloomington: Indiana University Press, 1955-1958). This work could be appended to take account of categories such as disability, same-sex relationships, implications of race.

9. David W. Marcell, "Poor Richard: Nixon and the Problem of Innocence," in *American Character and Culture in a Changing World: Some Twentieth Century Perspectives*, ed. John A. Hague (Westport, Conn.: Greenwood Press, 1979), 325-26. Retold in David W. Marcell, "Fables of Innocence," in *Handbook of American Folklore*, ed. Richard M. Dorson (Bloomington: Indiana University Press, 1983), 73-78.

10. Stith Thompson, "Sickness or Weakness," *Motif-Index*, 940.

11. Robert A. Orsi, "'Mildred, is it fun to be a cripple?': The Culture of Suffering in Mid-Twentieth-Century American Catholicism," *The South Atlantic Quarterly* 93:3 (Summer 1994): 547-90. This quotation is from p. 564. Like the Duffy article, this one makes no distinction between illness and disability and thus raises the level of ambiguity surrounding suffering.

12. Lee Sturma, "Flannery O'Connor, Simone Weil, and the Virtue of Necessity," *Studies in the Literary Imagination* 20:2 (1987): 109-22. This is also noted in Jeffrey J. Folks, "'The Enduring Chill': Physical Disability in Flannery O'Connor's Everything That Rises Must Converge," *University of Dayton Review*, 22:2 (Winter 1993-1994): 81-88. For other literary sources see also: Leonard Kriegel, "Disability as Metaphor in Literature," *Kaleidoscope* 17 (1988): 6-14; Nicholas Ranson, "Dickens and Disability: David Copperfield," *Kaleidoscope* (Summer/Fall, 1986): 11-15.

13. Gray Henry, "Even at Night, the Sun is There," *Parabola* 18 (Spring 1993): 60-65. Quotations in text from pp. 62 and 65.

14. Police Officer Steve MacDonald was shot while on duty and suffered paralyzing spinal cord injuries. He remains in a wheelchair with assisted life-sustaining facilities. When this occurred, his wife, Patti, was pregnant. Their baby, Connor, was born later, and the MacDonald family has been held up as a model by both the government of the city of New York and by Cardinal O'Connor and the Roman Catholic Archdiocese Diocese of New York. The analogy between the MacDonald family and the Holy Family has been cited extensively in the New York City area.

15. Mary Maples Dunn, "Saints and Sisters: Congregational and Quaker Women in the Early Colonial Period," *Women in American Religion*, ed. Janet Wilson James (Philadelphia: University of Pennsylvania Press, 1989), 27-46.

16. For historical examples of ambivalence based on ambiguity toward people with disabilities in American culture, see John Duffy, "Franklin Roosevelt: Ambiguous Symbol for Disabled Americans," *The Midwest Quarterly* 29 (Autumn 1987): 113-35.

17. One can only wonder what the turn of the millennium will bring regarding the search for inclusive community. There are several contemporary examples of the search for traditional values or utopias. One is the rise of cultic activity. There are now 4500 documented groups that might be categorized as cults. Another is the middle-class movement toward deliberate simplicity. Yet another is the return to "family values" exemplified by PromiseKeepers.

18. From *The Child's Book of Folklore*, ed. Marion Vallat Emrich and George Korson (New York: Dial Press, 1947). "Frog went-a courtin'" came on the Mayflower and is 350 years old.

19. The Ewe occupy much of Eastern Ghana and Togo and have often played the role of peacemakers among other tribes and language groups. In Ghana they are outnumbered by the Asante but, interestingly, during the time of Nkrumah predominated in the military, probably as a result of their peacemaking history. Stories of oppressed populations often feature an underdog who lives by wit or trickery rather than by domination. The story of the tar baby in the American South is one such example. Another is the golden goose, which causes people who try to steal it to stick to itself so the thief is revealed.

20. Charles Neely, *Tales and Songs of Southern Illinois* (Menasha, Wis.: George Banta Publishing, 1938).

21. A heartening modern example of this was published in 1992 by the Woodbine House, Special Needs Collection. In Clara Widess Berkus, "Charlsie's Chuckle" a small town boy with Down Syndrome accidentally invades a town council meeting and converts a bickering town board into a jovial cooperative group. The town celebrates Charlsie with a parade and special day.

22. Clifton Johnson, "The Twist Mouth Family," Memoirs of the American Folklore Society XVIII (Published by the *Journal of American Folklore*, 1905), from Clifton Johnson, *What They Say in New England; A Book of Signs, Sayings, and Superstitions* (Boston, 1896).

23. "Folklore from Maryland," by Annie Weston Whitney and Caroline Canfield Bullock, Memoirs of the American Folklore Soc, XVIII, *Journal of American Folklore* (1925).

24. Keith Cunningham, 58.

25. Cunningham, 59.

26. Dallies are turns of a rope used by riders of cutting horses. One "dallies the rope" around the saddle horn. After cutting a herd and isolating a calf or heifer you "take your dalllies." This refers to pulling up the rope by winding it around the saddle horn. It can cause burns, abrasions, or even loss of fingers if caught incorrectly. A true cowboy never wants to let go of the rope.

27. Clifford R. Schneider and Wayne Anderson, "Attitudes Toward the Stigmatized: Some Insights from Recent Research," *Rehabilitation Counseling Bulletin* 24: 299-313.

28. Keith Cunningham, "This is the Story They Tell Me: Legends in Paradise," *International Folklore Review* 4: 81-89.

CHAPTER NINE

"WE HAVE THIS MINISTRY": ORDAINED MINISTERS WHO ARE PHYSICALLY DISABLED

Albert Herzog

O rdained ministry is a vital component of the church. Any consideration of disability in the service of God must include an examination of the contributions made by the ordained ministers who are physically disabled and their potential for increased participation in the proclamation of the Word, the administration of sacraments, and the provision for the ordered life of the church.

Yet the ordination of persons with disability has been fraught with challenges from a variety of directions. Biblically and ecclesiastically, past and present, the church has challenged the right of persons with disabilities to seek ordination. Leviticus 21:17-23, barring anyone "blind or lame, or one who has a mutilated face or a limb too long, or one who has a broken foot or a broken hand, or a hunchback, or a dwarf, or a man with a blemish in his sight" (vv. 18-20), has been used to justify exclusion from ordained ministry of those with physical disabilities.[1]

In the Protestant traditions, this response has been muted by the emphasis on the minister being primarily called by God to proclaim the Word. In place of the overt prohibition, today many denominational officials subtly question the practicality of ordained ministry for people with disabilities. They emphasize such issues as the limitations in fulfilling pastoral duties, problems in finding appropriate placement, and congregational acceptance. To be sure, there are instances of overt attempts to limit the presence of ministers with disabilities. In the early 1980s, the American Lutheran Church (one of the predecessors to the Evangelical Lutheran Church in America) sought to reject certain persons with disabilities as "unsuitable for ordained ministry."[2] However, for the most part, opposition to persons with disabilities in the ordained ministry has been in the form of discouragement—failure to provide placements and lack of support and cooperation from denominational hierarchies. Ordained ministry, especially parish ministry, is conducted under normative patterns that outline specific duties and expectations. Too often persons with disabilities who have sought to enter or continue in ordained ministry have been discouraged mainly because their "deviance" did not fit the normative expectations of parishioners—or so they were told, sometimes by the persons responsible for selecting, ordaining, and appointing candidates for ordained ministry.

Yet, despite resistance and institutionalized discouragement, there have always been and will continue to be ordained clergy with disabilities. Many persons who entered the ordained ministry without disability have become disabled during their years of service to the church. Additionally, as sociologist Gary Albrecht has reminded us, in contemporary society disability is produced at increasingly higher rates.[3] Although current research does not tell us the number of disabled persons serving in the past or present, it seems apparent that more people with disabilities are being called by God to serve the church.

What then is the impact on the church of the increased number of ministers who either become disabled after ordination or are disabled from the outset? Are there distinctive challenges that add to the dynamic nature of ministry and point to their approaches as new and refreshing for the church? Is there something about their ministries, in particular, that teaches the church about its character and mission?

In many ways, these questions parallel those posed as increased numbers of women have entered the pulpits of mainline congregations.[4] Questions about gender-specific styles of ministry and challenges have been addressed by those who champion women's unique contributions to the church and by those who worry about women's ability to juggle the demands of clergy life. Whether or not women have a common ministry style or face common challenges as ordained ministers, their increased numbers and growing institutional power have raised new topics of conversation, have sometimes altered patterns of interaction, and have challenged traditional norms. The same is true for people with disabilities who are ordained ministers. Though my study revealed no one common style of ministry nor any single challenge faced by all ministers with disabilities, their presence within congregations and institutions altered taken-for-granted ministerial practices, necessitated increased attention to communicating across divergent expectations, and advanced discussion about the meaning and norms of clerical leadership. Attentiveness to adaptation and conversation is especially necessary in local church ministry where expectations about how and by whom tasks are done are altered by the presence of a minister with a disability. These different and unaccustomed ways of doing ministry affect how the minister with a physical disability is viewed by parishioners and how the minister views him or herself.

METHODS AND APPROACH

The study I draw upon here arose from my participation in a group of physically disabled United Methodist ministers who wondered if our experiences were characteristic of the population of ordained ministers with similar disabilities. Out of this collaboration came the plan for this interview study of ministers in The United Methodist Church who are physically challenged. The study was conducted in 1993 with the support of several churchwide groups interested in the future of ordained ministry by persons with disabilities. Ministers with visual, hearing, neurological, and mobility impairments were inter-viewed following a sampling procedure based on ministerial status, seeking representation from full members and ordained elders, local pastors, and student local pastors.

The study sought to document how persons with disabilities in the ordained ministry respond to the demands of church ministry. In many cases persons with disabilities who are ordained ministers are at least partially successful at challenging these norms about who a minister should be, and most importantly, how ministry should be done. These stories need to be told so that it is possible to understand the nature of the obstacles faced and how they are handled or overcome. They also need to be told so that taken-for-granted prac-tices of the church, particularly preaching, worship, and pastoral care, can be challenged and placed in a new perspective.

Additionally, this chapter responds to the notion that persons with disabilities who are ordained have something unique to share about ministry, namely their sensitivity to illness and the human predica-

189

ment, which one would presume is not as keen among the nondisabled clergy. In light of this book's focus on "disability in the service of God," exploration of this notion shows that ordained persons with disabilities are not simply unfortunates, victims caught up in a normative system, but rather persons whose presence in the ordained ministry and in church has something vital to say to the church about the nature of ordained ministry and the church. Though ministers with disabilities do not speak with a single voice or minister according to a single style, their presence in the pulpit and positions of denominational leadership enrich the perspectives of religious bodies and make the church more aware of the diversity in ordained leadership in its midst.

THE CONTEXT OF MINISTRY

Before discussing the interviewees' experiences of and views on ordained ministry, a review of their ministry settings is both helpful and necessary. Most ministers with disabilities were serving smaller congregations either as a single charge or joint charge, though some were located in nonparish settings, such as hospitals. Twenty-six ordained ministers were interviewed for this study. Twenty-four of the twenty-six ordained ministers were full members of their annual conference and ordained as elders in The United Methodist Church. One interviewee was a local pastor, and the other a student local pastor.

At the time of their interview, fifteen of the twenty-eight were serving as pastors of local churches, while two were serving as associate pastors. Three were serving as district superintendents; one had a special appointment to a social service agency; and one was a chaplain at a church-related home for older adults. Four were on disability leave; one was fully retired; and one was appointed to attend school with no pastoral assignment. Two of the pastors were serving congregations despite being officially retired.

Ten of the twenty-eight were female. The ages of those interviewed ranged from twenty-eight to seventy-seven. The disabilities experienced by these ministers included visual impairment and blindness, various types of mobility impairment, multiple sclerosis (MS), epilepsy, and speech impediment. The study also included ministers who were disabled as the result of heart ailments and back difficulties.

The circumstances in which these ministers served and their responses to their experiences varied dramatically. One woman pastor with epilepsy interviewed in her third year out of seminary had served a two-point charge in southern Idaho. Serving two congregations in a rural setting was extremely difficult for her since she depended on others to drive her around the parishes, to hospitals, and other church functions. Additionally in this rural area no local physician could adequately treat her epilepsy. At the time of the interview, she had recently been appointed as associate pastor in an urban congregation where she had a doctor relatively nearby. After the move, she also underwent an operation that relieved some of the symptoms of her disability.

An experienced woman minister who was blind had a quite different experience in a rural two-point charge. Although her superiors were at first reluctant to place her in a parish, she has successfully served a number of single and two-church parishes in rural and small-town settings in a midwestern state. At the time of her interview, she was serving a two-point charge and was receiving financial assistance for a driver-secretary to help her fulfill her pastoral duties. Still another woman pastor became disabled in her fifties as the result of complications from diabetes. She serves a single parish also in a midwestern state. According to her report, she has done rather well in performing her duties despite an impairment that limits her ability to move around the parish. She has also made some adjustments in how she conducts herself in worship.

Another participant in the study was a retired male in his early seventies who was serving an ethnic minority congregation whose building was not accessible to him. Nonetheless, he felt reluctant to ask his congregation to make alterations to its facilities. As a result, he often ministered by "proxy," allowing his parishioners to do his "leg work" for him. Another retiree had spent most of his career as a minister of Christian education, though he had served as a pastor for several years. During his ministry, he had accommodated his mobility impairment by moving to a warmer climate where he was more ambulatory. His decision to pursue ministry as a Christian educator was also, in part, an accommodation to his disability. He found the work physically less stressful, as he could do most of his work in meetings or via the telephone and other forms of communication.

Three ministers who were interviewed for the study were United Methodist district superintendents; one who was a church leader with a mobility impairment and another with a speech impediment were promoted after working for years as pastors. Their disabilities were not seen as stumbling blocks to promotion and service to the larger church. One district superintendent with multiple sclerosis was faced with the increasing difficulties of fatigue brought on, in part, by the strains of serving a large congregation. His bishop felt that the superintendency would be less demanding, and indeed this minister did find the demands of such a position to be less than those of pastoring. This experience helped him assist two other pastors with disabilities to face the difficulties of leaving the parish.

A few interviewees had faced difficulties in being placed. One was placed on disability leave immediately upon being ordained and had remained in this employment status. Another interviewee was recently placed on disability leave against his wishes. The ministry setting in which he was situated was being phased out; and since he was only a few years from retirement, his bishop decided disability leave was the only viable option. This incident followed a typical practice within The United Methodist Church of placing ordained ministers with disabilities on leave just prior to retirement.

Two interviewees held appointments in nonparish appointments. One, a paraplegic, was employed by a church-related retirement home as a chaplain. Although fully satisfied with his position and an active member of the annual conference, his description of his treatment after his injury indicates that he was directed away from parish ministry. The other serves as the director of a planned parenthood agency. She reports that she has learned to adjust to problems with increased visual impairment in both her management of the agency and her frequent participation in the pastoral ministry of the church.

FUNCTIONING IN MINISTRY SETTINGS

Whenever ordained ministers who are physically disabled serve in local church ministry, they are calling into question some norms under which pastoral ministry is conducted. One example is the norm that a minister assigned to do pastoral work must be able to communicate easily and widely. For a minister with a hearing impairment, the expected patterns of communication are altered. A sixty-one-year-old pastor describes how he responds to the challenges in communicating: "I have to be very careful of what I say in response to (an) interaction and I'm also very careful to watch very, very closely. I lip read and when someone talks to me, I guess I'm just twice as attentive as anyone else might be who could hear." For him, conversing with parishioners is a labor-intensive ministerial practice. Sometimes the challenge of conversing with his congregation is made nearly impossible when people forget or are unaware of his need to lip read. He reports that participation in larger meetings, even in the parish, can be frustrating when many people are speaking and interacting at the same time.

Mobility impairment presents its own challenges to norms for doing parish ministry and, in particular, the expectation that the clergy person will visit parishioners in their homes. Many homes are inaccessible to an individual using a wheelchair or other ambulatory aids such as canes or walkers. The inaccessibility of congregants' homes generally changes neither their desire to have pastoral visits nor the pastor's eagerness to visit them. Rather it makes innovation necessary. In the study, virtually every pastor with a mobility impairment made pastoral visits though they had to make some adjustments.

One seventy-year-old male who was retired and still serving as a pastor noted that pastoral calling became more difficult as he became older. When he became "slower," he didn't do much calling. "I did mostly hospital calling and things of that nature. I limited myself only to extreme emergencies, for hospitals and for home calling." Special in-home calls were made in cases of tragic deaths, but most pastoral work was done in hospitals, which are generally fully accessible. In order to compensate, he did a lot of telephoning.

Pastoral visitation similarly poses problems for the blind or visually impaired pastor. If, as for most of the visually impaired pastors interviewed in the study, the pastor is unable to drive a car, then other persons must be relied upon for transportation around the parish. Finding and affording a driver can be problematic. Some clergy must pay for this accommodation out of their own salary. Scheduling driver time to carry out regular visitation and making provision for transportation in emergency situations pose additional problems.

Not only the mechanics of making arrangements for transportation but dealing with the expectations of parishioners make pastoral visitation challenging. One forty-five-year-old pastor who had been in his present parish for six years noted that

> We came in explaining how [my disability] was going to affect my ministry and we worked those things out, and people were quite reasonably willing to work with that. Over the years, some people have become somewhat frustrated. They'd like more calling and visitation and that, but there are sighted pastors that do less calling than I do sometimes.

He also noted, "You know, I think it's one of those general expectations that people have that they want fulfilled, but I think it has been the primary area of difficulty and the frustration on the part of parishioners."

Pastoral calling can also be a source of tension for someone who cannot drive because of some other physical impairment. The female pastor with epilepsy, referred to earlier, noted that in her first church in rural Idaho she "had to make three or four phone calls to find someone who could drive me." In her new assignment as an associate pastor of a church in an urban location, she still cannot go whenever she wants. While she now has drivers assigned to her on given days, she commented that: "luckily, I work in tandem with another pastor and he's able to do most of the [pastoral calling in emergency situations]."

The vagaries of pastoral life experienced by able-bodied ministers as well as those with disabilities can be particularly complicating for ministers with certain disabilities. For example, for a minister without a disability being caught in a rainstorm during pastoral calls may be a nuisance; for a minister with a physical disability being exposed to the elements might bring on serious physical problems. Thus ministers with disabilities often must approach their daily schedule of visitation or meetings knowing that they must remain flexible. Accommodating their physical abilities and limitations means that they must pace their activities. Such pacing is both a challenge to their own vision of the minister who responds to all needs without regard for personal well-being and to the congregation's expectations of unimpeded access to the minister. But it may also highlight the necessity of certain ministries of the laity.

Responding to the congregation's expectations for pastoral visits, devising strategies to make visits in both emergency and routine situations, and attending to the physical limits that make visitation challenging proved to be common formidable tasks for ministers with disabilities. Though not insurmountable, these challenges sometimes created tension within the congregation and self-criticism within the pastor.

Worship is another arena in which congregational norms can clash with the innovations needed to accommodate a minister with a disability. The changes may be relatively minor. For example, one fifty-nine-year-old pastor on disability leave as the result of a heart condition noted that, toward the end of his active parish ministry, he had to stop in the middle of his sermon to catch his breath. Or alterations in the historic patterns of the congregation may be somewhat more dramatic. A former pastor with multiple sclerosis, who is now a district superintendent, noted that in his first service each Sunday he would sit on a stool and, then, in the second service, he would stand. This concession, however, was still too tiring. Sitting through the service was satisfactory neither to him nor to his congregation. Thus he accepted an appointment as a district superintendent, in part, because that position involves a great deal of desk work and meetings where he can sit down.

As with doing home visitations, accessibility proves to be a thorny problem when conducting worship services. Chancels are often the last space in the church building to be made accessible. One pastor with a mobility impairment had some of the churches he served build ramps to the chancel, enabling him to conduct worship and to preach.

Adjustments are also made in other areas of the worship life of the congregation. A forty-three-year-old female pastor with a mobility impairment noted that when baptizing an infant,

> I cannot stand and hold the child and baptize at the same time. I needed just to be seated, and so I had to make sure that there was a seat there. When it came to the point where the parent gave me the child, I was seated and therefore was stable and wouldn't have to worry about the possibility of falling or dropping the child.

In terms of the administration of the Lord's Supper, this same pastor notes: "If I try to handle the wine, because of the way I walk, I tend to slosh; so I let another person always be the person with the cup. Then I take care of the bread." Once again, a new ministry is, in effect, created and shared.

Communicating and accepting the limits of their personal stamina or abilities is another challenge faced by ministers with disabilities. One forty-four-year-old pastor with multiple sclerosis noted that "when [I am] fatigued with MS [I] typically drag a foot, and I'm more likely to be off balance and sort of fall. So I'm real uncomfortable maneuvering stairs or through territory with which I am not familiar." So she asks people to get things for her. She has also helped her parishioners to sense when she is fatigued and has invited them to freely tell her "go sit down."

However, some pastors are not comfortable with having others do tasks for them. One sixty-year-old pastor with visual and mobility impairments as the result of diabetes notes that

> I find difficulty within myself when I'm at the church going about work and people grab things from me because they think they need to hold it. They're being nice and I understand that, I appreciate that. But they need to let me do what I want to do. I walk into a fellowship group potluck with a hot dish, and they wrestle it out of my hands to take it because they think I can't walk across the floor with it.

While this pastor feels uncomfortable having parishioners do things for her, when she finds difficulty in other areas in ministry, she has learned that she must "let go." When she had difficulty navigating in the cemetery during a funeral, for instance, she "learned to just very quietly spot somebody I know and ask to take their arm and usually somebody thinks about it. That's very much appreciated."

Many of the interviewees mentioned the work load involved in being a pastor. One twenty-nine-year-old male with a mobility impairment as the result of severe arthritis, noted the

> sheer number of hours it takes to do an effective job of ministry. It does take a physical toll on me. Being out at night meetings after working a full day, that is very demanding, physically, and there are times that it does affect the quality of my ministry.

On the other hand, the heavy work load has necessitated that some ministers with disabilities develop new skills. One forty-year old male with multiple sclerosis reported that he has learned to manage his time more efficiently. He related that "it really forces me to consider seriously how I can extend the ministry of the church, not necessarily through my activities, but by enabling laity to take more of a role in ministry."

Enabling their congregations to accept a greater role in ministry was an oft-mentioned ministerial goal among the ministers in this study. A seventy-two-year-old retiree with a mobility impairment who still pastors a church noted that

> I'm the type of person [who's] perfectly comfortable doing things by proxy. In fact, I've learned the more you let other people do in the church, the happier the church is. This happens when you ask people to join in your ministry and to help you do the things you can't do.

In practice, however, most of the interviewees had not arrived at the point where they had systematically worked with their parishioners to develop a mutually shared ministry. One evidence of this is the expectation among most study participants that the pastor must do visitation; this view was so strong that energies appear not to have been channeled into innovative ways of doing this ministry.

A UNIQUE MINISTRY?

One issue that arose during the project was whether ministers with physical disabilities make a unique contribution to the church by their effective service in the ordained ministry. In answering this question it is important to keep in mind that day after day these interviewees labor. They preach, lead worship, teach, administrate, and provide pastoral care for those under their charge. They are serving parishes of various sizes, administering and providing oversight to several congregations, and conducting specialized ministries. Their presence as effective servants of the church is sufficient not to warrant emphasis on unique contributions.

Nevertheless, the interviewees felt that they did make a unique contribution to the church. Most important, they believed that they are particularly sensitive to the needs of their parishioners during times of illness and crises. A sixty-one-year-old local pastor with a hearing impairment thought that people respond to someone who is wounded. "Here is a person," he stated, "who is not perfect. He has his own troubles. He is sick too. He has to go through different things and he's one of us."

Another pastor with a mobility impairment and with many years of experience in the pastoral ministry stated that

No matter what has happened to my life, especially since I've been a committed Christian . . . my enthusiasm hasn't diminished one touch. [This is] in spite of the fact of my growing inability [to get around]. But it's all in God's hands . . . excuse me, I'm not being presumptuous or anything, but [people] marvel at how I'm able to handle . . . all I have experienced. And I think that adds a great deal to not only this church but other churches that I have served as well.

The former pastor with MS who is now a district superintendent felt that he had been able to help pastors with disabilities take and accept disability leave. He stated:

It helps me, pastorally, because people have some sense that I can know what they are feeling and [with] what they are struggling. . . .They can see that I'm not just sitting over there observing, but I'm in there with them.

Another aspect of this distinctive ministry is helping others to be sensitive to persons with disabilities. Several of the interviewees reported talking about their disabilities with their parishioners. They felt it helped their parishioners to be more at ease with them as they performed their duties. This awareness carried over into pastoral care situations. One pastor was able to help a little boy whose father killed his mother and himself in front of the young son. When the pastor's own leg was amputated and the boy came to the hospital to visit, she told him "awful things happen to us and in our lives."

CONCLUSION

In this chapter, I have portrayed the perspectives of ordained ministers with physical disabilities by presenting their words and their perspectives on ministry, especially with respect to their conduct of ministry in the parish.

With few exceptions, these persons were relatively successful. Their calls had been recognized; they had received conference membership and had been ordained; they had performed their ministerial tasks having served (from their perspective) effectively in their assignments; and they had provided some new perspectives on how ministry is to be done. The views presented here are somewhat biased in favor of those ministers with disabilities who were in a position to have the opportunity to be known to the national church agencies, and in a position to respond to this research effort. Nevertheless, of primary importance in the material presented is that persons with physical disabilities can and do respond to the call to ordained ministry. They hear the Gospel as they are socialized into it from an early age; they struggle with what it means to be a servant and to test their call in the concrete experiences of actual ministerial situations. This itself may change any static image of the minister in the congregation.

Onslaught of disability during ministry does not dampen their call, and in some cases, it strengthens it. While there is some evidence from the interviews to conclude that ministers who are successful to begin with are well received after the onset of disability, those with disabilities prior to entering the ministry are also accepted and the church has used their gifts of service.

There can be no doubt that ministers with physical disabilities call into question the norms under which pastoral ministry is conducted. In these circumstances, accepted practices are examined and viewed from different perspectives. Given the limited scope of the research presented here, it is probably unwise to conclude that many congregations have developed new styles of doing ministry. With the movement of ministers from congregation to congregation, parishioners may alter their expectations for a time but then reassert their original expectations in the presence of a nondisabled minister. Such images of complete able-bodied clergy are reinforced by the general culture's fascination with youth, energy, and omni-competence.

Yet, when pastors with disabilities share their faith and skills with those under their care, there is the potential for engendering new perspectives on ministerial practice—especially for the upbuilding of the lay ministries. Such challenges were provided by those interviewed; and it is my profound hope that as awareness matures, more opportunities will be given to other persons with disabilities so that they may serve in the ordained ministry of the church.

---

1. See Sarah J. Melcher, chapter 2, this volume.
2. See Nancy L. Eiesland, *The Disabled God: Toward a Liberatory Theology of Disability* (Nashville: Abingdon Press, 1994), 69-87.
3. Gary L. Albrecht, *The Disability Business: Rehabilitation in America* (Newbury Park, Calif.: Sage Publications, 1992).
4. Compare Edward C. Lehman, *Gender and Work: The Case of the Clergy* (Albany: State University of New York Press, 1993).

CHAPTER TEN

BARRIERS AND BRIDGES: RELATING THE DISABILITY RIGHTS MOVEMENT AND RELIGIOUS ORGANIZATIONS

Nancy L. Eiesland

During the last two decades, people with disabilities have increasingly identified with the organizations and goals of the disability rights movement. According to a Harris Poll, more than 60 percent of people with disabilities actively support disability issues.[1] For many of the more than 48.9 million people with disabilities in the United States, this identification has translated into self-advocacy and collective action within the institutions of their lives, including education, law, business, medicine, and religion.[2] These advocates have sought full access, self-determination, and empowerment.

At a time when the number of people with disabilities is increasing and the support among these individuals for disability rights causes is growing, analysis of the movement's history and evolution is warranted. In this chapter, a thematic account of the significant changes within and brought about by the disability rights movement is related. Though the history of the movement can be framed in a variety of ways, here primary attention is given to the variations in and contests over the moral meaning of disability advanced within the movement. By the moral meaning of disability I intend both the values and understanding about disability and the commitments and strategies for social activism.

This history provides insight into the origins of the often distant and sometimes tense relationship between the leadership of the disability rights movement and many religious organizations, including those commissioned to serve people with disabilities.[3] Although certainly a generalization, this appraisal is widely accepted by activists for disability rights both affiliated with and independent of religious bodies. Good working relationships, fruitful coalitions, and personal friendships exist among members primarily affiliated with both groups; and some individuals work equally well within both groups. Yet difficult or cool relationships are relatively widespread, especially among leaders. Within this chapter, I explore this rift through interviews with activists and religious leaders, my personal biography and experiences among both groups, and analysis of the social dynamics involved.

As a person with a disability who has been active for more than a decade within the disability rights movement and in the church my entire life, I have found the misapprehensions on both sides to be personally frustrating and disturbing. My experiences and conversations with individuals representing both religious groups and disability rights organizations have convinced me that personal incompatibilities or localized incidents do not adequately account for the frequent lack of affinity.[4]

In other work, I have written about the theological sense I have made of my own experience of disability and God's relationship with people with disabilities.[5] Here I use my primary discipline, sociology, to explore the social and historical sources of the oft difficult relationships between religious groups and disability rights activists and organizations. In this work, my aim is not only to analyze the factors involved but also to provide resources for respectful engagement.

THE DISABILITY RIGHTS MOVEMENT: AN OVERVIEW

The history of the disability rights movement in the United States is not widely known, and it is obviously beyond the scope of this chapter to address it comprehensively.[6] However, a schematic historical account is vital for understanding the changing moral meaning of disability.

Setting the Stage

Though roots of the disability rights movement in the United States exist in the early twentieth century, most activists locate the inception of the contemporary movement in the late 1960s and early 1970s.

201

Nonetheless, a quick glance further back sets the stage for the movement's emergence.

In the United States, and indeed most of the Western world, the early years of the twentieth century afforded few opportunities for people with disabilities, who were generally viewed as objects of shame and disgrace. Parents, often following professional advice, concealed disabled children from society in their homes or in institutions.[7] Disabled adults were frequently stigmatized as well. Historian Hugh Gallagher recounted the prevailing attitudes of the 1920-1940s through the experiences of President Franklin D. Roosevelt as a person with a disability. Roosevelt compensated for society's negative attitudes by hiding his disability from the public.[8]

World War I and World War II marked advancements for people with disabilities. Federal rehabilitation legislation mandated treatment for disabled veterans. The Smith-Sears Veterans' Rehabilitation Act of 1918 sought to address the needs of returning veterans by establishing physical therapy and job training programs. However, graft, waste, and delay prevented much of the funding designated for these programs from reaching disabled veterans. The self-advocacy groups, such as Disabled American Veterans (DAV) and Paralyzed American Veterans (PAV), that these veterans founded were one source of the contemporary disability rights movement. These organizations sought to replace the commonly held view that people with disabilities were helpless or "on the dole" with a more positive image of the returning hero seeking to contribute to the peacetime economy.

However, the stereotype of people with disabilities as nonproductive and pathological was dominant through the 1950s and continued to influence medical and legal practice long thereafter.[9] In fact, the return of successive waves of disabled veterans resulted in the massive growth of rehabilitation medicine and social policy. This rehabilitation regime—advantageous though it was for many individuals with disabilities who were aided in efforts to increase physical function and to adapt workplaces and work patterns—institutionalized a view of disability that has come to be called the "medical model."

Beginning in the nineteenth century physicians had increased their cultural power to define disability primarily by focusing on individual defect and pathology. With the growth and development of rehabilitation professions and facilities, physicians established themselves as treatment directors. Nurses, therapists, social workers, and other health care professionals were viewed as assistants who helped direct patients' lives. Patients, on the other hand, were generally seen as passive recipients of treatments dispensed by expert professionals. The experts made the decisions and informed patients of those decisions. Under the medical model, medical practice and theory became *the* defining authority in the lives of people with disabilities. The moral meaning of disability was indistinguishable from the values and treatments of medical science. It was objection to moral and practical implications of the medical model that stimulated the independent living movement, a grass-roots movement of people with disabilities.

Living Independently

According to sociologist Ralph Turner, "A significant social movement becomes possible when there is a revision in the manner in which a substantial group of people, looking at some misfortune, sees it no longer as a misfortune warranting charitable consideration but as an injustice which is intolerable to society."[10] As a social movement, the disability rights movement resulted from changes in the meaning of disability and the strategies for improving the lives of the disabled. Advocacy groups associated with various impairments, such as blindness, deafness, multiple sclerosis, quadriplegia, and paraplegia, began forming independently of one another beginning in the 1960s.[11] One particularly influential early effort focused on the goal of independent living for people with severe physical disabilities. Building on earlier efforts to deinstitutionalize the disabled, the independent living movement delivered a critique of the political, social, and moral foundations of institutionalization, particularly the dominant medical model of disability, and advanced alternative frameworks for construing their experiences.[12] Also criticized were religiously-based care facilities, which activists often found particularly offensive because of the combination of the medical model and a view of charity that often resulted in segregationist care.[13] During the early stages, the primary paradigm proposed by activists emphasized self-determination as the primary objective.

The independent living movement can be traced to Ed Roberts, who was sometimes called the father of the movement. A quadriplegic at fourteen and dependent upon an iron lung to breathe, Roberts broke United States educational barriers when he became the first person with such a significant disability to enroll in college; he entered the University of California at Berkeley in 1962. "Helpless Cripple Attends UC Classes," wailed one headline.[14] However, motivated by Roberts, a dozen other severely disabled men and women also enrolled at Berkeley. Together, the "rolling quads," as they came to be called, advocated and received ramps on campus housing, set up a twenty-four-hour emergency wheelchair repair service, and hired attendants to help with personal care. This group not only sought and gained educational access, they wanted access to the resources that would help them to live independently while enrolled and on the job after graduation.[15]

From Berkeley, the independent living movement spread around the country and eventually the world. Independent living activists were primarily concerned with controlling those domains of experience where private life becomes public, in particular, medical treatment, educational decision making, and housing. This perspective posited people with disabilities not as patients or clients but as educated and responsible consumers. Independent living proponents, such as Roberts, rejected traditional treatment approaches as offensive and disenfranchising and demanded control over their own lives. For example, they contended that when people with physical disabilities needed physical assistance with self-care, individuals should retain their own personal prerogative to hire and fire people who provide attendant care. The moral meaning of disability had begun to shift significantly.

In addition to control of medical treatment and personal care support for independent living, the movement sought to improve access to education for all people with disabilities. This effort was begun earlier by parents of children with disabilities, whose lobbying was, in part, responsible for the passage of Education for All Handicapped Children Act of 1975 (now the Individuals with Disabilities Education Act). This legislation inaugurated the process of "mainstreaming," or integrating students with disabilities into general education classes in order to address the requirement of "least restrictive environment." Many parents of children with disabilities and proponents of independent living contended that when children and adults with disabilities are not allowed to attend regular schools because of physical, attitudinal, and legal barriers, these children have been denied the possibility of self-sufficiency. At the college and university level, people with disabilities, including Roberts and "the rolling quads," began lobbying institutions to provide assistance that would enable them to complete degree programs, live in dormitories, and participate fully in college life. The goal was integration into mainstream society and individual control of the resources that would make that possible.

In order to facilitate independent living and to advocate access, Roberts and associates first established the Berkeley Center for Independent Living, which became a model for Centers for Independent Living (CILs) around the nation. CILs served as clearinghouses for information about service providers, products, and technology and provided common ground where individuals from disability-specific groups could forge coalitions for advocacy. What began as a grassroots movement became institutionalized nationally in 1978 with the Congressional establishment of Centers for Independent Living in ten states to support the concepts of independence and self-advocacy for people with disabilities. In 1996, there were more than three hundred independent living centers, a majority of which are staffed and governed by persons with disabilities, which operate in the United States.[16]

In addition to serving as a catalyst for legislation facilitating the independence of persons with disabilities, the independent living movement also served as a primary force in reshaping the way rehabilitation professionals generally viewed persons with disabilities.[17] Through market forces and legislation, the independent living movement introduced reforms in practice and was the impetus for new analytic paradigms for the care of people with a wide range of disabilities, including person-centered planning now used extensively among people with developmental disabilities.[18] Further, persons with disabilities were increasingly recruited for careers in rehabilitation where they worked cooperatively with consumers to design the most appropriate approach to address needs of assistive technology, employment training, remedial education, and independence.

The independent living movement, while it contained the seeds of future emphases on civil rights and disability culture, primarily launched a full-scale critique of rehabilitation policy and practice that defined people with disabilities as passive recipients of care and public and/or private charity. In a myriad of small and large battles, people with disabilities advocated for more control of the goods and services necessary for their survival and for integration into society. The independent living movement has been foundational both in the history of the disability rights movement and in its ongoing assertion of the agency and individual authority of people with disabilities.[19] This emphasis sometimes led to clashes with religiously-based facilities caring for people with disabilities. What some religious leaders saw as their duty in caring for the weak in obedience to scriptural mandates, independent living activists sometimes interpreted as enforcing dependency and custodial care for more complicated moral, social, and economic reasons.[20] Activists argued that without individual control and access to medical care, education, personal attendant services, and housing, people with disabilities could not enter the public sphere to lay claim to their rights as citizens.

Focusing on Civil Rights

The focus on civil rights followed from the gains won by the independent living movement, both in raising consciousness among people with disabilities and the general public and in putting more resources for self-care within individuals' reach. In prompting far-reaching reexamination of widely held assumptions that disability was caused solely by a medical problem located in a person's body, the movement generated more expansive attention to political, social, and environmental barriers for individuals with disabilities. These barriers included inaccessible buildings and public spaces, inadequate housing and transportation systems, and employment discrimination. The disability rights movement set its sights on bringing down these barriers and achieving civil rights protections.

As the movement expanded its focus, increasingly a minority group framework for understanding the experience of people with disabilities became the foundation of the political process of gaining civil rights.[21] The "minority model" asserts that discrimination against people with disabilities is rooted in the beliefs and values of the dominant culture. Activists argued that the behavior, self-concept, educational achievement, and economic success of people with disabilities can be understood only by viewing people with disabilities as a minority group who are subjected to discrimination found in their social environments.[22]

Arguing that the problem of disability is not located in the bodies of people with disabilities, but rather in the body politic that fails to treat fairly its minorities had several effects. First, it provided a political and philosophical framework for bridging the various disability-specific concerns of advocacy groups. Even more than a common commitment to independent living, the minority model highlighted the commonalities that people with disabilities shared, i.e., potential for or actual experience of discrimination on the basis of disability. Second, the effort to "account for" disability turned even further away from the examination of the individual physical pathologies toward analysis of society. For our purposes, this turn resulted in increased interest in the role of religion, particularly Judaism and Christianity, in shaping social views of disability. Though detailed analysis of the religious roots of bias were rare, it became commonplace within the movement to cite Christian or "Judeo-Christian" foundations of American culture, generally, and textual proofs from the Hebrew Scriptures and the New Testament, in particular, when giving accounts of the social sources of negative stereotypes and discrimination of people with disabilities. Thus the emergence of the minority model coincided with heightened negative views of Christianity among many advocates. Finally, the minority model made plain the precedents of the disability rights movement in the African American civil rights movement. While parallels had long been drawn between the disability rights movement and other civil rights movements, including the women's movement, the definition of people with disabilities as a disadvantaged minority helped legitimate by association its calls for civil rights. Disability activists, in part, capitalized on the moral authority of the African American civil rights movement to gain popular and political support. Further they followed the lead of earlier civil rights workers as they shaped the type of legislation that came to be the focus of the disability rights movement.

Beginning in 1983, the National Council on Disability recommended that Congress include persons with disabilities under civil rights law. This approach was a logical outcome of the acceptance of the minority model of disability. Scotch notes that during the 1970s the minority model became the accepted definition of disability as it was written into federal legislation, such as Section 504 of the Rehabilitation Action of 1973. "In the 1970s, federal definitions of disability were specified with the assistance of disability rights advocates, and in several cases they were actually written by representatives of movement organizations."[23]

The goal of passage of civil rights legislation was achieved when the Americans with Disabilities Act (ADA) was signed into law in July 1990 after extensive lobbying and public demonstrations, including the occupation of the Capitol rotunda by the advocacy group ADAPT. ADA stated that Americans who are disabled "are a discrete and insular minority who have been faced with restrictions and limitations, subjected to a history of purposeful unequal treatment, and relegated to a position of political powerlessness in our society."[24] The ADA is largely modeled on the Civil Rights Act of 1964. Designed to provide a clear national goal of eliminating discrimination against people with disabilities, ADA broadened the scope of federal civil rights laws to include people with disabilities and augmented previous discrimination laws based on race, sex, national origin, and religion. Through ADA, people with disabilities won civil rights protections in the arenas of employment, telecommunications, transportation, and public accommodations. However, because segregation of people with disabilities is often enforced by physical barriers such as stairs (as opposed to "Whites Only" signs), the authors of the ADA included provisions unique among civil rights acts. For example, ADA's concept of reasonable accommodation requires employers to modify the work environment for their disabled employees, unless such modification poses an "undue hardship" requiring "significant difficulty or expense." The disabled employee must, of course, be "otherwise qualified"—that is, capable of doing the job despite his or her disability. However, the ADA exempts from its provisions religious groups, private clubs, and private homes.

The efforts that culminated in the exemption of religious groups were a source of tension with disability rights activists. William Bentley Ball speaking for the Association of Christian Schools International opposed passage of ADA because of the expense Christian schools would incur and the concern about separation of church and state.[25] Other religious groups lobbied hard for exemption from the mandates of ADA and were relatively quiet in their support of the civil rights legislation.[26] Particularly distressing for many activists was the immunity of church-operated day care programs.[27] Without ignoring issues of church/state separation, many activists found too many religious groups' approach to ADA to be self-interested. As one activist

208

interviewed for this chapter stated, "If they [religious leaders] had been for us before, we could have been understanding. There were some legitimate fears, but the way they got so 'NIMBY' just got me disgusted." While many religious groups did support passage of ADA and have voluntarily complied with some aspects of the law, the activism of those religious leaders who testified against the bill or who spent their political capital primarily to gain exemption from its provisions further alienated many disability rights activists. Some saw parallels with some white religious leaders' failure to support the African American civil rights movement.

Thus when the main focus of the disability rights movement became the passage of civil rights legislation, the natural exemplar was the Civil Rights Act of 1964 and the Civil Rights movement that led to its passage. People with disabilities were understood as a distinct minority whose claims to full and equal participation in society had been ignored and thwarted. Disability rights activists took pages from the organizing manuals of the earlier Civil Rights movement; they also found legitimacy in its moral witness. Lines of support and opposition were often starkly drawn. When religious bodies sought immunity from the legislation, their moral authority as promoters of justice and the integrity of their commitment to full inclusion for people with disabilities was called into question by many within the disability rights movement.

Building a Culture

Though passage of the ADA certainly did not conclude activism for legal rights since the regulatory framework and litigation were yet needed to secure the legislation's impact, for many in the disability movement the victory had been won. Their efforts entered a new phase. Increasingly attention was turned directly to changing cultural representations and celebrating new portrayals of people with disabilities.

By defining people with disabilities as a discrete minority group, the movement had also begun to legitimate a distinct disability culture.[28] If people with disabilities were a minority group, they also had a minority culture, with its own art, literature, and insider language, as well as political, economic, intellectual, and social networks. In fact, the critique of dominant able-bodied culture and advancement of a distinctive minority culture had long been occurring in the movement—though not typically with the single-mindedness now seen. This perspective was particularly evident in the Deaf community, which saw itself as a distinct linguistic as well as cultural minority.[29]

One widely publicized example of Deaf cultural politics occurred in 1988 when students at Gallaudet University, a university in Washington, D.C., for people who are deaf or hearing-impaired, launched the Deaf President Now (DPN) movement, protesting the University's Board of Directors decision to offer the presidency to a hearing person. The DPN movement, which closed the University for a week, captured worldwide attention and increased awareness about deafness, deaf people, and their language and culture. The actions of students eventually prompted the hiring of a deaf man as the university president.

Among activists within the wider disability movement, protests also characterized the effort to assert cultural power and positive disability identity. For example, during the early 1990s demonstrations engulfed telethons, especially Jerry Lewis' Muscular Dystrophy Association telethon, whose paternalistic portrayal of people with disabilities and pandering to the fears and pity of able-bodied viewers were repudiated. Commenting on the impact of telethons in a journalistic face-off with Jerry Lewis published in *Vanity Fair*, historian and activist Paul Longmore said:

> Four major telethons—Easter Seals, the Arthritis Foundation, United Cerebral Palsy, and the M.D.A.—are the single most powerful cultural mechanism defining the public identities of people with disabilities in our society today, mainly because they reach so many people. . . . The message of telethons is that whatever condition people with disabilities have, that condition has essentially spoiled their lives, and the only way to correct that is to cure them. The message of the disability-rights movement is that it's possible to be a whole person with a disability.[30]

Through protests such as these, positive-identity cultural politics and celebration of the cultural distinctives among people with disabilities became the dominant focus of the movement. This shift within the movement—from disability rights to disability culture—is described by Longmore, who wrote:

> Beyond proclamations of pride, deaf and disabled people have been uncovering or formulating sets of alternative values derived from within the deaf and disabled experiences. They involve not so much

the statement of personal philosophies or life as the assertion of group perspectives and values.[31]

In the move toward disability culture, the moral meaning of disability was again altered. A defiant cultural stance, or "in your face" approach as it was described in a *New York Times* article, led to other very public controversies about the meaning and value of disability.[32] In 1996 and 1997, the controversy surrounding the F.D.R. Memorial galvanized people with disabilities and alerted the able-bodied public of the significant focus on disability culture within the movement. Advocacy organizations, like the National Organization on Disability (NOD), have argued that failure to represent President Roosevelt's disability both obscures history and ignores contemporary concerns. Jim Dickson of NOD rallied disability rights activists, saying "The symbolism of exclusion will exist years from now, unless we act."[33] Despite protests by disability rights groups, on May 1, 1997, the F.D.R. Memorial opened without Roosevelt's wheelchair visible. The protests have, however, prompted President Bill Clinton to ask memorial planners to design a statue of F.D.R. in his wheelchair to be added to the site. Cyndi Jones, in an editorial in *Mainstream,* wrote:

> Of all the issues that are critical to the disability community, why did the FDR Memorial ignite us? He was one of us, and yet the Memorial wasn't going to acknowledge this. We were still invisible. If we didn't win this battle of how FDR was portrayed, years from now no one would remember that one of the greatest Presidents who served this country through a tremendously difficult time, did so from his wheelchair.[34]

The protest by Gallaudet students, demonstrations at telethons, and the controversy over the F.D.R. Memorial underscore the development of cultural views of disability within the movement.

In addition to public protests, the primary venues for promoting these alternative cultural representations, values, and self-portrayals within the movement were the disability press, the Internet, and disability studies, as an academic interdisciplinary field. In the popular disability press, beginning in the 1980s, magazines like *Mainstream* and the *Disability Rag* (now *Ragged Edge*), had focused on the politics of identity and self-naming and published articles written by disabled individuals. One of the most important results of these debates and the emergence of an independent disability press was a revolution in the traditional antipathy to being identified as a person with a disability into pride in both individual and group strength. Increasingly the disability press ran editorials, poetry, and stories that had as their theme—"disabled and proud."

The growth and expansion of the Internet in the late 1980s and early 1990s also promoted the development and dissemination of disability culture. In addition to those specifically dedicated to political activism, many websites included more artistic, social, and humorous content. According to Jack Nelson, "perhaps the most important aspect of people with disabilities joining into the virtual community [of Internet] is simply that for the first time in their lives many find themselves being able to belong SOMEWHERE, a place where they fit in."[35] For people with disabilities the Internet made possible an entirely new level of organizing, connecting activists with an interested but not necessarily politicized on-line population. The range of concerns addressed by activists also expanded; on-line dating services, chat rooms, support groups, and technology updates proliferated. The Internet also made possible a direct mass communication of disability culture through websites, such as *Disability Cool*, which defines disability culture as

> pride in being who we are and translating our pride into changing the way media portrays us. It's revelling in sharing common experiences and enjoying the company of one another. It's recognizing the role we have as legitimate members of society and the value of our lives. It's being proud of our history and not feeling isolated. It's buying products developed and sold by other people with disabilities with our symbols on them.[36]

In addition to communication by the disability press and via Internet, other media—such as documentary films by and/or about people with disabilities, such as "When Billy Broke His Head and Other Tales of Wonder" and "Eden," anthologies of short stories and poetry, memoirs, art exhibits, and wheelchair ballet performances—have contributed to building a disability culture.

Finally, on campuses scholars have advocated for institutionalization of disability studies as an interdisciplinary field, similar to women's and African American studies. Early efforts to establish the field were often led by intellectuals, such as Carol Gill and Irving Zola, with long-standing ties to the disability rights movement. Many early proponents of disability studies had been trained in medical sociology or rehabilitation psychology and challenged the assumptions of these disciplines in line with developments within the movement. In establishing disability studies, scholars have argued that the field is not at base constituted essentially, i.e., not only people with disabilities may contribute to it, but rather disability studies is a critical theoretical field of inquiry to which able-bodied individuals may also make important contributions.

The foundation for disability studies as an interdisciplinary field was firmly laid with the inauguration of scholarly journals, such as the *Disability Studies Quarterly,* founded by Zola in 1982, and *Disability, Handicap and Society,* founded in 1986, and the establishment of academic guilds, like the Society for Disability Studies in 1986. In 1987, David Pfeiffer wrote:

> The field of Disability Studies is a vigorous one, examining issues in a socially relevant way. Disability Studies is on the frontier of knowledge. With its social and personal relevance, it is in a unique position to contribute to the development of academia and, through it, to the future.[37]

Today, disability studies courses are known to be offered through anthropology, economics, political science, English, psychology, and sociology departments at more than forty institutions of higher education in the United States and Canada.[38] Additionally, readers on disability studies prepared for classroom use have appeared.[39]

Though advances in disability studies scholarship have been made, its place within curricula of colleges and universities has not yet been firmly established. The case of Rosemarie Garland Thomson, associate professor of English at Howard University, has illustrated the problem. According to disability culture activists, Thomson experienced difficulty in obtaining promotion to tenure primarily because disability studies was not deemed a legitimate academic field at Howard. Thomson noted in an interview that the questions regarding disability studies "[echo] the unwillingness of some English departments to recognize African-American and women's studies as legitimate fields of inquiry."[40] Though painful for the parties involved, such battles may result in further publicity for the field as a whole and greater clarity regarding its place in the academic curriculum.

Although the main thrust of the contemporary movement of people with disabilities has been toward positive-identity politics and the establishment of a publicly recognized disability culture, debates about both the viability and existence of a distinct disability culture have raged within the movement. These debates reveal considerable internal diversity of opinion—uncommon during the days of civil rights advocacy. Some advocates see the assertions of disability culture as unnecessarily separatist and advocate greater attention to integration in dominant able-bodied culture. Others see the culture-building efforts of recent years as a distraction from the more important work of legislative redress. Though disability culture is now the primary focus of the movement, its support is not uniform among movement activists. Personally, I view this diversity of views as an important opening within the movement. Rather than a supposedly monolithic disability "community," it highlights the disability movement as constitutive of multiple disability publics—where concerns and divergent opinions can be openly aired without questioning the person's loyalty and commitment to the overall goals of the movement.

Within religious communities, however, debates about the viability and/or existence of a distinct disability culture have been curiously absent. Though discussion of the special case of the Deaf community has occurred, for the most part religious groups have not advanced particularly religious analyses of the focus on disability culture within the movement. This silence is due in part to organizational considerations. First, during the late 1980s and 1990s when advocacy for disability culture was heating up, many mainline Protestant denominations were closing their offices serving people with disabilities because of denominational downsizing. In 1981 most Christian denominations in the United States had nationally sponsored programs for people with disabilities; by October 1994 all but two major denominations had closed or consolidated their disability offices.[41] As a result, most denominations simply had no paid professional whose job it was to communicate with secular disability groups, establish consistent religious presence within the movement, and interpret changes in the movement to denominations and local congregations. Though many individuals at the local level, and a few among national leaders, maintained ties and worked within the movement, many denominational leaders and local congregations simply lost touch with movement developments. Among those religious bodies that retained national personnel addressing disability issues, often much of their focus has continued to be on gaining physical access to congregational facilities and employment rights for ministers with disabilities. An unintended consequence of exemption from the provisions of ADA has been that many religious bodies now occupy much of their time with concerns viewed by many disability rights activists as largely resolved with the passage of ADA. Religious groups and the disability movement were simply out of step.

Second, especially during the ascendancy of disability culture within the movement, many local and national religious organizations have been restrained because of their constituencies and goals. Many religiously-based disability organizations are primarily oriented to congregations, serving needs of bodies inclusive of both able-bodied and disabled members. In the appendix to this chapter, a sample of religious organizations serving people with disabilities is categorized according to each group's primary constituency and mission.[42] Organizations were classified into four groups on the basis of their mission statements: groups providing services primarily or exclusively to congregations; organizations providing direct services to individuals with disabilities; professional associations for disability workers; and advocacy groups. Groups that identified their mission principally as directed toward change of public attitudes, religious critique of the social circumstances of people with disabilities, advancement of civil rights, or improvement of disability culture were classified advocacy groups.

Of the forty-five groups listed, nineteen identified the local congregation as their primary constituency and highlighted their mission of providing services to promote access and inclusion of people with disabilities into local religious bodies. Fifteen groups emphasized in their mission statements their aim to provide religious services directly to people with disabilities; and four were professional associations. Seven organizations identified as their primary constituency people with disabilities and as their objective advocacy of attitudinal change, independent living, civil rights, and/or disability culture. Organizations whose constituency includes both people with disabilities and the able-bodied generally promote an integrationist agenda, advocating the inclusion of people with disabilities by emphasizing commonalities with able-bodied individuals. For many religiously-based disability groups, seeing the congregation—inclusive of both

215

people with disability and the able-bodies—as their primary constituency mitigated against strong support for a distinct disability culture.

While religious resources can be garnered to support both integrationist and minority culture perspectives, as has been the case with the theological works within the women's and African American movements, contributions by religious organizations to this debate within the disability movement have been largely missing. Religious groups that see their mission primarily to integrate congregations have missed the opportunity to advance their theological justification within the disability public sphere.

CONTESTING THE MORAL MEANING OF DISABILITY

Since its inception, activists and participants in the disability rights movement have sought to establish themselves publicly as the legitimate social and moral interpreters of disability. This movement marks the first time that large numbers of people with disabilities have advocated a view of disability that differed significantly from those offered historically by religious groups. Thus, one source of the rift between the disability rights movement and many religious organizations is their conflicting claims related to the moral meaning of disability.

During the 1700s and early 1800s, the moral meaning of disability was primarily in its representation of divine favor or disfavor. As such, religious organizations had primary authority for interpreting disability within the culture and for treating disability through spiritual means. Though present in earlier interpretations, the moral meaning of disability shifted again in the late 1800s as it was construed in medical and economic terms. Under the medical model, the primary authority for interpreting disability shifted to medical professionals who certified legitimate recipients of state-designated economic aid. However, religious groups maintained significant authority in interpreting disability, in part through their charitable actions. Many medical facilities for people with disabilities were run by religious groups and supported by charitable giving within denominations.

The disability rights movement emerged as an effort to promote independent living—as a social value and practical reality—and to counter the medical model of disability and the ideology of charity, which many argued had resulted in segregation, custodial care, and permanent infantilization of people with disabilities. Not surprisingly, religious groups often became targets of criticism as administrators of custodial care facilities for the disabled.

Later activists and disability studies scholars saw many stereotypes of people with disabilities as rooted in the Christian and Judeo-Christian culture of the United States. Some scholars in disability studies interpreted the historical and textual sources of Judaism and Christianity as univocal in their denunciation and marginalization of people with disabilities. For example, a 1996 article in *Social Work,* a research journal, related: "Although Judeo-Christian philosophy did not advocate killing, people with disabilities were ostracized and stereotyped. Disability signified 'sinner' to the ancient Hebrews, and people with disabilities were thought to be possessed by evil demons."[43] The Hebrew Bible and the New Testament do, indeed, contain deeply problematic texts that have been terrorizing for people with disabilities—as addressed by Sarah Melcher, Simon Horne, and Colleen Grant in this volume. However, disability studies scholars have not often delved deeply into the use of these texts in religious communities. Instead, criticism tends to be general, leaving unaddressed the particularities of religious and cultural milieus in which such stereotypes emerged.[44] Another quotation illustrates: "Many people, including the disabled, still believe the traditional myths about the disabled. Some of these negative attitudes have their origins in ancient religious beliefs that regarded the disabled as devil possessed, or as corporeal manifestations of family guilt."[45]

Relations among disability activists and religious groups were not bettered by the conduct of some religious bodies in the lobbying efforts for the passage of ADA. For activists, the civil rights legislation was morally equivalent to the "Emancipation Proclamation" or the Civil Rights Act of 1964. In lobbying for exemption, religious groups were viewed to occupy precarious moral ground and revealed that they did not see the minority group of people with disabilities as comparable to that of African Americans. Instead of siding firmly with people with disabilities against social injustice, religious groups were perceived by many in the disability rights movement as self-interested and timid.

Finally, even as many religious groups came to accept and even support the minority model of disability and the moral value associated with that definition within the movement, conflict and tensions

217

persisted. Now the culprit was often lack of information and communication. As denominations closed their offices or consolidated their efforts for people with disabilities, communication links were shut down; and official denominational presence within the organizations of the disability rights movement was curtailed. Additionally, as the focus of the movement shifted toward disability culture as a central rallying cry, the majority of religious groups that identified their constituency as congregations—including both people with disabilities and the able-bodied—were silent, indicating neither support for the cultural approach nor offering theological critique.

HISTORY AS PERSONAL STORIES

Though an analysis of the history of the disability movement helped expand my understanding of the social sources of tension among disability rights activists and religious groups and their leaders, my personal experience had long since disclosed the intimate details of the problem. As a person with a life-long disability, growing up in the church exposed me to a wide range of religious responses to disability. These folk theodicies are summed up in the familiar remarks: "You are special in God's eyes. That's why you were given this disability"; "Don't worry about your pain and suffering now, in heaven you will be made whole"; and "Thank God, it isn't worse." I was told that God gave me a disability to develop my character. But at age 6 or 7, I was convinced that I had enough character to last a lifetime. My family frequented faith healers with me in tow. I was never healed. People asked about my hidden sins, but they must have been so well hidden that they were misplaced even by me. The religious interpretations of disability that I heard were inadequate to my experience. Nonetheless, I found my Christian faith sustaining me, even as its interpreters often failed to address my experience.

In high school in the early 1980s, I learned about an investigative reporting contest sponsored by the President's Commission for the Employment of the Handicapped (PCEH). As I began researching, I discovered that in my rural North Dakota town, I would not even be be able to get into the courthouse to register when I was old enough to vote the next year. As a result of writing an essay about the inaccessibility of rural county-seat courthouses, I won a trip to Washington, D.C., where I became acquainted with the disability rights movement, which was seeking legislation that would promote access for people with disabilities. Back in North Dakota, far from Washington, I organized a letter-writing campaign for legislative change. Later as a local disability activist and college student, I sought ramps into the University of North Dakota library and accessible parking spots in front of my class buildings among other things.

The disability rights movement and activism addressed my experience, but it did not always give me answers to my more personal questions about the spiritual meaning of disability. For a long time, I experienced a significant rupture between my participation in the disability rights movement and my Christian faith. The movement offered me opportunities to work for change unavailable in religious organizations, but my faith gave a spiritual fulfillment that I found elusive in the movement. In my local congregation, members were sympathetic to my particular needs, but unconcerned about the plight of people with disabilities as a group. Within the church, sometimes even other people with disabilities were uninterested in political matters. In the rights movement, fellow participants saw religion as damaging or at least irrelevant to their work.

Striking to me during the interviews conducted for this chapter was the unanimity of opinion among disability activists regarding relations between the religious bodies and the disability rights movement. Confirming my own experience, all viewed the rupture as deep and thorough-going. To be sure, activists acknowledged the importance of spiritual beliefs and values in helping them face the challenges of their lives. However, the individuals I interviewed did not associate their spiritual resources with particular religious groups or traditions. Their spirituality was eclectic and self-defined; whereas they saw religion as orthodox and defined by leaders.

Criticism of religion, usually Christianity, fell into three primary categories: personal renunciation of past wrong-doing by religious individuals and groups, critique of the religious roots of stereotypes about people with disabilities, and reproach of religious groups serving people with disabilities that are not controlled by people with disabilities and that maintain a service provision rather than an empowerment model.

Stories of religious abuse are ubiquitous in the disability movement. At most gatherings of people with disabilities that I attend, individuals recount detailed, personal stories of discrimination or insult at the hands of religious folk. Sometimes I have told my own stories. The accounts are heart-wrenching. Tammie, a woman born blind, spoke of an aunt's accusation, directed toward her mother but interpreting Tammie's existence.[46]

> Mom told me that Aunt Lou confronted her after delivery asking her if I was my daddy's. "Did you sleep with someone else? Why else would she be blind? God probably made her blind so she didn't have to look at your sin while she was in the womb." And she's not a crazy religious fanatic or anything. She just came up with this thing.

Other accounts have the indictment leveled directly at the person with a disability. One account published in *The Disability Rag and Resource* in an article entitled, "Disability for the Religious," is both dramatic and frighteningly commonplace:

> I remember a fragile, frightened looking 20-year-old who told me that her grandmother had proclaimed her "possessed by the devil." Took her to an exorcist. Her voice and hands trembled as she went on to say that her seizures had continued. "Then Grandmother said 'take her away—PUT HER AWAY.'"[47]

Punctuating personal experiences of the article's author and acquaintances is the repeated multiple-choice question: Disability—it is (a) a punishment; (b) a test of faith; (c) the sins of the fathers visited upon the children; (d) an act of God; (e) all of the above; (f) none of the above. In the article, religion—here intending Christianity—is portrayed at best as irrelevant and at worst and most commonly as detrimental to people with disabilities.[48]

An interview with Annette, a thirty-seven-year-old white activist, revealed that the result of ignorance and mistreatment was her personal loss of faith after her diagnosis with multiple sclerosis:

> I find nothing there [in religion] that helps me anymore. In fact, I find that most the religious people who I meet want to turn back the clock when people with disabilities "behaved" themselves and made their primary reason for being thanking anybody who helped them. As far as I can tell a lot of religious groups still have that view of what we should do. We're always supposed to prove that we're deserving of their help. I'm tired of it.

These personal renunciations of religious beliefs, groups, and individuals are, I believe, attempts to wrest from religion, variously defined and specified, the power to define the moral meaning of disability. The stories of religious abuse among people with disabilities are political speech, intended to make a claim about injustice and failure of recognition. Too often in religious groups the political character of these narratives is not recognized. Instead well-intentioned individuals often attempt to comfort the narrator by asserting that the religious views expressed in the story are not shared by them, or that they are increasingly uncommon in religious circles. However, since these accounts are political, comfort or appeasement is not their aim. Rather their aim is solidarity with the project of the narrator, that is, transformation of the moral meaning of disability.

My interviews also revealed the prevailing view among activists that Judeo-Christian interpretations of disability account for the negative cultural representations of people with disabilities. Eileen noted, "The Bible is full of that junk. You can't seem to turn a page without some crippled guy being told he's in sin because he can't walk; or a blind person having a demon thrown out." Todd, a parathlete and activist, reported:

> I know for a fact that the Bible has all kinds of stuff about people with disabilities being helpless and pitiful. Just turn on the TV some night and watch those guys, preaching and telling all the people in wheelchairs to come forward and be healed. You think that helps us gain people's respect for what we can do?

Another source of criticism of religion, and Christianity in particular, is the perceived paternalism of many religious organizations serving people with disabilities. Leroy, a twenty-three-year-old African American activist, said that though he finds some support in local churches, he is not upbeat about his experience with religious groups serving the disabled:

> In my own church, I don't have to fight all the battles of racism as well as the disability ones. There I can just educate people about being disabled. But really in some of the groups that I've seen you've got to get people smarter about disability—since they've got this idea that we're stupid and that they need to tell us what is really good for us—and deal with the racial stuff, too. I say, why bother?

Warren, a person with paraplegia whose activism began only in the past year, articulated his frustration.

> I've got a real problem with people telling me that they want to help me, but don't want to listen to what I need help with doing. Even worse, the [religious groups] have got to clean up their own house. For years, they have told people with disabilities that we are "second-class citizens" or demon possessed. They've got to get a grip.

Among leaders of religious groups dedicated to disability concerns, frustration about the difficult relationship is prevalent as well. Though the religious leaders with whom I spoke were more likely to depict the relationship as more cooperative and less strained than did disability activists, they, too, found aspects of the relationship frustrating. LeAnne, who works with a denominationally-affiliated office for people with disabilities, commented,

> I think for the most part we work really well together. For some folks who are just hostile to religion, there isn't anything we can do. It's like they paint us all with the same brush. They think Christianity is bad for people with disabilities who want to better themselves.

LeAnne also expressed some frustration at the challenge of her job, made more difficult by staff and financial shortage. "I always feel torn. There's too much here for one person to do."

Garrett, himself a person with a disability who works in a Protestant activist organization, stated,

> I've always got to bridge to people from the activist side. It's hard but it's part of the job. They've got reason to distrust religion, because we're not always too good. I've got to work with church groups to get them to change their attitudes and with disability groups to get them to see the change that's happening in some churches. I know it's slow, but it's happening.

Jonah, who is the administrator of a Christian group home for people with developmental disabilities, indicates that sometimes the difficult relationships between activists and religious leaders are simply because they "don't talk the same language." He said,

We're out here trying to teach someone how to use the bus and deal with the physical stuff like getting them to shower. The activists are talking about making sure people can make all the decisions in their lives. What about those who can't do that? What have they got to say about them? Nothing.

Jonah contended that the disability activists were not in touch with the reality of the lives of many people with disabilities and, therefore, did not speak for the clients at his group home.

The lack of communication is made worse when religious leaders perceive that their work is noticed only when something goes wrong. Several interviewees noted that activists seldom appreciate the work they do; instead they are likely to criticize religious groups for being paternalistic. Questions about the control by people with disabilities over the organizations offering their care raise strong feelings for religious leaders. For many, serving people with disabilities is a vocational calling and suggestions that their motivations and practice may not be in the best interest of those individuals can be deeply wounding. Increasingly, however, religious leaders support inclusion of people with disabilities in the leadership teams of their disability organizations whenever possible. These changes have been brought about by the influence of the disability movement and its impact on rehabilitation policy generally.

One person who has discussed these changes within religious life is Marilyn Bishop, administrator for the National Council of Churches Committee on Disabilities, who writes:

A new wave is coming—and it combines the questions of *who* speaks about the role of religion in the life of people who are disabled and just *what* does religion have to say to people who are disabled. The rise of [disabled] leaders raises important questions about the future leadership of the disability movement within organized religion. The advocacy movement within religion has been led primarily by people without disabilities, but with experience and compassion for the issues of justice for people who are disabled. With the advent of new, vital leadership by people who are disabled, what will the role of the previous leaders be?[49]

These are challenging questions that must be explored within religious communities and in conversation with activists within the disability movement. Though some religious leaders see their work as unrelated to the movement, such attitudes do not adequately understand the historical and social contextual framework for all service of God. The disability movement has at its core contested the moral meaning of disability, declaring people with disabilities to be a minority group with a distinct culture. Whether or not they agree with this definition, religious leaders ignore the moral implications at their peril.

FURTHER FOUNDATIONS FOR RESPECTFUL ENGAGEMENT

For people interested in promoting respectful engagement, knowledge of history is vital. The history in question is not only the history of religious bodies' treatment of people with disabilities, but also the history of secular organizations by and for people with disabilities. Ignorance seldom promotes mutual understanding and cooperation. Among disability studies scholars' increased attention to religion is necessary. Established in 1995, the Disability Studies in Religion Consultation in the American Academy of Religion is promoting greater awareness of disability among religion scholars; however, no similar increased attention to religion is found within the annual meeting bulletins of such organizations as the Society for Disability Studies. Careful social and historical analysis of the relations among religious bodies and people with disabilities can provide the means for specifying the practices, images, and beliefs that promote inclusion and those that do not.

Elsewhere I have called for denominations, as part of their commitment to justice, to fund disability offices and full-time religious activists.[50] During times of financial difficulty, temptations exist to eliminate services to constituencies without strong political presence or whose numbers appear to be small. Such actions are, however, short-sighted. The population of people with disabilities is growing rapidly. As Baby Boomers age, the numbers will be further inflated. Religious groups must not only serve the direct physical and spiritual needs and concerns of people with disabilities in the pew and pulpit, they must also make their presence felt in the disability movement. Disability offices at denominations and in ecumenical organizations can and do establish that link. They cannot be sacrificed.

Finally, theologians, ethicists, and liturgists must continue to address the claims of the political speech of activists within the disability movement. If the moral meaning of disability is under consideration, then moral leaders must speak out. Unambiguously increasing the profile and presence of people with disabilities within religious groups also begins to address the participatory inequalities that are deeply rooted there. The future for participatory equality within denominations and congregations and better relations among activists and religious groups is, I think, bright. However, these goals will likely be achieved only as people attend to their history, recognizing that the disability movement is part of the history of religion in the United States, examining the moral claims about disability advanced by activists and religious leaders, and investing resources that will promote better communication and continued mutual education of activists and religious bodies and leaders.

APPENDIX

A SAMPLE OF RELIGIOUS ORGANIZATIONS
SERVING PEOPLE WITH DISABILITIES

Service Provision (Congregation)

Board for Parish Services, Ministry with Persons Who are Disabled
    (Lutheran Church-Missouri Synod)
Center for Ministry with People with Disabilities
The Christian Church Foundation for the Handicapped (Church of
    Christ)
The Christian Reformed Church: Committee on Disability Concerns
Ephphatha: Ministries with Persons with Handicapping Conditions
    (Evangelical Lutheran Church in America)
Educational Ministries, American Baptist Churches, U.S.A.
Episcopal Awareness Center on Handicaps
LEHIYOT "Becoming" Advisory Committee (Union of American
    Hebrew Congregation)
Lutheran Library for the Blind
Lutheran Special Education Ministries (Formerly Lutheran School
    for the Deaf)
Mennonite Developmental Disability Services (MDDS)
The Mill Neck Foundation, Inc.: A Lutheran Family of Organizations
    Serving Deaf People

Ministries to the Blind and Handicapped (Assemblies of God)
National Catholic Office for Persons With Disabilities (NCPD)
National Christian Resource Center on Mental Retardation
National Federation of Interfaith Volunteer Caregivers, Inc.
National Jewish Council for the Disabled
Pathways to Promise: Interfaith Ministries and Prolonged Mental
    Illness
Committee on Accessibility, United Synagogue of America (The
    Association of Conservative Synagogues in North America)

Service Provision (Persons with Disability)

Catholic Association of Persons with Visual Impairments (CAPVI)
Catholic Guild for the Blind
Catholics United for Spiritual Action (CUSA)
Christian Record Services (CRS)
Deaf Culture Ministries (DCM) (Assemblies of God)
Faith and Light, U.S.A.
The Gospel Association for the Blind, Inc.
John Milton Society for the Blind
JAF Ministries
L'Arche Communities
Lutheran Braille Evangelism Association (LBEA)
Lutheran Braille Workers, Inc. (LBW)
Mark Seven Deaf Foundation
National Catholic Office for the Deaf (NCOD)
Victorians Missionaries: National Shrine of Our Lady of the Snows

Professional Associations

American Association of Pastoral Counselors (AAPC)
American Association on Mental Retardation-Religion Division (AAMR)
Association of Jewish Special Educators
Church Interpreter Training Institute (CITI)

Advocacy Groups

The Healing Community
International Catholic Deaf Association
International Lutheran Deaf Association
Jewish Guild for the Blind

226

The Lutheran Institute on Aging (LIA)
The National Council of the Churches of Christ in the USA:
Committee on Disabilities
National Organization on Disability: Religion and Disability Program
(NOD)

1. Louis Harris and Associates, *The ICD Survey of Disabled Americans: Bringing Disabled Americans into the Mainstream* (New York: International Center for the Disabled, 1986).
2. According to the *U.S. Bureau of the Census, Americans with Disabilities: 1991-1992*, more than 23.5 percent of Americans over age 15 have a disability.
3. Throughout, my references are primarily to Christian groups, though occasionally Jewish groups and traditions are mentioned.
4. This research is based on informal, open-ended interviews with disability rights activists and leaders of religious groups serving people with disabilities, conducted in 1997. Ten disability rights activists and seven leaders of religious organizations working with people with disabilities were interviewed. Generally, the interviews were completed over the phone, but some were face-to-face. These interviews were supplemented with other informal conversations with other contacts.
5. Nancy L. Eiesland, *The Disabled God: Toward a Liberatory Theology of Disability* (Nashville: Abingdon Press, 1994). See also Nancy L. Eiesland, "Things Not Seen: Women with Physical Disabilities, Oppression, and Practical Theology," in *Grounding the Subject: Feminist Practical Theologies in Context,* ed. Denise Ackermann and Riet Bons-Storm (Louvain, Belguim: Peeters, 1998).
6. Numerous book-length accounts of the history are available. For a readable general history, see Joseph Shapiro, *No Pity: People with Disabilities Forging a New Civil Rights Movement* (New York: Random House, 1994). Other works focus on the experience of particular groups, especially Deaf. See, for example, Harlan Lane, *When the Mind Hears: A History of the Deaf* (New York: Knopf, 1984) and Oliver Sacks, *Seeing Voices: A Journey into the World of the Deaf* (Berkeley: University of California Press, 1989). Still others highlight social policy changes, Claire H. Liachowitz, *Disability as a Social Construct: Legislative Roots* (Philadelphia: University of Pennsylvania Press, 1989) and Steven L. Percy, *Disability, Civil Rights and Public Policy: The Politics of Implementation* (Tuscaloosa: University of Alabama Press, 1990).
7. J. Lenihan, "Disabled Americans: A History," *Performances* (November/December 1976-January 1977): 1-69; David Rothman, *The Discovery of the Asylum: Social Order and Disorder in the New Republic* (Boston: Little and Brown, 1971); and Frank Bowe, *Handicapping America: Barriers to Disabled People* (New York: Harper & Row, 1978).
8. Hugh G. Gallagher, *FDR's Splendid Deception* (New York: Dodd and Mead, 1985).
9. Paul K. Longmore, "Uncovering the Hidden History of People with Disabilities," *Reviews in American History* (15): 355-64.
10. Ralph H. Turner, "The Theme of Contemporary Social Movements," *British Journal of Sociology* (December 1969): 478.
11. Richard K. Scotch, "Disability as the Basis for a Social Movement: Advocacy and the Politics of Definition," *Journal of Social Issues* 44 (1988): 159-72. Clearly numerous disability specific groups had existed long before the 1960s. Scotch, however, contends that a rise in advocacy rather than direct service provision groups occurred in the 1960s.
12. For an excellent account of deinstitutionalization, see David J. Rothman and Sheila M. Rothman, *The Willowbrook Wars* (New York: Harper & Row, 1984).
13. Margaret A. Winzer locates the religious origins of the separation of people with disabilities in the Middle Ages. She writes: "The cloistering of disabled persons seemed a natural outgrowth of the monastic impulse, and, in the context of these dark times, it proved advantageous, as it protected them from the dangers confronting them in general society" (Winzer, "Disability and Society Before the Eighteenth Century: Dread and Despair," in *The Disability Studies Reader,* ed. Lennard J. Davis [New York: Routledge, 1997], 89). Winzer notes that early hospices for the blind were often built on monastery grounds. With the rise of widespread fear of witchcraft and

227

Satanic possession, people with disabilities were confined against their wills in these facilities so as to be under the observation of religious leaders. For an account of the growth of custodial care facilities in nineteenth century America, see Rothman, *The Discovery of the Asylum*.

14. Joseph P. Shapiro, "Others Saw a Victim, But Ed Roberts Didn't," *U.S. News and World Report* (March 27, 1995): 6-7. Ed Roberts died in 1995.

15. Shapiro, *No Pity*.

16. Fred Pelka, "Fire in the Belly: Just How Independent is the Independent Living Movement?" *Mainstream* 4 (1994): 35-38. A 1990 study of centers shows that the typical independent living center (a) has been in operation fewer than ten years; (b) has a staff fewer than ten people, more than half of whom are persons with disabilities; (c) has an executive director and at least two to three other staff involved in center management and (d) is governed by boards of directors, more than half of whom are persons with disabilities. See Q. Smith, L. Richard, M. Nosek, and L. Gerken, "Education and Training Needs of Independent Living Center Managers," *Rehabilitation Education* 5 (1990): 101-11.

17. Ibid.

18. Gerben DeJong, "Independent Living: From Social Movement to Analytic Paradigm," *The Psychological and Social Impact of Physical Disability*, ed. R. P. Marinelli and A. E. Dell Orto, (New York: Springer, 1984).

19. Wendell argues that the social authority of medicine to define the experience of the disabled and chronically ill is again on the rise. She cites among the reasons for this increase in the development of increasingly sophisticated genetic screening and prenatal diagnostic techniques. See Susan Wendell, *The Rejected Body: Feminist Philosophical Reflections on Disability* (New York: Routledge, 1996).

20. See Michael Oliver, "Disability and Dependency: A Creation of Industrial Societies?" in *Disabling Barriers—Enabling Environments*, ed. John Swain, Vic Finkelstein, Sally French, and Michael Oliver (Newbury Park and London: Sage Publications, 1993). See also Michael Oliver, *Understanding Disability: From Theory to Practice* (London: MacMillan, 1996).

21. Edward D. Berkowitz, *Disabled Policy: America's Programs for the Handicapped* (London and New York: Cambridge University Press, 1989).

22. Michelle Fine and Adrienne Asch, "Disability Beyond Stigma: Social Interaction, Discrimination, and Activism," in *Perspectives on Disability*, ed. Mark Nagler (Palo Alto, Calif.: Health Markets Research, 1988), 61-74.

23. Scotch, "Disability as the Basis for a Social Movement," 168.

24. Americans with Disabilities Act, 101st Congress (1990), 2nd Session, 3. U.S. Statutes at Large, vol. 104, 329.

25. William B. Ball, "Should the Senate Approve the 'Americans with Disabilities Act of 1989'?" *Congressional Digest* 68 (December 1989): 295, 297.

26. Mary Jane Owen, "What Does ADA Mean to U.S. Churches?" *Disability Studies Quarterly* 15 (Summer 1995): 58-59.

27. Religious organizations with fifteen or more employees are not exempt from Title 1 employment protections of ADA.

28. See Robert Brannon, "The Use of the Concept of Disability Culture: A Historian's View," *Disability Studies Quarterly* 15 (Fall 1995): 3-15.

29. The Deaf culture (capitalized) is seen as distinct from any disability culture. In fact, many Deaf leaders do not view deafness as a disability, but rather as a cultural distinction. For a careful discussion of the emergence of Deaf culture and the tensions with leaders in the disability rights movement see, Harlan Lane, "Construction of Deafness," in *The Disability Studies Reader*, ed. Lennard J. Davis (New York: Routledge, 1997), 153-71; Edward Dolnick, "Deafness as Culture" *The Atlantic Monthly* (September 1993): 37-51.

30. Quoted in Steven E. Brown, "A Celebration of Diversity: An Introductory, Annotated Bibliography of Disability Culture," *Disability Studies Quarterly* 15 (Fall 1995): 36.

31. Paul K. Longmore, "The Second Phase: From Disability Rights to Disability Culture" *Disability Rag and Resource* 15 (September/October 1995): 6-7.

32. Douglas Martin, "Eager to Bite the Hands That Would Feed Them," *New York Times* (June 1, 1997): Section 4, 1.

33. Jim Dickson, "FDR Memorial Battle Presses On," *Ragged Edge* 18 (March/April 1997): 9. See also John R. Woodward, "The Roosevelt Memorial: Whose Version of History," *The Disability Rag*

and Resource 16 (September/October 1995): 49-50, 53; and Cass Irvin, "My Own Private Roosevelt," *Ragged Edge* 18 (January/February 1997): 24-29.

34. Cyndi Jones, "FDR Still Brings Us Together," *Mainstream* (June/July 1997) internet edition.

35. Jack A. Nelson, "The Internet, The Virtual Community, and Those with Disabilities," *Disability Studies Quarterly* 15 (Spring 1995): 15. See also T. Raine, "Hooked on Chat and Other Goodies: Adventures On-Line," *Disability Rag* 17 (November/December 1995): 9-12.

36. See Disability Cool website at http://www. geocities.com/HotSprings/7319/discool.html. See also the website for the Institute for Disability Culture at http://www.goodnet.com/ onaroll/culture.html.

37. David Pfeiffer and Karen Yoshida, "The Teaching of Disability Studies: Results from a Survey of SDS Members," *Disability Studies Quarterly* 14 (Spring 1994): 8-11.

38. Ibid., 9.

39. See Davis, ed., *The Disability Studies Reader* (New York: Routledge, 1997); ed. Elaine Makas and Lynn Schlesinger, *End Results and Starting Points: Expanding the Field of Disability Studies* (Portland, Maine: The Society for Disability Studies and the Edmund S. Muskie Institute of Public Affairs, 1996).

40. Rosemarie G. Thomson, "Tenure Battle Questions Legitimacy of Disability Studies," *Ragged Edge* 18 (July/August 1987): 5. Thomson is the author of *Extraordinary Bodies: Figuring Physical Disability in American Culture and Literature* (New York: Columbia University Press, 1997).

41. Reported in Valerie Stiteler, "Embracing Those Unwelcomed: The Role of Christian Initiation in Excluding Persons with Disabilities from Participation in Public Worship and Community Life," *Disability Studies Quarterly* 15 (Summer 1995): 44-50.

42. This listing is intended to be representative not exhaustive.

43. Romel W. Mackelprang and Richard O. Salsgiver, "People with Disabilities and Social Work: Historical and Contemporary Issues," *Social Work* 4 (January 1996): 7.

44. See also, Beatrice Wright, *Physical Disability: A Psychological Approach* (New York: Harper & Row, 1960); Gary Albrecht, *The Disability Business: Rehabilitation in America* (Newbury Park, Calif.: Sage Publications, 1992); and H. Livneh, "On the Origins of Negative Attitudes toward People with Disabilities," *Rehabilitation Literature* 43 (1982): 938-947. For an exception to this generalization, see Winzer "Disability and Society Before the Eighteenth Century."

45. P. Israel and C. McPherson, "Introduction," *Voices from the Shadows*, ed. G. F. Matthews (Toronto: Women's Press, 1983), 14.

46. Pseudonyms are used throughout.

47. P. J. Majik, "Disability for the Religious," *The Disability Rag and Resource* 15 (November/December 1994): 24-25.

48. For my letter to the editor, see "Another Choice from Religion," *The Disability Rag and Resource* 16 (January/February 1995): 46.

49. Marilyn E. Bishop, "Religion and Disability: A New Wave," *Disability Studies Quarterly* 15: 55-56.

50. Eiesland, *The Disabled God*, 95.

PART IV.

PRACTICAL THEOLOGY

Practical theology bridges, on the one hand, the social sciences that see their primary tasks as description, interpretation, and sometimes explanation and, on the other, theology that understands its crucial tasks as moral suasion, normative judgment, and religious reflection. Practical theology is a vehicle for pragmatic, socially informed moral and theological analysis. Practical theology that underscores the particularity of our circumstances also reveals the situated character of our struggles with God and as God's people. In this section, authors explore the practical theological implications of placing people with disabilities at the center of inquiry.

In Chapter 11, H. Dean Trulear highlights the peculiar eclipsing of people with disabilities within many African American congregations and advocates a reinvigorated ethic of hospitality. Vereene Parnell (Chapter 12) addresses the experiences of two worshiping communities responding to the reality of AIDS/HIV in their midst. Though their responses differ, these congregations transform their identities as they risk enacting God's acceptance of people with HIV/AIDS. Such transformations in congregational life are not easily achieved. Brett Webb-Mitchell (Chapter 13) describes the too frequent failure of Christian education programs to incorporate people with disabilities, particularly cognitive ones, into the ordinary educational mission of the church. He proposes a model for crafting responses that are open to the dynamic life of the church and to altered understandings of the educational capabilities of people with disabilities.

Finally, Helen Betenbaugh and Marjorie Procter-Smith (Chapter 14) consider public prayer when the experiences of people with disabilities are central. Advocating a reclamation of lament as a healing narrative, they offer a powerful example of such a prayer for public use.

CHAPTER ELEVEN

TO MAKE A WOUNDED WHOLENESS: DISABILITY AND LITURGY IN AN AFRICAN AMERICAN CONTEXT

Harold Dean Trulear

In this chapter, I view the issue of liturgy and disability in the African American church context against the backdrop of the shifting social stage on which the drama of African American life is rehearsed in contemporary society.[1] In other words, just as one can trace the history of advocacy for the rights of the disabled through the twin foci of cultural ethos and social engineering/legislation, so too does this issue in the Black community call for contextualization in light of the changes in African American culture on the one hand, and the reshaping of Black institutions on the other. As the ritual of Black worship constitutes the primary context for the mediation of meaning in the Black Christian community, it makes sense to look at worship practices in light of these changes in the social order.[2]

African Americans with disabilities are persons whose marginality to the mainstream of American society lies anywhere from the double jeopardy of race and disability to the quadruple jeopardy of race, disability, class, and gender. The percentage of African Americans with one or more disabilities is nearly twice that of white Americans (14 to 8 percent). At the same time, "an African American with a disability is more likely to be female, to have less than a high school education, and to be unemployed."[3]

But as one African American female advocate for the disabled has put it, "When it comes to disability, . . . it doesn't matter what ethnic group you are; we have a culture all our own."[4] Therefore, the concept of marginality can be quite helpful in looking at the African American disabled community in that marginality not only serves as a historical paradigm for the Black community but also allows for the disabled within that community to be seen as a "marginality within a marginality," thereby enabling us to investigate the veracity of assertions by the Black church's commitment to justice and equality.

African American Christianity has historically defined itself in light of the power relations extant in American society. As such, it has engaged in a quest for individual and communal wholeness in the face of being oppressed and marginalized by the larger society. This fundamental problematic of African American Christianity causes Black Christians to struggle consistently with images of wholeness and well-being that are either in contrast with or consistent with (but never ignorant of) definitions of wholeness proffered by the normative gaze of American society.[5]

Among African Americans the question, "What must I do to be saved?" always implies the prior interrogative, "What does it mean to be saved?" The meaning of salvation—or wholeness—has most often pointed to a theological anthropology that stands in contrast with the definitions of Black humanity ascribed by the dominant society; e.g., the affirmation that one is a child of the King serves as a response to societal assertions that one is, at best, inferior or defective humanity or, at worst, not even human.[6]

However, the press for integration during the Civil Rights era and the subsequent development of a significant presence of African Americans in the mainstream of American life has led to a new, albeit tenuous, consensus concerning the place of Blacks in the American social ethos in general and a series of subtle yet detectable shifts in theological anthropologies in particular.[7] Marginality, while still present, has been redefined in light of a more fluid interchange between the Black community and the larger society, leading to the development of an institutional life that reflects a more centrist understanding of Black life. Salvation, in keeping with the shift in consensus, now embraces much more of what it means to be a part of the power structure than what it means to be over and against American racism and classism.

This reflects the impact of uncritical integration on the African American community as a whole and on the life of the Black church in general. In moving toward the center of the American mainstream, however, the church has begun to adopt much of the ethos and ethics of the exclusivist practices of the very society against which it has struggled for centuries. Much of this can be traced to a failure to discern distinctions between inclusion and transformation as realizable social goals. An inclusivist or integrationist ethic does not carry within it an inherent critique of the injustice of the social arrangements beyond the exclusion of the group in question. An ethic of transformation raises questions about the nature of social arrangements itself, beyond the simple injustice of one marginalized group in particular. Protest movements that strive only for inclusion will prove their right to belong often through appeals to the same symbol systems that have undergirded what I call the majoritarian culture. They will also make concession to the majoritarian culture in the quest for integration due to the sheer hegemony of the system itself.[8]

This Black church has been part of a movement of social protest that has focused far more on integration than transformation. Therefore, it has adopted and made concessions to much of the dominant culture's ethos. The church has become less welcoming and hospitable to the stranger; it has rendered members of its own community invisible. Yet within its historical ethic, what Peter Paris has called the Black Christian Tradition,[9] there lies the power for a truly inclusive fellowship that offers reconciliation between differing parties and critiques definitions of human wholeness that are atomistic, discriminatory, and exclusivist. It offers a definition of human wholeness that is fundamentally communal, and within that communal ethic posits the notion of egalitarianism—a further critique of power relations in the larger society. It is within the context of worship that these themes are most clearly and regularly rehearsed.

We understand worship in the African American context as the primary venue for the mediation of meaning for Black Christians. The ritual of Sunday morning enables the congregation to develop an interpretive scheme through which they can understand the everyday life-world, their own humanity—corporate and individual—and the reality of the providence and parenthood of God.[10] Melva Costen makes a similar point when she offers that the unique history of African Americans, their experience as people who were "enslaved, marginalized, denied respect and oppressed by the very people who introduced them to Christianity" moved them to create "communities for refuge" where it was discovered "that the separate environments were conducive to authentic communication with God and each other."[11]

The worship tradition of African Americans has offered the strongest resistance to uncritical inclusion into the American mainstream. As such it offers the clearest statements on human wholeness and the reality of the covenant love of God, manifest in God's presence in the struggle of the people. This tradition proffered the idea of the ultimate triumph of this union of God and people over the forces of oppression and dehumanization. The focus of this chapter will be three primary dimensions of the church's ritual through which the historical ethical resources of African American Christian worship both critique contemporary practice and offer hope for a new ecclesiology with respect to the inclusion of persons with disabilities. First, the ritual of the church includes the preaching of the Word, i.e., the telling of the story encased and encoded in the various images central to liberation. The church's ritual also includes music and dance, which are elements that called the whole of the congregation to rehearse their corporate identities as children of God and as human beings. Third, in light of the struggle for wholeness in the face of racism and oppression, the worship service was the context for the creation of "sacred space" where "freedom could be sought and experienced."[12] I will argue that these signal dimensions of the Black worship tradition contain seeds for a liberatory praxis for the Black church and its ministry with disabled populations.

PREACHING POWER

The preaching tradition of the Black church must be interpreted against the backdrop of power relations within the church itself. The Black preacher has historically exhibited social control over his (and sometimes her) members that functions as both bane and blessing. It points both to the strength of a leadership tradition and to the struggle with egalitarian norms within the church. The Black Christian Tradition—the parenthood of God and the kinship of all people—has had its strongest manifestation with respect to matters of race and the protest against racial exclusion. Similarly, it has found expression in the ethics of love and forgiveness within the church context itself.[13] Yet, as womanist theologians have been quick to remind us, this tradition has not been inclusive and egalitarian with respect to women's roles in church and society. And we still await a good theological critique of power relations within Black churches, especially with respect to the relationship between clergy and laity.

The call for an internal power critique of the contemporary Black church reflects a shift in understandings of community within the church. The historical role of pastor in the Black church has always carried considerable authority. It is in the preaching event that much of this authority is exercised, as the pastor is charged with providing primary images for the process of meaning construction.[14] One could assume a strong commitment to egalitarian relations within the laity. However, as Blacks participate in increasingly structurally differentiated spheres and institutions in our society, such a notion of differentiation and difference becomes part of the church and congregational ethos as well, exacerbating the extant power differences between leadership and laity.[15] If this is the case, we would expect the differentiation of groups such as the disabled to be reflected in the organization of the church in general.

The important question becomes, then, "Who are the laity?" This question is both empirical and theological. It is empirical because it forces us to look at who actually comes to church. It is theological in that it bids us look at our definition of the body of Christ to see if we have a truly inclusive notion of the church, or whether there are populations for whom Christ died that are notably absent from the church. The question here is this: Has the Black church, with its history of representing the spirit and soul of a marginalized people in American society, now become an institution that similarly marginalizes other people?

The biblical paradigm of the Babylonian exile is instructive here. The children of Israel had been brought out of bondage to Egypt and charged with creating a covenant society of devotion to God and care for humanity. When their ways began to reflect those of the oppressors from whom they were set free, as well as the surrounding societies and their institutions of structural dominance, they were forced into exile. The strain of their situation in Babylon provided the context for renewal, as they offered repentance for their failure to keep covenant and recaptured their sense of a marginalized, peculiar community in covenant with God.

Similarly, the Black church finds itself in a situation of exile. Historical marginality is threatened as a primary locus of the faith community, while integration moves Black Christian identity closer and closer to the mainstream of American culture. Some people with disabilities would identify with their cultural faith community if the attitude of that community toward their disability were not a barrier to full participation in the life of the church.[16] As such, they experience themselves cut off from their community of origin, marginalized by the marginalized. The church's claim to be a just institution is critiqued by its own inability to come to terms with difference within the community and full inclusion in the life of the church.

In one scenario, two Black Baptist churches, only blocks apart, with strong middle-class memberships and years of history, investigated the possibility of making their facilities fully accessible. One church succeeded, embarking on a remodeling campaign to make the church facilities fully available to people with disabilities. The other church succeeded only in installing a used stairlift to get people up the stairs to the nave and sanctuary, but not downstairs to enable them to use the bathrooms or fellowship hall. The primary difference between these congregational responses lies in the situation of the pastoral family of the successful church. The pastor's wife was a paraplegic. When asked by his less successful colleague what led to the church's success, the pastor at the accessible church replied tongue-in-cheek, "I guess the people just got tired of seeing the pastor struggling to push his wife up and down those steps in a wheelchair."[17]

The relationship between the church and disabled persons calls for investigation of the relationship between physical difference and marginality. The Black church has a long tradition of giving special attention to physicality. This attention has come in two forms. First, the existence of the Black church reflects white American and historical European aversion to the physical appearance of Blacks, thereby making one of the church's missions the affirmation of that appearance—blackness—as the *Imago Dei,* the image of God. Second, traditional African American worship has placed a premium upon free bodily demonstration of the presence of the Spirit (or Spirit possession). Put simply, the first order of business is the celebration of the body. The goodness of the Black body is affirmed in the first case and the dance of the Black body in the second.

The Black church must seek ways to affirm the goodness of the Black body that is disabled. On the one hand, it is the affirmation of the divine gifting of all persons that critiques the sentiment expressed by one interviewee, "Many people think that because I have an orthopaedic disability, that I must have a mental one as well." This view asserts the relative worthlessness of a person based on perceived ability to function and be productive.[18] T. J. Wright notes that this dilemma is enhanced for African Americans whose status as disabled and minority can become so stigmatized that it can obfuscate any positive perception of individual gifts and abilities.[19]

On the other hand it involves the search for positive images of Black bodies that are steeped in the worth of the individual. Images such as the Christology constructed by Nancy Eiesland in *The Disabled God,* where the risen Christ interacts with followers while incarnate in a body with visible scars and marring, are helpful.[20] They push the Black church right at the heart of its theological construct: images of Jesus, the marginalized one, the outsider, the one who is the only one who "knows the trouble I see." Black Christians have long held the tension between Jesus as Lord and Jesus as fellow sufferer. But the tension itself bespeaks a theological problem. In holding together bipolar images of Jesus, we miss the opportunity to see how the seeming opposite attributes form a whole of their own, thereby reducing the tension inherent in the dichotomizing of Christ.

In its stead, Eiesland's image of a strong and wounded Christ offers the church the opportunity to explore its own woundedness and brokenness, at which point the exclusion of any form of brokenness becomes untenable. But this means a shift from historical Black populist notions of a resurrected Jesus that are fundamentally triumphalistic toward a vision of Jesus as he embraces the margin, not to be crucified a second time, but to show dignity and brokenness to occupy the same ground. Eiesland suggests that even in the resurrection, Christ is part of a marginalized community. His triumph over the grave is not necessarily the conquest of the oppressors in the mainstream, but rather the redefinition of the mainstream to an inclusive community headed by the Christ, himself having a wounded, imperfect body.

Another helpful image is offered by Douglas Sullivan, a student at Colgate Rochester Theological Seminary during the time of activism leading up to and including the passage of the Americans with Disabilities Act in 1990. Sullivan, in a lecture given to fellow students and faculty in Christian Ethics, noted the parallel between the story of Jesus' healing of the man with the withered hand in Mark 3 and the account of the God's dealing with Moses in the Exodus narrative.

In both cases, asserts Sullivan, God/Jesus calls the individual to "stretch forth your hand." In Moses' case, he responds, and the definitive liberating event occurs in the life of Israel. In the case of the man with the withered hand, he responds and his healing restores him "into the midst" (Mark 3: 3) of the community. By identifying the man with the withered hand with Moses, Jesus gives people with disabilities a restored sense of self-esteem and a belief that they, too, can be leaders in the liberation experience of the people of God (cf. Grant, chapter 3).[21]

This same theme is rehearsed by Reverend Charles Williams, a seminarian who was blinded in an accident after a successful career in business. "When I entered the Black church as a visually impaired person," he notes, "I was brought to a seat to sit down, and this was where I was expected to stay." Williams was seen as someone with nothing to offer, after all "a visually impaired person couldn't [be expected] to teach a sighted person to read."[22] Williams contends that the Black church only acknowledges the disabled either in its bulletin and/or announcement list of "sick and shut in" or as examples of God's miraculous activity in healing. There is no recognition of the dignity of the disabled within the context of their current state. "My mission," he says, "is to take my experience as a disabled person and not just be led to a chair, but help lead the church with direction."[23]

Laverne Nichols of Inglis House echoes this theme. She recasts the traditional image of the Black church missionary in her testimony. Nichols tells the story of a visiting minister who came to her church prior to her disabling illness. He prophesied that "four people here are going to be missionaries. He named the names," she continues, "and I was one of them. . . . When I got here [Inglis House], I realized that this is my missionary place where I can go around and work for the Lord."[24] For Nichols, her sense of calling as a missionary, serving from her vantage point as a person with a disability, provides a model of the wounded Christ, stricken, yet active in ministry—wounded yet whole.

The importance of these images for African American worship is in the power of story and orality in church ritual. Put simply, the preached word remains the centerpiece of Black worship.[25] This ritual event carries the primary responsibility of naming experience in the world and shaping the identity of the people of God. The images that emerge from the lips of the Black preacher become definitive for congregants as they attempt to make sense of their world and take their place in it.[26] Therefore, the first order of business in African American ritual and disabled persons is for the pastor to "preach it," that is, to assist the congregation in the development of images of Jesus and the people of God that are more radically inclusive and empowering through creating and nurturing of images that reflect the wholeness of those wounded by disability. We must preach that people with disabilities are created by God in God's image and called to be active participants in the liberative activity of God through Jesus Christ. In other words, preach it.

THE WORSHIPPING BODY

In considering the next elements, music and dance, we again face issues of body. In making a joyful noise unto the Lord is the clear invitation to act out the freedom proclaimed through the music by the involvement of bodily participation. Whether in raising hands, clapping, swaying, or dancing, we expect bodily expression in many Black church worship contexts. One primary activity in the more demonstrative ritual forms of Black worship is called "shouting," an experience of the power of the Holy Spirit that is described as "religious ecstasy, or uncontrollable physical movements involving one's whole person." It is not uncommon to see worshippers "stand and dance or jump about involuntarily, or they may remain seated and swing their arms and legs convulsively."[27]

How then does the disabled person dance? Can a person "shout" in a wheelchair? If full expression of physicality is a hallmark of Black worship, then what room is there for the one whose full bodily expression is a reminder of both woundedness and wholeness? One response is to call for the "stretching forth of hands" in ritual, i.e., to call for the gifts of movement and physicality available to persons with disability during the worship service. A precedent exists for this in Black worship. When a physical response of standing is called for in a Black worship service, persons who are unable to do so raise their right hand as a sign of solidarity with those who are able physically to stand. This response is appropriate for persons with orthopaedic disabilities, temporary conditions such as broken bones or torn muscles, and even women expecting or holding a child. African American congregations have shown the ability to construct new rituals as the occasion arises (e.g., use of different instruments, development of tarry services,[28] and applause translated to "clap offerings"). As new images are created that point to the broken, wounded body of the risen Christ as a central theological symbol for imaging the body of Christ, the ways of symbolizing this "wounded wholeness" will become central to liturgical function.

In another sense, rituals of embrace and touch can be expanded to affirm the wholeness of wounded bodies. These rituals are not frenzied, as a rule, but they are danced. They involve the choreography of movement and are recognizable to the congregation as such. The challenge is to embrace physical difference within the body of Christ through the use of the passing of the peace, careful attention given to the orchestration of handshake rituals, such as the "right hand of fellowship,"[29] and the exploration of skills and technologies, such as sign language, speaker jacks in pews, and accessible altar rails. The effort toward full participation enables the church to rehearse its historical rhetoric of inclusion with integrity. At the same time, the presence of fully participating persons with disabilities becomes a symbol of the wounded nature of life for the whole congregation. As Charles Williams puts it, "I am there to remind the congregation of their imperfections and also the inevitability of death, when these bodies will stop functioning permanently."[30] This encounter gives the congregation the opportunity to reflect on new images of what it means to be whole. It is the audacious attempt to make a wounded wholeness.

CREATING SACRED SPACE

Melva Costen contrasts antiseptic worship space in which the realities of tenuous human existence cannot intrude with "sacred space."[31] The concept of sacred space in African American worship reflects years of tradition in which Black worshippers sought an environment of freedom—a context wherein "the personhood of every believer could be affirmed."[32] Seeking refuge from the oppression of the everyday life-world, African American Christians came to worship as a place where their freedom in Christ could be dramatically rehearsed, in contrast to the circumscribed identities enforced by the larger society.

Costen also suggests a clear connection between the sacred space within the worship tradition and the press for justice in the larger society. She offers that "the need for sacred space both evolved from and enhanced the opportunity for ministry," both in ministries of "pastoral care and nurture in the faith" and in ministries of social justice and liberation. "Inherent in the gospel message," she writes, "is a radical disapproval of the claim of power invested in a few who work vigorously to maintain the status quo."[33] Riggins Earl rehearses this theme when he notes that the birth of the Black church independence movement "symbolized a historical attempt on the part of black Americans to acquire their own institutional worship space."[34] Earl shows how the ethic of sacred space also creates the context for the ritual of the Civil Rights movement's mass meetings, i.e., the stage for the eschatalogical rehearsal for the actions of protest and justice in which Martin Luther King, Jr. and his followers engaged.[35]

The notion of antiseptic space becomes relevant when the connection between the theological freedom of sacred space and the social freedom of just space in the larger society is loosened. The church and its worship become haven without help, meeting without ministry, and refuge without redemption. To lose sight of the larger demands for justice in society and the church's call to ministry in this sphere is not only to reduce the freedom of the sacred space to an anesthesia against the pain and injustice of the larger world, but also to cease to join God in the work of social transformation. The haven works for those present, but they have ceased to be energized by the larger vision of a just world under the auspices of God. What began as a call for justice degenerates into group self-interests. The call for inclusion replaces the cry for transformation. The argument here is that the failure to create space for persons with disabilities in the African American worship experience is a clear indication that this process is underway.

Just as history records the ante-bellum African American Christians' critique concerning the incongruity of the founding fathers calls for liberty while holding slaves, apparent contradictions exist between contemporary African American rhetoric about justice spoken from pulpits of churches that are not handicap accessible, in congregations that make little or no provision for the visually or hearing impaired, and that have yet to examine their Christian education programs in light of the needs of special education. That which was once sacred space for African Americans to affirm their worth as human beings has become a place of exclusion for persons with disabilities. Williams' earlier comments about being shown where to sit—an act of relegation—are reflected in Jackie Sullivan's warning. "It is perhaps this inability to see people with disabilities as unique individuals which prevents them from being treated as human beings."[36] This irony stands out in contrast to the Black church as a place of human affirmation.

One place to begin, theologically, would be to give distinct visibility to those persons whose disabilities have relegated them to the margins. While special care needs have required that some live in specially equipped residences with trained health care facilities, physical separation can no longer legitimate the marginalization of the disabled. The body of Christ, wounded though it may be, stretches across physical boundaries to include those whose mobility is limited or who live in places like Inglis House. Inglis House residents, like Naudya Commack, are working to make visible the life and culture of disabled persons by taking initiative to develop programs that invite clergy and churches into their world. Commack, whose church, First African Baptist of Sharon Hill, Pennsylvania, picks her up and brings her to church regularly, works with Inglis House chaplain Scott Simmons in making contact with local clergy and churches "to see how aware they are and what they can do to make the church accessible or [develop] an outreach to those who can't come." The project is designed to gather feedback from area churches and establish dialogue between these congregations and the community of physically challenged persons both inside and outside the facility.[37]

Simmons points to another intersection of marginality and visibility—the situation of young Black males in his facility. The growing number of young Black males confined to wheelchairs due to street violence presents a new challenge to African American churches. Those churches that begin to give visibility to the physically challenged will discover the increased numbers of young Black males among them. The extant rage of "menaces to society" and their victims will constitute a voice with which those churches must reckon.[38] To hear these voices and to redefine our notion of the body of Christ in light of their authenticity promises real theological insight.

244

On the programmatic front, the obvious place to begin is for Black churches to examine their physical facilities. For the purpose of liturgical sensibilities, the efforts to accessibility might start with the sanctuary and nave and the entrance to the church itself. In many cases, this project will require significant creativity, especially for those congregations that are housed in historical buildings.

The larger issue of contextualizing such efforts lies at the intersection of theology and will. If African Americans lay claim to a historical theology of justice, rather than a primarily self-interested ethic of inclusion, then the Black church will have to reexamine its own tendency to exclusivity born of myopia that threatens its vision. In affirming its historical liberation ethics of empowerment, the Black church must turn to the marginalized within its own ranks and receive their gifts as part of the overall liberation and empowerment of the community.

In a 1988 article entitled "Can Disability Be Beautiful?" Harlan Hahn noted that, like the African American community as a whole, persons with disabilities have lived in a milieu "that was not designed to accommodate [their] interests or needs . . . [they] experienced one of the highest rates of unemployment, poverty, and welfare dependency in the country." People with disabilities have "been sent to separate or segregated schools and . . . been prevented from interacting, or integrating, with their nondisabled peers in transportation, housing, and public accommodations by barriers and policies as rigid as the most restrictive practice of apartheid."[39] Hahn called for a movement among the disabled that would parallel the Black Civil Rights movement, including a call for the recognition of the beauty of persons with disabilities—a call for self-esteem within and justice without. When the Americans with Disabilities Act was passed in 1990, it echoed the great Civil Rights legislation of the 1950s and 1960s. Sadly, the institution most responsible for these Civil Rights gains was largely absent from these more recent events, either as an advocate for the marginalized within their own ranks or as a partner in the politics of coalition toward which Martin Luther King moved in his later years.

The historical ethic of hospitality[40] requires a contemporary response that opens the doors of African American churches to the marginalized within the Black community itself. Such a theological reclamation project will require the creation of a new sense of symbol, ritual, and gesture that mirrors the creativity of earlier eras. It will also require non-Black advocates for persons with disabilities to engage Black churches in the spirit of coalition politics in order for the fullest expression of the humanity of African Americans with disabilities to be realized in both church and world.

This embrace of the physically challenged offers African Americans additional opportunities to reject mainstream cultural ideals of what is attractive, strong, or whole. Embracing marginalized persons can remind us of our own marginality in matters of body and physicality. One must be cautious here to resist the gnostic solution, i.e., the advancement of the "strong character" and/or "mental capacity" of the disabled. Such an offering still negates the embrace of the body. Rather, the challenge is to provide the room for all bodies as dimensions of persons who are among the fellowship of the reconciled. In this way, new forms of Black ritual will be tied to the new consensus of community and body, but which are historically rooted in the tradition of the Black church ethics of love, inclusion, and hospitality.

---

1. Data for this essay has been extrapolated from a data base on African American congregational studies begun in 1984 as part of the project "Black Worship and Afro-American Identity," funded in part by grants from the New Jersey State Historical Commission and the Association of Theological Schools. Additional data came from subsequent ethnographic interviews with residents of Inglis House, a home for adults with disabilities located in Philadelphia, and interviews with persons involved in ministry with disabled populations. These interviews were conducted between January and June of 1996 by the author and by New York Theological Seminary student Patricia Lawson.

2. For a careful rehearsal of this theme, see especially William B. McClain, *The Soul of Black Worship* (Multi-Ethnic Center for Ministry, 1979); Wyatt Tee Walker, *Somebody's Calling My Name: Black Sacred Music and Social Change* (Valley Forge, Penn.: Judson Press, 1979); Melva Costen and Darius Swann, eds. *The Black Christian Worship Experience*, rev. ed (Atlanta: ITC Press, 1992); and Jon Michael Spencer, *Protest and Praise: Sacred Music of Black Religion* (Minneapolis: Fortress Press, 1990).

3. Frank Bowe, *Adults with Disabilities: A Portrait* (President's Committee on the Employment of People with Disabilities, 1992) cited in Reginald Alston, Charles Russo, and Albert Miles "Brown vs. Topeka Board of Education and the Americans with Disabilities Act: Vistas of Equal Educational Opportunities for African Americans," *Journal of Negro Education* 63:3: 349. This article also notes that "only 18 percent of African Americans with disabilities were employed in 1990, and they earned less than $10,000 a year on the average."

4. Interview with Antoinette Daniels, General Theological Seminary. Another interviewee, Naudya Commack, of Inglis House, described her sense of marginality within and without the Black community as being almost invisible. "It's kind of funny; they [other people] may pat you on the head or talk to the person with you, but don't talk to you."

5. Cornel West, *Prophesy Deliverance! An Afro-American Revolutionary Christianity* (Philadelphia: Westminster Press, 1982), 53-55.

6. In his *Christianity on Trial: African-American Religious Thought Before and After Black Power* (Maryknoll, N.Y.: Orbis, 1996), Mark Chapman reminds us that this idea was first analyzed by George Kelsey in *Racism and the Christian Understanding of Man*, (New York: Scribner, 1965). From there, authors such as James Cone were able to build theologies that reflected the need for such a response (see Chapman, *On Trial*, 126-28).

7. See Harold Dean Trulear, "The Black Middle Class and the Quest for Community" *The Drew Gateway* 61:1: 44-59.

8. This has been called adaptation in Parsonian social theory, and while much debate has occurred in the years since Talcott Parsons penned his theories of social change, the force of his analysis in this revision of Max Weber's concept of the routinization of charisma still carries weight. See Talcott Parsons, *The Social System* (New York: Free Press, 1951), 525-35.

9. Peter Paris, *The Social Teaching of the Black Churches* (Philadelphia: Fortress Press, 1985), 10. He defines this as the nonracist vision of the church historically expressed in the African Methodist Episcopal Church motto of "God our Father, Christ Our Redeemer, Man Our Brother" and given contemporary witness in the idea of "the parenthood of God and the kinship of all people."

10. Harold Dean Trulear, "The Lord Will Make a Way Somehow: Black Worship and the Afro-American Story" *Journal of the Interdenominational Theological Center* 13:1: 89.

11. Melva Costen, *African American Christian Worship* (Nashville: Abingdon Press, 1992), 14.

12. Ibid., 37.

13. See especially Riggins Earl's treatment of this issue in "Under Their Own Vine and Fig Tree: The Ethics of Social and Spiritual Hospitality in Black Church Worship," *The Journal of the Interdenominational Theological Center* 14:1&2: 181-93.

14. See Henry Mitchell, *Celebration and Experience in Preaching* (Nashville: Abingdon Press, 1990), 18-19; also Harold Dean Trulear, "The Sacramentality of Preaching" *Liturgy* 7:1: 17-18.

15. Ida Rousseau Mukenge, *The Black Church in Urban America: A Case Study in Political Economy* (Lanham, Md.: University Press of America, 1983), 77-112.

16. Two interviewees attend predominantly white churches in their denomination precisely because of congregational attitudes toward disability. When Antoinette Daniels first visited her parish, she was asked by the pastor how she could be made more comfortable. Her reply was that the church could remove two sets of pews. When she returned the following Sunday, the pews were removed, allowing her space to sit closer to the front. She remarked, "In a Black congregation, they would have had to go through a whole lot of people, deacons and decision makers. Here, they just got it done because the commitment is there." When asked if she were to find a Black congregation that was fully accessible (not just to the nave and sanctuary, but also to the bathrooms and altar rail) she eagerly responded that she would join. Similarly, Joan Jones of Inglis House posited monthly visitations from her parish priest, accessibility of the church edifice, and the parish's commitment to pay for public para-transit between her residence and the church as clear evidence of that congregation's care for her and others with disabilities.

17. Interview with a pastor whose point was that the congregation was motivated to remodel the church because of their concern for him. This reflected some measure of concern. At the same time, like many congregations, they struggle with the larger egalitarian vision and with the fullness of compassion for the marginalized in society. Members of the other congregation declared that this was not an issue for them, since they had no people with disabilities. "Well, guess why not?" responded Antoinette Daniels in her interview.

18. Daniels interview. Adds Lucille Williams of Inglis House, "We have a mind. Instead of looking at the (wheel)chair, look at us, the whole person. We know what's going on in the world. I got my education (A.A., B.A.) right here (at Inglis House)."

19. T. J. Wright, "Enhancing the professional preparation of rehabilitation counselors for improved services to ethnic minorities with disabilities," *Journal of Applied Rehabilitation Counseling* 19:4: 4-9.

20. Nancy L. Eiesland, *The Disabled God: Toward a Theology of Disability* (Nashville: Abingdon Press, 1994), 98-105.

21. Douglas Sullivan, "Healing, Self-Esteem and Empowerment: Stretching Out the Hand in Mark 3:1-6," lecture given in Introduction to Christian Ethics at Colgate Rochester Divinity School, March 1990. I credit Sullivan; his wife, the Rev. Jackie Sullivan; and my father, Harold H. Trulear, retired professor of special education at Antioch University, for initiating my own interest and stirring my conscience in this entire arena.

22. Interview with Minister Charles Williams, January 1996.

23. Charles Williams interview.

24. Interview with Laverne Nichols, Inglis House.

25. This can even be true (though not necessarily always) for Black churches with ministry to the hearing impaired. At one such church, Society for the Helping Church in inner city Philadelphia, the preaching event, both aurally and signed, stands as the signal event of worship. Here preaching is both aural and visual, especially considering the demonstrative style of Black preaching.

26. Trulear, "The Lord Will Make a Way Somehow," 1. This is not to say that the congregation brings nothing of its own experience to the worship event. Rather, the preacher must be well acquainted with the life experience of congregants in order to craft sermons that relate clearly to them. In that regard, the preacher becomes an interpreter of experience. See especially Henry Mitchell, *Celebration and Experience.*

27. Costen, *African American Christian Worship,* 48. Bishop John Bryant, of the African Methodist Episcopal Church and a leader of its charismatic or neo-Pentecostal wing, affirms the practice, while disputing the idea of its being uncontrollable or involuntary. He argues that just as one can choose to sing or pray while in worship, one can choose to shout. "Why must we always assume that when someone gets up to dance for the Lord that they have to be 'out of their mind'?" From remarks given at the "Consultation on African American Worship Traditions Research Project," Interdenominational Theological Center (November 1987).

28. The tarry service was developed as a service within the service as part of the ritual of Black Pentecostal worship. It usually follows the sermon or altar call, and is an invitation to persons to seek the "baptism of the Holy Spirit" usually manifested by speaking in tongues.

29. The right hand of fellowship is used in many churches as the final ritual act for the reception of new members. New members traditionally line up across the front of the congregation, while the pastor, ministers, officers and sometimes other members make their way to the front to shake hands with each new member. This final initiation ritual can be orchestrated to be fully inclusive of disabled members, both new and established.

30. Williams interview.

31. Costen and Swann, *Black Christian Worship,* 38-39.

32. Ibid., 15-32.

33. Ibid., 125-26.

34. Earl, "Under Their Own Vine," 187.

35. Ibid., 188-191; see also Costen and Swann, *Black Christian Worship,* 126. See also James Evans, *We Have Been Believers* (Minneapolis: Fortress Press, 1992). While not treating worship per se, Evans does argue that the whole of the Black freedom movement, indeed the whole concept of freedom for African Americans, is rooted in the theological image of the free God, and the press for Blacks to seek and create the space in the larger society in which to live their lives.

36. Jackie Sullivan, paper presented in fulfillment of requirements for "Introduction to Christian Ethics," Colgate Rochester Divinity School (May 1990).

37. Commack interview.

38. Interview with the Rev. Scott Simmons, chaplain at Inglis House, Philadelphia, Pennsylvania.

39. Harlan Hahn, "Can Disability Be Beautiful?," *Social Policy* 18:3 (Winter 1988): 26.

40. Earl, "Under Their Own Vine," 192-93.

CHAPTER TWELVE

RISKING REDEMPTION: A CASE STUDY IN HIV/AIDS AND THE HEALING OF CHRISTIAN LITURGY

Vereene Parnell

Liturgy is a way of coming to rest in the heart of the cosmos. Liturgy is how a people becomes attuned to the way things are—the way they really are, not the way they appear to be.[1]

The body of Christ has AIDS. While institutional Christianity struggles to defend itself from liberal detractors on one hand and ultra-conservative advocates on the other, academic theologians make peace with new philosophical quietisms. But no matter how apt HIV/AIDS may be as a metaphor for debilitated and debilitating institutions, we cannot afford to appropriate the language of disability for purely literary purposes. Quite literally, the body of Christ has AIDS—in all its denominations, in every geographic region, in ivory towers and mahogany pulpits, in folding chairs and soup kitchen lines. The disabling effects of this pandemic are real, and a clever turn of phrase will not bring about the revolution in health care, public education, and basic human compassion our suffering world so desperately needs. But a heartfelt transformation of liturgy, a radical expansion of the inclusivity of our table fellowship might accomplish just that. It has been known to happen.[2]

Anthropologist Ronald Grimes challenges the popular stereotype that casts liturgy, in general, and Eucharist, in particular, as a museum piece, a reliquary preserving the dry bones of primitive superstitions and antiquated spiritualities. Like the skeletal remains of giant dinosaurs that haunt museums of natural history, overpowering space that might hold a different host, these brittle bits are treasured primarily as reminders of how things *were*. But Grimes would have us believe that liturgy brings us heart-to-heart with the beauty and the terror of "the way things are—the way they really are." If he is correct, we should

249

expect contemporary Christian liturgy to confront participants with a church that is dying in a world that is dying from apathy, from ignorance, from AIDS.

By and large, Christian liturgical practitioners and participants have avoided the risk of intimate contact with human disability, in general, and the effects of HIV/AIDS, in particular. We have done this most heinously by demonizing the vulnerable, but also by succumbing to the hypnotic rhythms of liturgical routine and the social conspiracy of denial. We numb ourselves to the cries for justice and healing that echo through our own communities and religious traditions. But our resistance is breaking down. Slowly, the body of Christ is reclaiming its place as a locus of healing and transformation for all God's people by embracing its role as wounded healer. The liturgies birthed from such wounded bodies challenge and empower us to risk brutal honesty for the sake of tender possibility.[3]

This chapter builds upon the theological foundations laid by field work done in 1995-96 with two very different worshipping communities. The first, University Friends Meeting (Quakers) in Seattle, Washington, working with members living with full-blown AIDS, developed a model of care that is now being imitated throughout the Religious Society of Friends and reproduced throughout the United States. Across the geographic and liturgical map, the Episcopal Church of the Redeemer in Morristown, New Jersey, transformed its rectory into interim housing for individuals and families left homeless because of the pandemic, as a memorial to its first member to die from an AIDS-related illness. In intensive interviews with members of these two faith communities, my theological co-conspirators and I began to articulate some of the insights gained through intimate contact with the body of Christ at risk, diagnosed, dying and—just possibly—rising again to a new life of wholeness and healing.[4] This essay explores the broad and ever-spiralling implications of those initial theological reflections for the worship life of one congregation.

I begin this essay with a brief history of the Church of the Redeemer, including its first encounter with HIV/AIDS. Then, using Sharon Welch's *A Feminist Ethic of Risk* as an interpretive lens, I review theological concepts that emerged in conversation with Quaker and Episcopal dialogue partners and relate these concepts to subsequent liturgical transformations at the Church of the Redeemer. Rather than focusing on AIDS-specific worship services, I will explore the subtle but powerful connections between the congregation's theological response to HIV/AIDS and its "regular" liturgical practices.[5]

THE BODY OF CHRIST IN TIME

The inclusive-language liturgy currently celebrated at the Church of the Redeemer each Sunday condenses the Nicene creed into two theologically juicy lines: "Jesus is Lord, and we are the body of Christ." While most Sundays any number of feminists would be willing to debate the first phrase, the second is sung with gusto. Both feminism and gusto are relatively recent developments at this worship site. In 1988, Redeemer was a dying congregation. Having lost touch with a long history of faith-based political activism, thirty to fifty souls huddled around liturgical half-measures in a cold stone building waiting for the last candle to burn out.

The Church of the Redeemer was founded in 1852 by twenty-nine members of St. Peter's Episcopal Church of Morristown. Although details of the split are somewhat sketchy, the fire that warmed the hearts of these twenty-nine pioneers seems to have been both liturgical and political—the senior congregation's enthusiasm for the more Catholic inclinations of the Oxford Movement and lack of enthusiasm for the abolition movement. In any case, Redeemer quickly developed a strong support base among the working class and politically active residents of Morristown. In 1885, when the Diocesan Standing Committee sought to formalize the class distinction between the congregations by dividing Morristown into two distinct parishes, the younger church literally moved itself uptown, dragging the building and all its accoutrements up a hill, through a swamp to its current site three blocks from St. Peter's, two blocks closer than the senior parish to the town green—the center of social, commercial, and religious life in Morristown.

With a congregation that reached 700 members by the end of the Great Depression, Redeemer's new Parish House served as an active community center, open twenty-four hours a day. The church sponsored Morristown's first Boy Scout troop and was the first church in the northern New Jersey area to offer meeting space to Alcoholics Anonymous groups, a number of which still use the Redeemer facilities. The political and liturgical changes that swept the nation during the 1960s and 1970s affected Redeemer as well. The decision to host

251

civil rights meetings cost the church membership and financial support during the 1960s. A decade later, Redeemer's members actively participated in the denominational process of revising the 1928 Book of Common Prayer, an experience that split many Episcopal congregations across the United States. Almost immediately after the 1974 "irregular" ordination of eleven women to the Episcopal priesthood, Redeemer's pastor, F. Sanford Cutler, invited Nancy Wittig, one of the "Philadelphia Eleven," to be the first Episcopal woman to celebrate Eucharist in the greater New York metropolitan area.

As in many Protestant and Catholic congregations, membership at Church of the Redeemer dropped dramatically in the later 1970s and early 1980s. By the mid-1980s the congregation was very small and very tired. Further liturgical reforms were embraced halfheartedly, and political action became almost exclusively the rector's concern.[6] I believe that this fading energy and commitment at the Church of the Redeemer and in many liberal congregations during this period can be attributed to what feminist ethicist Sharon D. Welch calls "cultured despair."

In *A Feminist Ethic of Risk,* Welch addresses the ironic fact that systems of oppression are perpetuated by good, well-meaning people. She attributes this participation in systemic evil to a misguided understanding of responsible action derived from an ethic of control prevalent in Euro-American culture and politics. Within this ethic,

> we assume that to be responsible means that one can ensure that the aim of one's action will be carried out. To act means to determine what will happen through that single action, to ensure that a given course of events comes to pass.[7]

This romantic image of decisive and effective action, derived more from the American Western than from political reality, crumbles in the face of complex social issues, such as those encountered in the HIV/AIDS pandemic and, more broadly, in the disability rights movement. According to Welch, the most common responses to the failure of simple, unilateral action are either escalated coercion or a retreat into cynicism and despair.

Welch's description of the phenomenon I prefer to call "privileged" rather than "cultured" despair exposes the dynamics behind the apparent unconcern of well-meaning but "temporarily able-bodied" believers to the issues and injustices so eloquently expressed by disability and HIV/AIDS activists.

> The cultured despair of the middle class is ideological: it masks the bad faith of abandoning social justice work for others when one is already the beneficiary of partial social change. . . . Becoming so easily discouraged is the privilege of those accustomed . . . to having a political and economic [and medical and architectural] system that responds to their needs.[8]

If the pain is not our own and the solution is not immediately obvious, even the compassionate often surrender the suffering before us to the category of inevitability. We wish the world different but despair of concrete action.

Lenten prayers at the Church of the Redeemer, in part, confirm Welch's observations. "We have acted out of our fear and ignorance. We have remained silent when we could have spoken out. We have cooperated with systems of injustice. We have failed to claim our potential as your children."[9] The harshness of Welch's diagnosis is tempered by the hopefulness, clarity, and practicality of the ethical change of heart she proposes. In response to the ethic of control and the climate of cynicism and helplessness it fosters, Welch formulates an "ethic of risk" that contains three key elements: "a redefinition of responsible action, grounding in community, and strategic risk-taking."[10] These three elements parallel the transformations experienced by the Redeemer congregation when HIV/AIDS breached the line of privilege protecting the cultured despair that was, in fact, destroying their once-vital church community. In 1988, Rev. Philip Wilson accepted the leadership of a church that knew it was dying.[11] For almost two years, the new rector desperately searched for vital signs. He looks back on this tremendously disheartening process. "I jumped on every idea that came along. Nothing worked."[12] Then Eric Johnson came home to die.

Eric grew up at Redeemer, the church his parents, Bill and Anne Johnson, still call "home." "Church is the people . . . and these people are family," Anne told me. Bill sang in the boys choir during his youth and credits the community he found there with saving him from an otherwise unhappy and chaotic childhood. Anne was raised in a neighboring parish in the same diocese and joined Redeemer a few years after she and Bill were married. Anne and Bill had not been surprised when Eric "came out" to them when he called to tell them that his lover, Luis, had just died from AIDS. When Eric was diagnosed, the Johnsons turned to the Redeemer family just as they had done in other times of personal crisis.

The news did shock some long-time friends, but in *most* cases, church members put their own homophobia on the back burner or transformed it through engagement and compassion. In the difficult and confusing months that followed Eric's homecoming, Redeemer members became "the constant, . . . the familiarity in the midst of all the newness and change."[13] They visited Eric and his parents at home, brought homemade soup and bread to hospital waiting rooms. They sent notes of love and support. Bill's lack of surprise at this behavior is disarming. "It's what churches do," he told me with unshakable conviction.[14] In this matter-of-fact response, Philip Wilson found the heartbeat he had been looking for, a faint but steady rhythm that would revive and transform an entire congregation. The Church of the Redeemer met the stranger in their midst and recognized him as their own.[15]

Eric died on June 6, 1990. A few months later, the vestry voted to convert Redeemer's beautiful old rectory into transitional housing for individuals and families left homeless because of HIV/AIDS. During the next few years, Redeemer sponsored AIDS "buddy training" and organized the first AIDS Walkathon in Morristown, which raised money for renovations and start-up costs for the Eric Johnson House. A number of AIDS activists who had felt marginalized in other faith communities found a new spiritual home at Redeemer, and they told their friends. Fearing that Redeemer was becoming a "gay" church, a few long-time members did move to more traditional parishes, but many old Redeemer families stayed on, and slowly the church began to grow—in numbers and theology. "Because of Eric," said Philip Wilson, "a whole new group of people found Redeemer, intent on making this a place where people were free to be whomever God intended them to be."[16]

In spite of the rainbow flag out front and the buses that leave from the parking lot for the annual Pride march in New York City, the Church of the Redeemer has not become a "gay" church. The "whole new group" Wilson described defies simple demographic characterization. They are straight and gay, multiethnic, trans-generational, apparently able-bodied and obviously otherwise, united by the commitment to worship where people are free to be who God intends and are empowered to live that freedom more responsibly. A commitment to social justice and human compassion in one area has quickly spread to others. The local soup kitchen and food and clothing banks are housed at the church, which also hosts the Interfaith Hospitality Network (a "floating" shelter for homeless families) six weeks a year. Men's groups and women's groups grow in their own ways, and the Racial Inclusivity Team continues to evolve. Youth programs are expanding, taking on their own outreach ministries. The Lesbian and Gay Support Group met regularly for several years before disbanding, in part, so members had more time to take active roles in the general governance of the church and in other outreach ministries. The AIDS Ministry Team remains among the most active of Redeemer's community services. After opening the Eric Johnson House as an independent not-for-profit organization, they began work on an AIDS Memorial Chapel, dedicated in November of 1995. Their next project is a monthly interdenominational HIV/AIDS healing service.

This lush and well-established growth inspires and is inspired by Redeemer's liturgy. Along with a growing commitment to inclusive language, special holy days have been instituted that celebrate the liberation struggles of African Americans, lesbians, gays and bisexuals, women, and people in recovery. There have also been modifications to the liturgical calendar, redefining the long "Ordinary" season between Pentecost and Advent in order to extend the celebration of the Spirit at Pentecost and incorporate two newly created "Green" and "Creation" seasons, discussed in more detail below.

The Church of the Redeemer did not succumb to cultured despair. Nor did it fade into monotoned mediocrity. Like certain first-century gatherings along the Sea of Galilee and beyond, Redeemer has become a motley crew, a "come-as-you-are party," according to one of the signs facing Morristown's most upscale shopping district, "a liberation community in the Episcopal tradition." So far, the Episcopal tradition has survived the shock, but it has not survived unmoved. At the 1996 Diocesan Convention, the Church of the Redeemer was awarded the Bishop's Banner for Congregational Excellence. In reminding convention delegates of this congregation's unique contribution to the Episcopal Church, to the Diocese of Newark, and to the community of Morristown, Bishop John Spong praised Redeemer for refusing to make "an idol of the past," courageously risking "the death of that which no longer carries meaning in order to experience a resurrection into that which does." He pointed to the vibrant interdependence between the congregation's worship life and outreach ministries, commending Redeemer for becoming "an ecclesiastical haven for those who have felt themselves to be outside the scope of traditional religious care [and] for those who want their worship to issue directly in concrete action."[17] The second half of this chapter focuses on this relationship between inclusivity, worship, and social action—the risk of making meaning that continues to result in something we might well call resurrection for the Church of the Redeemer.

THE BODY OF CHRIST AT WORSHIP

In my interviews with worshipping communities confronted by HIV/AIDS, three theological concepts suggesting a renewed understanding of church repeatedly surfaced—corporeality, corporate accountability, and courage. These concepts parallel the ethical transformations invoked by Welch as antidotes to privileged despair—the redefinition of responsible action, grounding in community, and strategic risk taking. And all of these intersecting ethical imperatives find material expression in the liturgical life of the redeemed Church of the Redeemer.

Ritualizing Responsible Action as Attention to Corporeality

Sharon Welch suggests that the ethic of control is, in part, an attempt to escape our limitations by retreating into the relative privileges offered by class, gender, race, and, we would add, temporarily "able" bodies. But because the HIV virus refuses to be confined to easily scapegoated populations, AIDS confronts us with these limitations over and over again. We are all "at risk," and there are no perfect solutions, no easy miracles or carefully timed resurrections. Cries of God-forsakenness echo across the theo-ethical landscape, yet the cavalry fails to arrive. The ethic of control begins to crumble. When wrestling with "the Trickster AIDS," Quaker artist and AIDS activist Nani Paape identifies "the most important thing" as "the willingness to be imperfect and do it anyway."[18] This willingness to

256

risk imperfection often comes, as it did for the Church of the Redeemer, in response to an immediate, physical crisis.

When Christian theologians speak of the corporeality of the body of Christ we speak of embodied immanence, of *incarnation*, a term most commonly interpreted as a unique and spiritually cataclysmic event, a singular noun: the Incarnation. But a very different understanding emerged in conversation with my theological co-conspirators in Morristown and Seattle, an understanding more intimate, but equally cataclysmic. For those touched by HIV/AIDS or other disabling conditions, incarnation is an ongoing imperative, a continuing physical process, an ever-present call and response.[19]

The real meat fleshing out this concept of incarnation is *real meat*, corpo-reality, from *corpus* meaning body (not only of texts), like "corpse" and "corpuscle," body and blood, the scene of the crime, the stuff of passion, death and Eucharist. Theories of "the body" titillate academic writers these days. They proliferate in contemporary philosophies and philosophical theologies.[20] In some cases, the people who spoke with me about their experiences with AIDS and church rattled the bare bones of these oddly abstract theories of flesh. In others cases, these colleagues put real meat on those bones. But over and over again, our conversations began and ended with two points—the absolute necessity of taking the physicality of human life seriously and the unqualified obscenity of all attempts to romanticize that corpo-reality.

HIV/AIDS forces an acute attention to physical detail, for better and for worse. The gentle touch of a lover's hand, the smell of spring air, the bad harmonies of good friends singing "Happy Birthday" vigorously off-key vie for time and energy with the less welcome aspects of life incarnate in the HIV/AIDS pandemic—complex drug regimens, major shifts in food tolerance, basic mobility issues, blindness, incontinence, dementia. Abstracting and/or romanticizing the body, considering either the joys or the sorrows of incarnation alone, is unimaginable in the day-to-day context of HIV/AIDS. A congregation living and working within the pandemic becomes intimately involved in what Nancy L. Eiesland calls "the 'mixed blessing' of embodiment."[21] (See also Patterson, chapter 6.)

The joy of this incarnate mix pervades the Church of the Redeemer's worship life, which celebrates a re-valuation of sensuality in many ways. Every Redeemer liturgy approaches sense-ability through an ironic twist of architecture that flirts with parody. Redeemer's liturgies, which seem perfectly suited to the worship-in-the-round styles of the late '60s and '70s, unfold in a very traditional, very Anglican stone church complete with stained glass windows imported from Mother England and scrupulously maintained by a raucously American congregation. This juxtaposition of high church and something liturgical conservatives might view as high camp could strike purists on both sides of the aesthetic/ideological aisle as odd, but not so the congregation's current wardens, Rob Liotard and Lily De Young. Both experience the rootedness in liturgical and aesthetic history provided by the building as contributing a sense of empowerment and even entitlement to Redeemer's overt and implicit critiques of that tradition. The church sees itself as a locus of radical reformation standing firmly and rightfully within Anglican Christianity, which it seeks to reform by bringing bodies back to the church and corporeality back to the corpus.[22]

This revaluation of incarnation as the site of ethical action includes the affirmation of a broad range of healthy and respectful expressions of human sexuality, ritualized in the blessing of same-sex couples and the baptism of children born to or adopted by lesbian or gay parents. But this is only one aspect of redeemed corporeality celebrated by this worshipping body. The liturgical seasons themselves, some created at and for the Church of the Redeemer, echo the complexity of life incarnate, beginning with pregnancy themes at Advent and ending with the Creation season, a celebration of the Cosmic Christ and incarnation in its broadest context. This new liturgical season, developed at Redeemer, takes its thematic cues from three patron saints, Francis of Assisi, Elizabeth Barrett Browning, and Chief Seattle, the Native American (and Episcopalian) hero. Rector and liturgist, Phillip Wilson, scores this and other Redeemer liturgies for all the senses. Fall colors drape the sanctuary, reinforcing the smell of dry leaves and wood fires outside, and one of the basic elements of creation—earth, air, fire, and water—is presented with the eucharistic elements each week. The Prayers of the People for the Creation season affirm humanity's place in the web of life and recall the responsibility connected with that relationship.

Leader: We stand before God and each other, confessing our abuse of creation and praying for its healing and ours:

We have forgotten who we are. We have alienated ourselves from the unfolding of the cosmos. We have turned our backs on the cycles of life. . . . We have sought only our own security. We have distorted our knowledge.

People: Now the land is barren. The waters are poisoned, and the air is polluted . . . We ask forgiveness. We ask for the gift of remembering. We ask for strength to change.

Leader: We seek the healing of creation and each other. We join with the earth and each other: to bring new life to the land, to restore the waters, to refresh the air . . .

All: (Sung) Earth's crammed with heaven, and every living thing afire with God.[23]

Music plays a particularly important role in Redeemer's worship life. More than half-a-dozen Hymn Team members rework old songs and contribute new ones, often bringing to voice the trials and celebrations of the invisible and the silenced. Reworked standards include liberation versions of the un-Redeemerly classics "Just as I Am" and "How Great Thou Art," an ever expanding repertoire of verses for "Simple Gifts" and "Amazing Grace" and some fairly cheeky rewrites of such unlikely profeminists as Thomas Aquinas and St. Paul. Original compositions include a full liberation mass (in progress) and children's Christmas pageant, as well as countless original pieces on women's journeys, creation spirituality, recovery, and social transformation.

Colors, sounds, and smells establish resonances within our own bodies, but corporeality embraces a different intimacy as well. Repeatedly, my partners in this project brought me back to the flesh-on-flesh experience of incarnation, an embodied encounter requiring an embodied response. The Passing of the Peace at the Church of the Redeemer is such an encounter. Visitors are welcomed warmly, while old friends hug, kiss, cajole—and console. An essentially joyous part of the service, the ten to fifteen minutes of apparent chaos is also where parishioners meet and share the sorrows of embodiment in the sobs of a grieving friend; the temporary relief of a family sheltered and fed; the cruelty of disease and disability of all kinds; and especially, the holes, the gaps, the aching, empty wounds created in the body when one of its members is released—late or soon—from the mixed blessing of corporeality. When responsible action is redefined ethically and liturgically in terms of incarnation, salt tears blend with boisterous laughter; but frequent sermons on suffering challenge the too-common Christian fantasy that pain is in-and-of-itself glorious or salvific.[24]

Liturgy as Corporate Accountability:
Grounding Responsible Action in Communities of Dangerous Memory

Nani Paape and my other "informants" warned repeatedly that life with the Trickster AIDS is rarely glorious. It is clumsy and painful, a trial and error process, first and last an exercise in humility and mortality, which requires an acute attention to the particularities of incarnation, to the specifics of each unique corpo-reality.[25] In this sense, all incarnations, even The Incarnation, are appropriately unique, but never exclusive. The challenges of need and desire are too great for any single response. Always particular, incarnation is also necessarily *corporate*— from the same root as corporeal: body, blood, passion, but complexified, bodies of Christs, a plural plural.

Welch's emphasis on community not only reinforces this plurality but also illuminates its temporal nature. While an ethic of control seeks to effect change through immediate and unilateral action, the transformation of systemic violence envisioned in an ethic of risk requires the work of present-tense communities of solidarity as well as a clear sense of connection to traditions of resistance that precede and inform our efforts and that will continue building on the partial victories we achieve. The AIDS pandemic illustrates these points perfectly. The medical, moral, and logistical complexities that arise during a single human encounter with HIV/AIDS easily deconstruct omni-helpful saviors, one-stop redemptions, and even church as constituted by these monolithic concepts. Responses to the pandemic must be multifaceted, drawing on the diverse talents present in our contemporary communities and on our rich history of corporate responsibility. From before church became church, the Jesus movement was a collective, many individuals, each with unique gifts and unique needs. If, as the African proverb suggests, it takes a village to raise a child, it also seems to take a world of incarnations to face the Trickster AIDS.

In *Worship as Theology: Foretaste of Glory Divine,* Don E. Saliers calls liturgy "an intensification of social being before God."[26] He goes on to characterize corporate worship as (1) doing God's work in the world, (2) recalling who God is and who we are with God, and (3) "identifying the world to itself" in all its beauty and terror.[27] I would like to suggest that Saliers' second point serves as a prerequisite for the other two. Liturgical honesty—liturgy's ability to identify the world to itself and attune us to the way things really are—seems to rest on a congregation's ability to know itself as a unique collection of individuals standing together before God and the wider community in a long and courageous tradition of faithfulness.

This recognition of corporate identity, the many parts as well as the gathered whole, shapes the worship life at the Church of the Redeemer in a variety of ways. First, Redeemer knows itself to be a congregation in recovery. While the parish itself regains its theological strength after what might be described as a long illness and individual parishioners struggle with HIV/AIDS and other chronic or disabling diseases, many of its members are also healing from addictions and/or from various forms of physical, emotional, and sexual abuse. Anniversaries of recovery are recorded along with anniversaries of marriages and blessings, and a special liberation Sunday celebrating these journeys inaugurates Lent, the traditional Christian season of self-reflection.

Redeemer recognizes itself as a community of individuals who have been marginalized, oppressed, and shamed because of who they are. Lesbians, gay men and bisexuals, women and poor people in general, racial and ethnic minorities, the physically and emotionally challenged, like those in recovery from addiction and abuse, have been uniquely associated with sinfulness by certain segments of the wider religious community and have often deeply internalized their role as scapegoat for a violently broken world. Therefore, the language of sin is used sparingly and with great care in worship at Redeemer, even as the priest, Worship Committee, and congregation struggle to find new ways to acknowledge our shared human capacity for inflicting pain. Confession, outside the Lord's Prayer, is currently included in worship only during the seasons of Lent and Creation. In both cases, confession addresses the specificity of sin, acknowledges shortcomings rather than engenders shame, and describes concrete ways to mend broken relationships.

The Lenten liturgy abandons traditional themes of guilt and sacrifice for Rainer Maria Rilke's advice on patience and self-reflection.

That advice, so much more easily quoted than lived, "to be patient toward all that is unsolved in your heart and to love the *questions themselves*" reflects the organic nature of growth and healing and echoes Welch's warning against simple solutions—without condoning complacency. Rilke goes on, "the point is, to live everything. *Live* the questions now. Perhaps you will then gradually, without noticing it, live along some distant day into the answer."[28] The absolution during Lent, offered first by the priest to the congregation and then by the congregation to the priest, forgives the partiality of our answers, affirms the project of life, and supports the connection between God, self, and community. "Be you well assured that God forgives and accepts you. Forgive and accept yourself. Forgive and accept others, and be free."[29]

Finally, Redeemer knows itself to be a community of diverse theological orientations, welcoming Buddhists, Quakers, Unitarians, and Jews to the Communion table. "The only requirement," the invitation assures, "is that you be hungry." Corporate cohesiveness is found in ortho-praxis, right practice, rather than in orthodoxy, right belief. Still, the community continues to claim a place in the Christian tradition. Don Saliers calls liturgy "a school for remembrance and praise."[30] The Christianity re-membered each week at the Church of the Redeemer stands within a particular sacred history informed by the stories of prophecy and liberation recorded in the Hebrew Bible, continuing through the wanderings of the peasant teacher Jesus of Nazareth, into the late twentieth century and beyond. This grounding in an ongoing tradition of resistance calls us to a watchful and strategic patience, acting where we can, remembering that we are never alone in celebration or defeat, and trusting that our actions now contribute to fullness in time.

Worship and the Courage to Risk: Finding the Beat

I began the work shared here with the story of a new pastor searching for the pulse of a dying congregation. I ended each interview with the same question: "Where do you find the heart—to do this amazing work, to take these enormous risks, to live with the threat of physical, emotional, and spiritual death every day?" The answers varied, but a persistent image began to emerge. From its first recorded usage, Paul's phrase "the body of Christ" was a peculiarly heady term, serving most often to reinforce hierarchies it may have been coined to destabilize. Again and again, I heard that if Christ is indeed the "head" of the church, then Christ is misplaced and the church is in trouble. My theological partners in Morristown and Seattle consistently pointed to a more centrally-located organ.

Since "corporeal" and "corporate" both derive from the Latin root *corpus* or "body," there is a movement of recapitulation in the terms I have used thus far, a double rhythm, like that of a healthy human heart—not the bosomy, bloodless stuff of greeting cards, but a strong and many-chambered muscle that does not negate the contribution of talking heads, but rather centers, grounds, and vivifies all the members of the body. My work with Episcopalian and Quaker bodies of Christs concretized for me Rita Brock's understanding of heart, which, used unsentimentally, carries rich connotations:

> it . . . is the center, innermost region, and most real, vital meaning and core of our lives. The human heart is symbolically the source of emotions, especially . . . love, empathy, loyalty, courage. The profoundest intellect lodges in our heart where thought is bound with integrity, insight, consciousness, and conscience.[31]

Without slipping into anti-intellectualism, Brock reminds us that "knowing by heart" is knowing at the deepest, most embodied level. When we know by heart, thought and feeling—especially love, empathy, loyalty, and courage, the third aspect of Welch's ethic of risk— combine in one incarnate movement, as close and steady as our own breath. At last I heard the answer to my final question. "Where do you find the heart?" Just there, at the center of things, where you'd expect it to be.

Sharon Welch invokes Johann Baptist Metz's phrase "dangerous memories" to describe stories that inspire us to "take heart" and to take risks. Dangerous memories are not salves for cultured despair. They are its antidote. Such stories form the heart of Redeemer's liturgy—individual stories shared on special holy days throughout the year, Green season[32] celebrations of freedom struggles beginning with the Exodus, and finally, the corporate story of the body of Christ celebrated each week in the Eucharist, Christianity's heart of hearts.

According to Don Saliers, the eucharistic celebration involves a "double process of memory"—calling participants to remember what Christ gave for the world and calling God to remember what God has yet promised to give. Implicit in this double movement of human gratitude and divine promise is a third remembering, made quite explicit at Redeemer. This third re-calls the congregation's own responsibility for the covenant of incarnation, past and future. The most powerful liturgical recognition of this hearty responsibility comes at what traditionally has been the most jealously-guarded eucharistic moment. At Redeemer, the consecration of the elements is a shared blessing. The priest narrates the story, but the priest and congregation together recite the words of institution. The orchestration is simple, but the effect is inexpressibly profound. This is—potentially—memory at its most dangerous.

Far from fostering complacency or nostalgia, ritual participation in past victories—and defeats—becomes "dangerous" in a radically redemptive sense when, and only when, it fuels continuing resistance to and transformation of institutions and ideologies of oppression.[33] The liturgies that resurrect and re-incarnate such stories speak a new world into being. They are, themselves, according to Saliers, "eschatological acts," bringing about the reality they describe.[34] "Gather us by this Holy Communion into one body in your Son Jesus our Christ. Make us a family of praise and celebration." By the time the bread is broken, the eucharistic prayer is answered in fullness, but the work of corporate incarnation has only just begun.

Through such eschatological acts, the Church of the Redeemer has, de facto, resurrected the eucharistic concept of "transubstantiation." No longer at issue—for most communicants—is the transformation of bread and wine into flesh and blood, rather the substantial transformation of the very incarnate body of Christ, the church, through sharing of the ritual meal at the altar, on the soup kitchen line, in the formal dining room or front porch of the Eric Johnson House, in members' homes or hospital waiting rooms. The bodies of Christ multiply like loaves and fishes, becoming flesh and blood, creative spirit, beating heart, a community of extraordinary and everyday saints once more.

CONCLUSION: THE CHURCH ALIVE

According to philosopher Alfred North Whitehead, "The world lives by its incarnation of God."[35] Lives and, perhaps, also dies. This is quite literally true in the HIV/AIDS pandemic. Ostracized individuals and morally bankrupt faith communities will live or die by the ways we incarnate God in this crisis. HIV/AIDS is neither an act of divine judgment on homosexuals, drug addicts and hemophiliacs, nor an act of divine grace for a dying church. HIV/AIDS is a disease and a particularly loathsome one. AIDS is never salvific. People with AIDS are not our Paschal lambs or our good deed for the day. AIDS—like all other sources of pain and suffering, like war and cancer and sexual violence and racism—is an urgent appeal to each and every one of us to open our lives and our work to creative transformation, however we name that holy risk. This pandemic, like the others that precede, swirl around, and will surely follow it, calls church and academy, individuals and communities, to incarnate courage and compassion and healing—corporeally, corporately, heartily—and to learn to recognize that same divine incarnation in the faces, hearts, and minds of individuals, communities, and academies around us.

1. Ronald L. Grimes, *Beginnings in Ritual Studies,* rev. ed. (Columbia, S.C.: University of South Carolina Press, 1995), 51.
2. This essay is lovingly dedicated to the memory of Eric Johnson whose story follows; Claude Branque, my beloved brother, teacher, and member of University Friends Meeting of Seattle; and Richard Smith, my dear friend and member of the Church of the Redeemer, Morristown, who died from complications of AIDS the morning this chapter was first presented.
3. For an excellent treatment of the many strategic connections between HIV/AIDS and broader disability issues, see *The Disability Rag & Resource* (March/April 1994).
4. Vereene Parnell, "The Body of God at Risk: Ecclesiology and AIDS." Paper presented at the annual meeting of the American Academy of Religion, Philadelphia, Pennsylvania, November 18-21, 1995.
5. For examples of HIV/AIDS-specific liturgies and information on the religious response of African-American communities to the pandemic, see *Who Will Break the Silence: Liturgical Resources for the Healing of AIDS* (New York: The Balm in Gilead, 1995).
6. The parish history through 1986 is taken from the congregation's 1987 self-study undertaken as part of the search process for a new rector.
7. Sharon D. Welch, *A Feminist Ethic of Risk* (Minneapolis: Fortress Press, 1990), 3.
8. Ibid., 15. Bracketed additions are my own.
9. From the "Order of Worship for Lent, Holy Eucharist, Inclusive Language Rite," Church of the Redeemer, Morristown, N.J.; the Rev. Philip Dana Wilson rector and liturgist.
10. Welch, *A Feminist Ethic,* 20.
11. From the 1987 congregational self-study, 3.
12. Philip Dana Wilson, interviewed by author, Morristown, New Jersey, June 10, 1995.
13. Anne Johnson, interviewed by author, Morristown, New Jersey, August 16, 1995.
14. Bill Johnson, interviewed by author, Morristown, New Jersey, August 16, 1995.
15. Philip Dana Wilson, Advent Sermon [Photocopy], Church of the Redeemer, Morristown, NJ; November 29, 1992.
16. Ibid.
17. The Rt. Rev. John S. Spong, "Bishop's Statement to the Annual Convention of the Diocese of Newark, January 26, 1996," reprinted, *Crossroads: The Newsletter of the Christian Liberation Community at the Church of the Redeemer* (February 1996): 2.
18. Nani Paape, "AIDS Care Among Friends: A Care Committee's Story," *Friends Journal* (January 1994): 15-17.
19. Embodiment is a central theme in most liberation theologies, including but not only theologies of disability. See Nancy L. Eiesland, *The Disabled God: Toward a Liberatory Theology of*

Disability (Nashville: Abingdon Press, 1994); Emilie M. Townes, ed., *A Troubling in My Soul: Womanist Perspectives on Evil and Suffering* (Maryknoll, N.Y.: Orbis Press, 1993); Carter Heyward, *Touching Our Strength: The Erotic as Power and the Love of God* (San Francisco: HarperCollins, 1989).
20. See Luce Irigaray, *Speculum of the Other Woman*, trans. Gillian C. Gill (Ithaca: Cornell University Press, 1985); Julia Kristeva, "Stabat Mater," *The Kristeva Reader*, ed. Toril Moi (New York: Columbia University Press, 1986); Alison M. Jaggar and Susan Bordo, eds., *Gender/Body/Knowledge: Feminist Reconstruction of Being and Knowing* (New Brunswick, N.J.: Rutgers University Press, 1989). For theological treatments, see note 19 and also Mark C. Taylor, *Erring: A Postmodern A/theology* (Chicago: University of Chicago, 1984).
21. Eiesland, *The Disabled God*, 22.
22. Robert Liotard, interviewed by author, Summit, New Jersey, September 28, 1995; Lily DeYoung, interviewed by author, Summit, New Jersey, October 5, 1995.
23. From the "Order of Worship for the Creation Season, Holy Eucharist, Inclusive Language Rite," Church of the Redeemer, Morristown, New Jersey; the Rev. Philip Dana Wilson rector and liturgist.
24. This warning cannot be overstated. Inspirational stories from the pandemic and from other arenas of human suffering often flirt with the suggestion that people with AIDS and/or other people in pain are Christ figures or that the presence of HIV/AIDS is or can be a Christ event for a congregation. While I believe that this line of reflection opens a number of interesting theological doors, we must be meticulously careful not to commit ourselves to a theological relationship that once again equates suffering with redemption. Persons with AIDS do not die for their sins or for the sins of the Church. AIDS is not redemptive; it is not the agent of creative transformation. Human response to HIV/AIDS, the embodied response of real people, real members of the body of Christ can be redemptive of persons, communities, and theological traditions.
25. Nani Paape, interviewed by author (telephone), Seattle, Washington, October 22, 1995.
26. Don Saliers, *Worship as Theology: Foretaste of Glory Divine* (Nashville: Abingdon Press, 1994), 26.
27. Ibid., 27-28.
28. Rainer Maria Rilke, *Letters to a Young Poet*, rev. ed., trans. M. D. Herter Norton (New York: W. W. Norton, 1954), 35.
29. From the "Order of Worship for Lent."
30. Saliers, *Worship as Theology*, 31-32.
31. Rita Brock, *Journeys by Heart: A Christology of Erotic Power* (New York: Crossroads, 1988), xiv.
32. The Green season follows Redeemer's extended celebration of Pentecost and precedes the Creation season. It celebrates growth at the corporate level, particularly the histories of liberation movements, taking its themes from the Passover seder and from the African American freedom movement.
33. Welch, *A Feminist Ethic*, 154-55. From Johann Baptist Metz, *Faith in History and Society: Toward a Practical Fundamental Society* (New York: Seabury Press, 1980). A blessed, but human, institution, the Church of the Redeemer continues to struggle with transformation at these many levels.
34. Saliers, *Worship as Theology*, 17.
35. Alfred North Whitehead, *Religion in the Making* (New York: Macmillan, 1926), 156.

CHAPTER THIRTEEN

CRAFTING CHRISTIANS INTO THE GESTURES OF THE BODY OF CHRIST

Brett Webb-Mitchell

I was lost in the labyrinthine maze of classrooms and worship space in a prosperous urban, mainline denominational church where I was teaching an evening class. I came to the very end of a dark hall, buried deep in the basement, and could go no further. Here, one last door to a classroom remained. Like all the other doors in this large church, it carried a professionally carved plastic sign. This one read, "Special Education."

Educated as a music therapist, special educator, and anthropologist, I am a bit of an untamed theological cynic when it comes to the place and presence of people with disabilities in the church. This room and its location within the church provided the impetus I needed to write this chapter. If architecture reflects certain social or cultural themes, then which of these were being revealed in the spatial design and its uses in this church?[1] I believe that the presence and placement of this particular Special Education room is emblematic of what we Christians consider to be education in the church, and that this education replicates patterns and philosophies from the broader educational world, especially and primarily that in our public schools.

For example, in most public schools, the typical special education classroom is often segregated from all the other normal classrooms in the building. One strategy is to put the classroom in the front of the building near the administrators' offices so that these authorities may be alerted quickly in the event of an emergency. The other alternative is to distance the classroom as far away as possible from the rest of the school. For instance, many schools use mobile class-

267

rooms for special education, and while these may be attached to the primary school building, usually they are not. Schools with basements tend to locate special education classrooms there. The children placed in these segregated classrooms are seen by normal students only during times of integration designated by the school, as, for instance, during music class. In churches, these practices are echoed in the tendency to keep those who attend special education Sunday school before worship segregated in their classrooms throughout worship as well. This is because many in churches believe that people with disabilities like mental retardation will either not understand worship or will not act in socially appropriate ways during that time.

It is also instructive to consider how public schools and churches vary in the ways they are typically able to implement special education programs. In public schools, children with various disabling conditions can be segregated according to their individual disabilities, oftentimes depending upon age and grade appropriateness, but also keyed to staffing resources of special education-trained teachers and therapists. In churches, such differentiated classrooms are a luxury. Instead, people with various disabilities, including mental retardation, are often brought together in the same room, where the teacher and aide may not be well-versed in special education and thus depend solely upon the curriculum text for guidance.

Such patterns and practices remind us that the way Christians have educated disabled children and adults alike employs the same educational philosophy practiced in American public schools. Indeed, education in general in the church is woven from the same philosophical fabric as that in a public school setting. That is, educators in both settings hold in common specific philosophical presuppositions of modern thought, principally characterized by a strong distinction between mind and body. Thus, Christian education not only mimics the practices of the how, when, and where of American public education, it also focuses on the what we educate: the rational mind of the individual learner. The only differences between these settings lie in the content of the material in which students are being schooled.

To challenge this practice, I suggest both that we restore "body"— namely the body of Christ—as the primary context in which we educate Christians, and that we reiterate the truth that education of Christians is a community practice of the mind, body, and spirit of Christ. As I have suggested above, the church's practice of "education" has been a false psychology that divides and creates a Cartesian duality between mind and body, with the preeminent mind serving as the pilot that steers the barge of body, all to the detriment of those who are disabled. I intend to show how Paul's understanding of the body of Christ offers a new way to reconstruct these matters, not only for the disabled, but for us all. Furthermore, I shall propose that any attempt to reimagine body must be accompanied by transformations in language, since the false duality is currently lodged in our speech.

Beyond this, I will suggest what some would consider a novel approach to educating—or better, crafting—Christians *as* Christians, regardless of their capabilities or disabilities, but depending upon the gift and measure of grace they have received by the Holy Spirit. My choice of the word *craft* is deliberate. I want to emphasize that Christians know their place in the body of Christ through gestures. In short, I hope to show that we need to educate Christians as if the church believed what Paul believed, namely that the church is literally the living, redemptive body of Christ upon this earth.

CRAFTING CHRISTIANS INTO THE GESTURES
OF THE BODY OF CHRIST

Some educational philosophers have suggested that the characteristics of public education described above may be labeled a modernist construction of education whose meta-discourse reveals a grand narrative. This narrative assumes we believe there are some universal and objective values we all agree upon, which are therefore generalizable unto all cultures of people throughout time. For example, right and wrong, good and bad are moral values that are shared among all people in all cultures as determined by many religions in a culture. As the social scientist Erik Erikson wrote in his book *Childhood and Society:*

> All religions have in common the periodical childlike surrender to a Provider or providers who dispenses earthly fortune as well as spiritual healing . . . an admission in prayer and song of misdeeds, of misthoughts, and of evil intentions, since all religions are constructed by human beings.[2]

Postmodern philosophers, critiquing such modernist constructions, argue from the position that there is no meta-discourse or grand narrative. Instead, there is a "plurality of voices and narratives—that is, for different narratives that present the unrepresentable, for stories that emerge from historically specific struggles." Postmodernist philosophy is attempting to situate what counts as reasoning and rationality within, rather than outside, the particular configurations of space, place, time, and power of a specific people.[3] Thus, in this view, there can be no universalisms in educational theory, no objective values free from the contingencies of time, place, and the story of a people.

Following this, my argument is that education, particularly education of Christians, is local rather than global. The telos of education, which shapes the rhetoric and thus the instruction of and about the telos, can only be comprehended and further constructed by the very contingencies of a community of people. As Christians, our convictions are borne of our belief that we are created in the image of God, and that out of deep and abiding love he sent his Son to this world. Such knowledge is sustained by our continuing communion with the Holy Spirit.[4] Beliefs and certainties of life shared among a people constitute and reconstitute what a people need to be taught in order to know, broadly speaking, that *this* is life.[5]

Therefore, while modern American public educational practitioners may assume that there are theories "out there" that they understand to be normative, universal, and generalizable to all people, disabled and nondisabled alike, those who are called by God and given the gift of grace to be teachers, *didaskaloi*, of Christians, believe and know otherwise. For we are a "peculiar" people who believe and live in the radical hope that we are created and called by God in Christ, and guided and sustained by the Holy Spirit, to be part of one another in the body of Christ.

It is because of this truth that we must practice what educational philosophers Stanley Aronowitz and Henri Giroux call a "border pedagogy" in the context of American society in the latter part of the twentieth century. Because the church is a specific culture, *in* but not *of,* the American culture, engaged in creating and recreating itself by God's Spirit, we must practice a pedagogy that is different from the knowledge/power relationship of domination in American society. As Christians, we are historically constructed and socially organized, guided by a certain code of conduct that explicitly announces the boundaries and therefore the freedoms of our existence as God's children—a code embodied in Scripture, remembered in the sacraments, and lived out among and within the Christian community. How we educate, and towards what ends, is mandated by who we are, namely God's children. Because we are God's, we are called to educate one another from within the conviction that the body of Christ matters. What would it mean to educate God's people as if the body of Christ actually mattered?

In the following section, I shall explore how adopting Paul's understanding of body as the body of Christ might alter our view of education in the church. My emphasis will be on the practice of crafting Christians into the gestures of the body of Christ. I want to invite the reader to consider the intricacies of such crafting, especially the need to continuously discern and negotiate the gestures of the church and how they might they be different in practice than those of the culture in which the church is located. Such a learning and practice of gestures is dependent upon a people whose life together is guided by the narrative of God's story and pre-figured by the telos of the journey, the kingdom of God. It is, in short, a craft dictated by the Gospel.

The Body of Christ

In I Corinthians 3:1-9, we read that while one may be planted by Paul and watered by Apollos, it is God who gives us growth. However, what is it that we are growing into? Paul presents us with various ways of thinking about who we are and where we belong—that we are being made a "building," with Christ as the sure foundation (I Corinthians 3:10, 11), or that we are God's household (Ephesians 2:19). For Paul, the context in which Christians are educated is the body of Christ. He actually believed that we are the body of Christ (see Romans 12:3-8; I Corinthians 12; Ephesians 4:15-16; Colossians 1:18-20).[6]

When Paul referred to the body of Christ, the construct of body was quite different from the merely physical, barge-like object that Descartes referred to in his work. In the Hellenistic and Judaistic culture that Paul lived in, the body was a way of describing the pattern of living in a culture, as suggested by references to the "body politic" of society. In the ancient world, the social body was itself a microcosmic reflection of the universe at large, for, to Plato, the cosmos is itself a tangible body, a "single, living thing."[7] As such, the body, both physical and social, is hierarchically arranged, with each part of the body representing various parts of society, with the human head, because it is spherical in shape, the most divine part of the body.[8] Even within this hierarchical arrangement, the body is described as being beautifully balanced. Finally, the social and physical body's boundaries are permeable, allowing "pneuma," "spirit," or the "stuff" of life to flow into and out of the body, carried by air. The growth of bodies so conceived is alive and dynamic.

It is from within this worldview that Paul writes to the early churches about being the body of Christ. Consider his description in his letter to the Romans 12:3-8:

> For by the grace given to me I say to everyone among you not to think of yourself more highly than you ought to think, but to think with sober judgment, each according to the measure of faith that God has assigned. For as in one body we have many members, and not all the members have the same function, so we, who are many, are one body in Christ, and individually we are members of one another. We have gifts that differ according to the grace given to us: prophecy, in proportion to faith; ministry, in ministering; the teacher, in teaching; the exhorter, in exhortation; the giver, in generosity; the leader, in diligence; the compassionate, in cheerfulness.

What is unique about this body, according to Karl Barth, is that it is unlike any of our romantic, sentimental, or moral notions of body as a self-contained, individual human personality, "as if it were so many cells within a body."[9] Instead, Barth insists that this is a particular body—the body of Christ—for that is where we encounter God in Christ, through the fellowship and communion among our neighbors.

Barth helps us to understand some of the characteristics of this particular body. First, what we do in this observable, varied, and peculiar body is not of our doing, but God's. We owe God our thanks for placing or assigning us to our part in the body, "each according to the measure of faith" (Romans 12:3). This is the God who transcends every individual, whether isolated or gathered in one whole. Second, the focus of education in this body is on being in fellowship with one another, in communion or community; for we encounter the one true God through our relationships with our neighbor. The body of Christ is not an aggregate of individuals—millions of "me's" and "I's" collected in a body. We can only know our oneness in Christ by understanding that we are members one of another (Romans 12:5).

Third, what the Christian community must do, by the grace given to us by God, is to discern what gift we have been created to perform and what gestures we are to practice in the manner of craft, within the body of Christ. Is it "prophecy, in proportion to our faith; ministry, in ministering; the teacher in teaching; the exhorter, in exhortation; the giver, in generosity; the leader, in diligence; the compassionate, in cheerfulness" (Romans 12:6-8)? Nowhere in this listing of grace-filled gifts is one person more important than another, though people have different gifts. Nor is there any suggestion that people need to have a certain I.Q. or E.Q. score,[10] be a certain alphabetic combination on the Myers-Briggs Type Indicator test, be able to read fast or not, nor move with some measure of dexterity in order to be the part of the body of Christ in the manner in which one is called. This is because one's ability to accomplish what is required as a member of the body is itself God's gift in the first place, made known in the context of the Christian community.

Gestures

Because we are individually members one of another—"body parts"—in the body of Christ, we must each practice the gestures specific to our part. For, like any body, if a body part is not exercised and moving, then there is a good chance for not only lethargy but also atrophy. And if it is practiced wrongly, then there is the great possibility of dislocation, not to mention a strain and possible broken-ness within the body.

A gesture is an act of mind, body, and spirit of Christian community that expresses or receives thoughts, ideas, or emotions. Such gestures range from speaking to someone, listening to someone else, or perhaps writing or typing. Gestures may be symbolic or signifiers, depending upon the intentional usage of hands and arms. Gestures involve a people's thinking or feeling or their being engaged by the Spirit of God; but they are enacted through the body, following the intent of mind and spirit.

Gestures are not an act of the individual, but are corporate in that they are learned and refined through the actions of a community. In

273

the case of the Christian community, learning and practicing gestures is an act of Christ's body, mind, and spirit. This is because we one are in the body of Christ. Therefore, it is Christ's body, mind, and spirit that is alive in and through us in Christian community.

Gestures have a history. The gestures we practice today were practiced and had meaning in a specific community before we were born. We can only know the meaning of a gesture by the stories of a community that practices the known gestures. Therefore, gestures are context- or community-dependent. Gestures make it possible for us to be in and relate to others in community. Every time one uses a gesture, one recreates the practice of the gesture once learned for and with others. Indeed, gestures, like stories, create community; and the community is ever recreated with the gestures that are practiced. In the gesture is the story embodied. This is why people who are anthropologists and speech therapists, philosophers of language and sociologists, and some theologians and this educator, are fascinated by the practice of gestures in human communities. Gesture, gesturer, and community are one.

Because Christians are the one body of Christ, "and individually we are members one of another," there are certain gestures that we practice in common and certain specific others that are unique unto the gift that we have received, according to the grace given to us. For example, in his letter to the Galatians, Paul writes that we are to have the "fruit of the Spirit" which is "love, joy, peace, patience, kindness, generosity, faithfulness, gentleness and self-control. . . . Bear one another's burdens, and in this way you will fulfill the law of Christ" (Galatians 5:22, 23; 6:2). What Paul is outlining are some of what Thomas Aquinas would later call the Christian virtues which, by their practice, shape and determine our character. Since such virtues as the love, joy, and peace of Christ are not "natural" to our being, they involve gestures that we must learn, and we learn them only in Christian community.

In addition, I would suggest that while we have been given the gifts of prophecy, ministry, teaching, exhortation, giving, leadership, and compassion, all for the building up of the one body of Christ, these gifts involve certain gestures that are to be learned from those other people in community who are our mentors in such gifts of God. For while God makes it possible for us to grow into Christ's body, God so wills that such growth involves human relationships, as God has chosen to use teachers in community to teach us the ways of Christ.[11] Learning and practicing both the shared or common gestures with the other members of the body, as well as the specific gestures that embody and identify our place among the membership with others in the body of Christ, is like learning a craft from a gifted artisan. We who are learners assume the roles and functions of apprentices, or indentured learners, in and among a guild of mentors who know the tradition, the story, the good of the craft, the gesture to be learned. We are learning these intricate gestures in order to achieve an excellence in a way of living together as the one body of Christ. The learning is not for hope of obtaining merits for the kingdom of God, but rather in thanksgiving for the gesture of God's gift of unmerited grace.[12]

Crafting Christians

Focusing on the practice of the gestures of the body of Christ prompts the church to consider that "knowledge" is not only knowing *what* is faith, hope, love, constancy, and perseverance; rather, knowledge of virtues must entail enactment in community. This approach presses us to address the more salient consideration—that the practice of gestures of the body of Christ make us, as Christians, faithful, hopeful, and charitable.[13] What is the point of knowing what faith, hope, and charity are if one is not trying to be faithful, hopeful, and charitable as the Holy Spirit calls us to be as Christ's body?

As Christians learn and practice the gestures of and in the body of Christ, our very character is being shaped and sustained by the practice of these virtues that inform and underline the gestures being practiced as the Christian community. Therefore, in learning gestures we are doing more than practicing just gestures qua gestures. For if gestures are an act of community, each gesture is an embodiment of a storied-knowledge, whose practice demands that we use the gestures with deliberative judgment. Aware that congregations and parishes in some way or another reflect the culture surrounding us, the subtlety of taste in exercising a gesture is also learned within the body of Christ. That gestures-as-Christian-practices shape and therefore determine the very character of Christians within the body of Christ is key to understanding this radically alternative pedagogy.

Teaching the gestures of the body of Christ is like initiating someone into the practices of a craft. The designation craft may be applied to furniture making, learning a visual art, building boats, or teaching and performing the piano. In medieval Europe, the term was even used to characterize intellectual inquiry, as in the liberal arts: this was considered the craft of the free person. [14]

In the craft tradition an apprentice first learns from a mentor. As we consider using this as a model for the learning of gestures in a Christian community, it is important to note that the apprentice is not an "empty box" or a "tabula rasa" in which beliefs are instilled or written. Rather, there is the assumption that the apprentice may hold certain interpretations or judgments, some of which will need to be eradicated or transformed. Or there may exist certain desires that must be drawn out of the person and into the good that is known only in the practice of the gestures of the body of Christ.[15] The mentor needs to understand that the apprentice has both a potential and need for learning these virtuous gestures as a member of Christian community. The hope or telos of such an apprenticeship is the competent use of gestures. It should prepare the apprentice to use certain gestures in various situations, using judgment to discern which gestures to use when and how, depending upon the circumstances.[16] These judgments require a certain sort of a *dialogue:* a verbal or gestural exchange about what one sees and hears, thinks and feels, in light of what one should see and hear, think and feel, given the character of the Christian community.[17]

Crucial to the teaching of Christian gestures is a mentor who crafts and disciplines the apprentice into the necessary knowledge, judgment, and taste, otherwise known as *phronesis.*[18] Mentors must teach when to apply which gestures and how to practice them, in Wittgenstein terms, as if one were walking upon rough, unexplored terrain or sailing in stormy seas. We, as mentors, are preparing apprentices to have a repertoire of gestures that they may use in safely navigating the rough terrain or the high seas.

Patterning Gestures of the "Good Work"

Practicing such gestures, we participate in crafting the very character of a person into the specific virtues of the Christian life. These make it possible for us to comprehend the excellence of living in Christian community with one another. This craft we practice is guided by the story of the community, as proclaimed in the Gospel, enacted in the celebration of the sacraments, and lived out in service among the diverse members of the body of Christ.

In the practice of gestures, we come to comprehend the good that we share in common: being created and called to be part of the Christ. Let me explain this in further detail. In the act of crafting the aforementioned Christian gestures, we are patterning the many members as the body of Christ. The term "patterning" comes from Paul's letter to young Titus, who was in the act of teaching on the isle of Crete. Paul writes that in teaching the younger men, Titus is to teach them with "what is consistent with sound doctrine . . . showing yourself in all respects a *pattern* (my translation) of good works, and in your teaching show integrity, gravity, and sound speech that cannot be censured" (Titus 2:6-8). The pattern of "good works" is Jesus Christ. Crafting gestures is the work of patterning the many members of the church and the gestures they are to practice into and as the body of Christ. And it is in the organic yet mystical body of Christ, of the church that serves Christ's Spirit, that "vivifies it by way of building up the body," writes biblical scholar Paul Minear.[19]

Another example of patterning may be seen in the practice of some physical therapists who work with young children with autism· or severe physical disabilities. The intent is to literally reconfigure or rewire the child's muscles and nervous system. Called "neuromuscular reflex therapy," this type of patterning involves promoting motor development through the repetition of primitive patterns of movement. It is effective in getting some children to begin crawling, usually a prerequisite for walking. It is known to require both a significant time commitment and a large group of caregivers, each concentrating on just one body part yet coordinating their work with the rest of the team.

What I am suggesting is that we consider something similar in patterning people into the Christian gestures that we are to perform as members of Christ's body. In this case, we begin by patterning a person out of an individualistic, modern sense of having a mind, body, and spirit that is one's own. This is the first habit that needs to be addressed. Then, through a kind of repatterning regimen comprising the entirety of the Christian community, we are all being crafted into the gestures of the mind, body, and spirit of the body of Christ. It is a patterning that calls for nothing less than a radical submission of individual members to the will of the Christian body. Such patterning will involve the broad spectrum of all members of the Christian body, regardless of limitations or capacities, morning, noon, and night.

Where does such patterning take place? We begin with baptism, a sacrament of the church in which we know "that our old self was crucified" with Christ, so that we know that "we will also live with" Christ (Romans 6:6, 8). We continue to be patterned into the gestures of Christian community during the Eucharist. In the sacrament of Holy Communion, we are patterned into the hope given to forgiven betrayers by Christ's sacrifice; we practice the ongoing gesture of "eucharistic living."

We pattern people into the gestures of Christian community when we practice other marks of being Christians. In Romans 12:9-21, Paul lists the gestures of being Christian, like loving one another with mutual affection, outdoing one another in showing honor, rejoicing in hope, being patient in suffering, persevering in prayer, contributing to the needs of the saints, extending hospitality to strangers. "Bless those who persecute you . . . Beloved, never avenge yourselves, but leave room for the wrath of God." If we are to live like this, practicing these gestures, it will come only through story-guided, story-constituted ceremonies and other rituals of Christian communities. We can only learn such gestures in a church that is engaged in the serious task of patterning our mind to think this way, our bodies to act in such a fashion, and our spirit to be eager and willing to become an instrument of Christ-like peace. It is the church that can help us to practice this "unnatural" gesture of peace, especially among our enemies: "If your enemies are hungry, feed them; if they are thirsty, give them something to drink; for by doing this you will heap burning coals on their heads."

EDUCATING AS IF THE BODY OF CHRIST ACTUALLY MATTERED

Writer Annie Dillard is known for asking what some would consider a bold question: "If Christianity is true, why on earth don't we act like it?"[20] In this article, I pose a parallel question: "What would educating or crafting Christians be like if we believed Paul's assertion that we are actually the redemptive, living body of Christ on this not God-forsaken earth?"

Understanding education in the context of the body of Christ has certain consequences and may raise some important concerns. First, taking Paul's conviction seriously makes one an outsider to what is normatively understood as education, where teaching and learning happen in a classroom outside and separated from the public square. When Thomas Aquinas and the monks before him created and constructed what we now call the Academy, they initiated a practice that still shapes and sustains the rhetoric of education today. As I have argued, the rhetoric by which both church and public schools now practice education assumes that the habits by which we pass on knowledge are normative.

A second consequence of taking Paul seriously is that it renders irrelevant the question of the place and presence of people with disabilities. That is, what one could or could not do was not relevant to the gift of grace given in Godly measure to the members of the body of Christ. What mattered was that the person was in Christian community, understanding that whose we are, rather than what I am, is the salient point of being in the body of Christ.[21]

Third, as mentor and apprentice engage in the craft of learning and practicing gestures in the context of Christian community, there is no longer an I or me separate from the other. Because we share being in this one body, having the mind of Christ and infused by the Holy Spirit, it means that someone else will be body for me if my body is unable to fulfill certain tasks as teacher, that someone else will be my voice of faithful conviction if I am unable to speak eloquently (as in the God-given relationship between Moses and Aaron), that some will have to believe for me when I find it hard to believe.

Finally, there is little or no need for such rhetoric of "able-bodied" and "disabled" because we, "though many, are one body in Christ, and individually . . . members one of another" (Romans 12:5). As Karl Barth wrote, what is important is that we live into the incomprehensible knowledge that we are members of the once-crucified-now-resurrected living body of Christ. Because of this, God has dealt to each one of us in his or her particularity gifts differing according to God's grace, which kills us in order to make us alive to him. We must understand that we, the body of Christ, must bow. And we all bow—even those who cannot stand for they are already bowed—as in one gesture, to the sovereign Lord of Creation.

---

1. Norris Brock Johnson, *Westhaven: Classroom Culture and Society in a Rural Elementary School* (Chapel Hill: The University of North Carolina Press, 1985), 22.
2. Erik Erikson, *Childhood and Society*, 2d ed. (New York: W. W. Norton, 1963), 250.

3. Stanley Aronowitz and Henri Giroux, *Postmodern Education* (Minneapolis: University of Minnesota Press, 1991), 69.

4. There needed to be some affirmation of the Trinity in this chapter.

5. Elizabeth Newman said something similar to this in her article, "Teaching Religion and Science," 2.

6. In writing about being the body of Christ, it is important to note that our Enlightenment notion/construction of the body, as constructed by such philosophers as Descartes, is radically different from the understanding of what is body in the plethora of world views when St. Paul was writing this description. Both Dale Martin, *The Corinthian Body* (New Haven: Yale University Press, 1995) and Peter Brown, *The Body and Society: Men, Women and Sexual Renunciation in Early Christianity* (New York: Columbia University Press, 1988) to name just a couple, describe in more detail both a Hellenistic concept as well as a Judaistic perspective on body that is unlike our Enlightenment-narrated, modern scientifically contrived notion of body.

7. Martin, *The Corinthian Body*, 23.

8. Ibid., 47.

9. Karl Barth, *A Shorter Commentary on Romans* (London: SCM Press, 1959).

10. E.Q. stands for an "emotional quotient."

11. John Calvin, *Institutes of the Christian Religion*, vol. 2, ed. John McNeill (Philadelphia: Westminster Press, 1960), 4.1.5.

12. Gestures change through time, given the culture often in which the church is located. In this regard, there is a diachronic "nature" to gestures, even in the body of Christ. For example, the gesture of shaking hands, or as in the practice of the Presbyterian Church, extending the "right hand of friendship" is a gesture that is derived from hand shakes in the sixteenth-century among the Dutch. There is no biblical evidence that Jesus and his followers shook hands. However there is evidence that in and among the Christians in the early church, there was the gesture of the holy kiss, which is not practiced as widely today among Protestant and Roman Catholic churches (I Corinthians 16:20).

13. Nancy Sherman, *The Fabric of Character* (New York: Cambridge University Press, 1991), 162, writes that "virtuous character is acquired through habituation of the non-rational part of the soul."

14. Alasdair MacIntyre, *Three Rival Versions of Moral Enquiry* (Notre Dame: University of Notre Dame Press, 1990), 61.

15. Joseph Dunne, "What's the Good of Education," *Partnership and the Benefits of Learning*, ed. P. Hogan (Dublin: ESAI, 1995), 74.

16. See Sherman, *Fabric of Character*, and MacIntyre, *Three Rival Versions* for more clarification on this point.

17. Sherman, *Fabric of Character*, 172.

18. In her book *Curriculum, Product or Praxis?* (London, N.Y.: Falmers Press, 1987), educator Shirley Grundy draws upon an Aristotelian concept of "phronesis," which is the knowledge, judgement, and taste that permits one to know what is the "excellence" of living with one another.

19. Paul Minear in Stanley Hauerwas, *In Good Company* (Notre Dame: University of Notre Dame Press, 1995), 23.

20. This quotation was found in an article on Dillard by Phillip Yancey, "A Pilgrim's Progress" in *Books and Culture* (September/October, 1995): 12.

21. There is the possibility that, within the specific context of the body of Christ, there may be a different understanding of what it is to be "able" or "not able" when it comes to, for example, an understanding of living morally.

CHAPTER FOURTEEN

DISABLING THE LIE: PRAYERS OF TRUTH AND TRANSFORMATION

Helen Betenbaugh and Marjorie Procter-Smith

P rayer is encounter and discourse with the Holy One, and as such it demands honesty and authenticity. How then are persons with disabilities to pray? In what ways does their embodied knowledge of difference, suffering, exclusion, and rejection shape their prayers before God in the midst of the community? How have the conventions of traditional Christian public prayer enabled or inhibited the full participation of persons with disabilities in public worship?

THE DISABLED BODY IN THE BODY OF THE CHURCH

We who raise these questions do so from different perspectives. One of us is temporarily able-bodied, having a limitation of vision that is correctable and not regarded socially as a disability, and one of us has used a wheelchair for twenty years as a result of a spinal fracture and post-polio syndrome. We use the term "temporarily able-bodied" as a reminder of the fragility of health. In the words of Kat Duff, "Illness, like death, is a universal experience; there is no privilege that makes us immune to its touch."[1] Any of us could become permanently disabled in a moment; and if we live long enough, we will each gradually become impaired in seeing, hearing, speaking, and mobility. We use the term "person with a disability" in this chapter to refer to individuals who have any physical or mental condition that is not readily correctable and is used by society to devalue and limit the activities of that individual.[2] Often these limitations are expressed by restrictions on the person with a disability's ability (or permission) to function or even be seen in public. William Rankin describes these limitations somewhat tongue-in-cheek as the "Five Rules of the World":

> One, you must have nothing wrong with you; two, if you do, you must get over it immediately; three, if you can't get over it, pretend you did; four, if you can't even pretend, just don't show up, because it is too painful for the rest of us; and five, if you insist on showing up, you should at least have the decency to be ashamed.[3]

The liturgical questions we raise have to do not with private or domestic prayer (often presumed to be the only or even the privileged domain of the person with a disability), but with the church's prayer in public gatherings, the very place persons with a disability are not able or allowed to participate. Together with the social unacceptability of the person with a disability in public gatherings (and especially in roles of leadership or other visible or audible roles), other theological principles affect the participation of persons with a disability in public prayer. The assumption that illness or disability is the result of sin or separation from God is deeply embedded in the biblical religions, as is the assumption that healing or recovery is the result of faith or virtue, either on the part of the one who is suffering or of those acting on her or his behalf.

This assumption finds expression most fully and clearly in traditional services of healing, as is made clear in the commentary on the healing services in the United Methodist *Book of Worship:*

> A Service of Healing is not necessarily a service of curing, but it provides an atmosphere in which healing can happen. The greatest healing of all is the reunion or reconciliation of a human being with God. When this happens, physical healing sometimes occurs, mental and emotional balance is often restored, spiritual health is enhanced, and relationships are healed.[4]

While the distinction between healing and cure is appropriate, persons with permanent disabilities may find in the suggestion that reconciliation with God brings about healing the implication that their disability is a result of separation from God.[5] Speaking on the

282

parable of the healing of the paralyzed man in Matthew 9, Kathy Black comments that

> Some people in the disability community feel that it would have been better if Jesus had healed the community of its common practice of ostracizing all those with disabilities. . . . If the community had been healed in this way, all the people Jesus did not cure back then and now could also have become an integral part of the community.[6]

Instead, healing services focus their energy on healing the individual, whose illness or disability is thus defined as the problem. These services, as published by mainline Christian churches in books of worship materials, normally include a prayer of confession with absolution, petitions for healing, and prayers of thanksgiving. In fact, these three types of prayer—confession, petition, and thanksgiving—mark the limits of public prayer in contemporary Christian worship whether they are oriented toward healing or not. Since prayer is intended not only to articulate the disposition of those praying but also to shape and form that disposition, then the normative attitudes of the Christian at public prayer are limited to penitence, requests for assistance, and gratitude.

These attitudes are precisely the ones most often demanded and expected of persons with a disability, particularly in public. They are frequently blamed for their condition, assumed to be always in need of help, and expected to be grateful for whatever help the able-bodied may wish to offer. They are certainly not supposed to demand anything. They are to be the object of prayer, never the subject—having their experience defined by others. In a Christian context, theological language is often used to reinforce such assumptions:

If only you had more faith/prayed harder/trusted in God more, you would be healed.

What did you do to cause this condition? Why is God punishing you?

There but for the grace of God go I.

Thus sin and its reverse, repentance/faith, are related to the disability as if they were causative: the disability is caused by sin, cured by repentance. But in the experience of the person with a disability, the connection is never so simple. Some persons do have culpability for the onset of their disabilities, when they themselves were the causative agents: driving too fast, playing with guns and other potentially lethal weapons, diving into an unknown body of water, trying sports maneuvers beyond their training and expertise, or abuse of drugs and alcohol. These and other acts may be directly or indirectly responsible for the person's injury and subsequent disability. Here guilt is a factor, and repentance a necessary process. A process in which the persons with a disability claim responsibility for their own self-destructive behavior is valuable not only because such a step is a necessary component of repentance and reconciliation, but also because it recognizes the person with a disability as a responsible agent. Such recognition is valuable in a context in which persons with a disability are normally treated as if they are helpless children.

On the other hand, a person with a congenital disability, or someone injured through the actions of others, is not primarily in need of repentance but is a victim of what Korean theologians call *han,* the burden of suffering at the hands of others.[7] The theological assumption that his or her suffering is punishment from God creates a burden of guilt and shame that reinforces the societal rejection of the disabled body as repulsive.

Paradoxically, suffering is also sometimes glorified, regarded as redemptive and a sign not of divine judgment but of divine approval:

God is testing you; be faithful/hold on and there will be some great reward for you or some great work that God has in mind for you.

You're being purified; one day you'll be one of the saints.

This is your cross. Be grateful, take it up, and follow Jesus.

You've done all your penance with what you're going through. Now you have *carte blanche* to sin all you want to—you've paid in advance.

Your disability is really a blessing in disguise; look at what you're doing now!

God never gives us a greater burden than we can bear.

The connection between suffering and salvation is particularly strong, and for Christians this connection is linked with the suffering of Jesus. However, the inevitable theological link between suffering and redemption has been questioned by contemporary theologians. Feminist theologians Rebecca Parker and Joanne Carlson Brown argue that "suffering is never redemptive and suffering can never be redeemed."[8] Kat Duff, in *The Alchemy of Illness,* makes it evident that if there is transformation, if dross does turn to gold, it is only after tremendous struggle.[9] Robert J. Schreiter argues that, "Suffering in itself is neither noble nor redeeming. It is essentially an erosion of meaning. It is an interruption and destruction of those fundamental senses of safety and selfhood without which we cannot survive as individuals and as societies."[10]

Disability and illness may be completely nonredemptive for some people, leading even to their deaths from suicide. Furthermore, the assumption that suffering is redemptive, or divine punishment, allows others to wash their hands, Pilate-like, leaving the possibility of redemption or judgment solely in the hands of God and the one suffering. This effectively insulates temporarily able-bodied individuals from the messiness of disability-related pain. It also allows these able-bodied persons to comfort themselves with the idea that the person with a disability is a romantic figure, ennobled by suffering, an idea that does not allow the person with a disability to express anger or make demands.

Similarly, prayers of thanksgiving often couch the thanks in forms that deny or glorify suffering. That persons with a disability are to be grateful whatever their "lot in life" is both a social and religious expectation; and like other assumptions about persons with a disability, it protects temporarily able-bodied persons from confronting the reality of suffering. There is a further issue with gratitude, especially the church's teaching that "it is more blessed to give than to receive." We all hear this from our earliest days in Sunday school. What it leaves out is perhaps implicit, but rarely perceived; giving requires a recipient, and the sacramental potential of the transaction is enhanced by a welcome taker. Persons with a disability must frequently ask for assistance of various kinds, and are thus often the recipients of the giving. All of this results in a crushing blow: one is guilty for not being a giver (and therefore blessed) and further guilty for being a taker. Such assumptions are abusive. People with disabilities need confirmation and affirmation of the fact that by their receiving they are simultaneously giving grace to the giver.

Finally, prayers of petition are most likely to objectify persons with disabilities. They are presumed to be in need of prayers (as well as other forms of "help"), but are not presumed to be capable of naming their own needs or desires for themselves. They are object, not subject.

285

But the assumption of temporarily able-bodied individuals that the primary need of persons with a disability is for "cure" is faulty. For many persons with a disability, the needs are a good job, a good intimate partnership, health and happiness for their children, success with their investments, and other "normal" desires. They have "made their peace" with their disabilities, have established medical care or have forsaken the medical establishment, have procured what mechanical and technological aids they need in order to function, and have established goals apart from being rid of their disability. At the same time, there are many others for whom cure is—and will always remain—the primary goal. Many of these persons enter research programs and focus their energies on regaining the ability to walk, to see, to hear, or to speak. Still others, whether newly injured and undergoing rehabilitation and therapy, recovering from illness, or in treatment for emotional illness, may need a "time out" period before they can resume "business as usual."

Prayers of confession, thanksgiving, and petition carry assumptions with them that inhibit the full participation of persons with a disability in the church's public prayer by reinforcing harmful assumptions about persons with disabilities. But in addition to these limitations, traditional Christian prayers frequently employ sensory and mobility language in ways that further the social and religious marginalization of persons with a disability. Most commonly, spiritual ability is identified metaphorically with physical ability. Consider, for example, the following prayer from the new *Book of Common Worship* of the Presbyterian Church:

> Give me, O my Lord,
> that purity of conscience
> which alone can receive your inspirations.
> My ears are dull,
> so that I cannot hear your voice.
> My eyes are dim,
> so that I cannot see the signs of your presence.
> You alone can quicken my hearing
> and purge my sight,
> and cleanse and renew my heart.
> Teach me to sit at your feet
> and to hear your word.[11]

By the logic of this and similar texts, sight, hearing, and mobility are all necessary (metaphorically or literally) in order to receive divine inspiration; and sensory clarity is equated with a clear conscience. Hymnody in particular, with its use of the metaphorical imagery of poetry, is laden with sensory and mobility language, all of which is used to describe the spiritual life and faith journey. For example, "Open My Eyes That I May See" and "My Faith Looks Up to Thee" associate physiological vision with spiritual insight. "Stand Up, Stand Up for Jesus" and "Rise Up, O Men of God" make the ability to stand a metaphor for religious courage. "I Want to Walk as a Child of the Light" and "O Master, Let Me Walk With Thee" associate physical mobility with discipleship.

A final inhibitor is the presumption in traditional forms of public prayer that the unison, single voice best expresses the unity of the assembly. Hence a printed or published prayer may be read in unison by the congregation, or a leader may offer (read or created extemporaneously) prayers on behalf of those assembled. This assumption fails to take account of the varieties of possible forms of address to God and privileges the spoken (and perhaps read) word over prayers signed, embodied, or otherwise expressed. Further, the preference for a single voice inhibits the expression of difference and cannot hope to encompass the varieties of experience found among persons with disabilities.

Temporarily able-bodied persons tend to reduce the diverse experiences of persons with disabilities into one archetypal model, thus excluding and nullifying countless stories and lives. There is no single model for living with a disability, no single way of "handling" or perceiving it. Persons with a disability are like those who are temporarily able-bodied: unique, individual, and in need of being heard and of participating in corporate, public life, both religious and secular. For some, coping means denial, trying to "pass," and fierce independence. At the other end of the spectrum are those for whom disability has given them the only unique identity they have ever perceived. They cling to their need to be "special" and therefore to the disability. All manner of differences fill in the distance between these two extremes.

Into this mix must be added the obvious fact that not all disabilities are of the same magnitude or evoke the same reaction from temporarily able-bodied persons. An amputee with a well-fitted prosthesis

287

may "pass," while Christopher Reeve's quadriplegia has made Americans aware of the catastrophic effects of high-level spinal cord injuries. Such persons require around-the-clock assistance for virtually every activity of daily living. And even within the life of a person with a disability there may be degrees of disability. A friend born without forearms or hands and also without one lower leg and foot says he never felt disabled because he had never experienced life or his own body any other way. But in midlife he suffered a torn rotator cuff as a result of a fall on ice, and suddenly felt enormously disabled.

Finally, inherent in unison prayer is the demand that all speak at the same speed and be in the same place in the text at the same time. This does not provide space for persons with visual difficulties, with speech deficit, with learning or cognitive disabilities, to read at their own pace. Conformity thus results in exclusion and in frustration as the person's disability publicly makes him or her unable to take part in a simple community activity. Thus corporate (of the "body") prayer excludes those whose bodies do not conform to the "corporate standard."

In corporate prayer, the body of the church constructs and maintains its relationship with God through direct address in speech and act. But in limiting its prayers to confession, petition, and thanksgiving; in employing sensory and mobility language as metaphors for spiritual values; and in privileging the unitary voice in prayer, the church has limited access to this process of relationship-building for persons with a disability. It has also constructed and maintained what Robert J. Schreiter has called "the narrative of the lie." Although Schreiter is dealing with the effects of violence on individuals and societies, his definition of the narrative of the lie is applicable to persons with a disability as well:

> Violence tries to destroy the narratives that sustain people's identities and substitute narratives of its own. These might be called narratives of the lie, precisely because they are intended to negate the truth of a people's own narratives. . . . The negation is intended not only to destroy the narrative of the victim, but to pave the way for the oppressor's narrative.[12]

We contend that the traditional Christian interpretations of suffering and disability foster, intentionally or not, the narrative of the lie by suggesting that suffering and disability are a result of divine

288

punishment or a result of sin; or that they are sent by God to test, refine, or bless in some paradoxical way; or that recovery and cure can be had by holding the proper faith or by praying in the proper way; or that suffering is redemptive in and of itself. Such a narrative destroys the complex and ambiguous narratives of persons with disabilities, limits the ability of those individuals to construct meaning out of their experience, and colludes with society's rejection of the disabled body as not "normal" or "beautiful."

The alternative to the narrative of the lie is resistance: "Not to accept the narrative of the lie means resisting the breakdown of our own narrative. . . . It is only when we discover and embrace a redeeming narrative that we can be liberated from the lie's seductive and cunning power."[13]

The process of resisting the narrative of the lie and discovering a redeeming narrative requires that persons with a disability claim their own voice as individuals and as a group, to lament suffering, to cry out against oppressors, to make demands of God and of the community in which they worship and pray.

> Silence is the friend of oppression and crying out names the perpetrator of the violence against us. Crying out gives voice to our pain and calls others to our side, to help us be restored to the larger social network. Crying out is an address, an appeal to God that what we face reaches beyond our ability to cope.[14]

Clearly in this context "crying out" is not limited to verbal speech, but encompasses any form of protest and resistance to the narrative of the lie. In prayer, protest and resistance are found in forms rarely used in traditional Christian prayer: lament, exorcism, and cursing. All of these prayers, found in Scripture and in ancient Christian rituals, are ritual means of saying no, of protest and resistance.[15] The recovery and development of such forms are necessary elements in the creation of a redeeming narrative in public prayer.

CHALLENGES TO THE BODY OF THE CHURCH

The internalization that follows a narrative of a lie is, in itself, paralyzing. Is there a way to empower persons with disabilities to resist the lie, challenge it, and move past it to hope and flourishing? Is there a way for religious communities to be healed of their practice of ostracizing those with disabilities? Requisite for empowerment and liberation is the discovery and embracing of a redeeming narrative. Therefore, persons with disabilities must challenge their temporarily able-bodied brothers and sisters in the church to offer hospitality, safety, and solidarity. These need to be offered by more than lovely sounding, though hollow, words of invitation and inclusion in worship bulletins, evangelism materials, or the parish newsletter. The offer must be a vital one, alive with the promise—and the delivery—of a journey shared in community. In this chapter we refrain from any language that implies persons with disabilities versus the church, believing that persons with disabilities are already part of the church. Instead, the complex issues center on giving voice to the heretofore voiceless, or indicating a willingness to learn, to be challenged, to begin trying to see ways in which the opportunity can be given for persons with disabilities to have a voice. To realize the promise of full inclusion of all in the church's prayer, a safe and hospitable environment must be provided.

The most obvious sign of the promise is the delivery of an accessible church campus, including all facilities and buildings. Most of all, it means an attitude of accessibility, that the staff and congregation are ready to welcome, to assist, and to listen. It should mean access to the chancel/altar area for lay and ordained persons with disabilities who are called to assume roles of leadership in corporate worship.

These physical signs challenge the economic commitment of the congregation as it wrestles with prioritizing budget items—ever increasing demands on frequently diminishing dollars. It is almost universally true that people who dismiss the need to spend dollars on access change dramatically when they or a spouse, parent, child, or close friend become disabled; then the personal becomes the political.

Time and patience are also requisites for the inclusion of persons with a disability in the worship and fellowship functions of the church. It takes conscious effort to allow more time and space around what happens in worship. Readers who use Braille texts, or who communicate using American Sign Language and require simultaneous voice translation; persons who move slowly; those with speech deficits all have voices that should be heard in worship. Likewise, all should take part in the movement to and from the rail for Communion if they desire—or the community should be prepared to wait while they are communicated in their places.

All of these areas of commitment mean change, the acceptance of diversity, and the willingness to experience ambiguity on a regular basis. Persons with disabilities push the boundaries of our theological understanding: What does it mean for a person who is mute to "have a voice?" What does it mean for a blind or partially sighted person to "see the light?" What does it mean for a person who uses a wheelchair or braces and crutches to "walk with the Lord?" What do these and others—persons with mental retardation, with emotional illnesses, with AIDS or cancer, with cerebral palsy, with no hands or arms—demand that we ask of God? And do we fear these questions and their possible answers? In a world of doing, what does it mean to value a person simply for being, regardless of the potential for ever doing anything grand or perhaps ever performing the simple tasks of daily living?

The ultimate call, then, is to a commitment of energy: energy that goes into dealing with the discomfort, perhaps even the pain, of having the boundaries of one's world pushed and stretched; energy that goes into fund-raising, into hands-on accessibility work, into a mode of patience and acceptance. Energy also goes into companionship with any person, temporarily able-bodied or with a disability, but which may require more expenditure in the first days and weeks of relationship with persons with a disability. For healing and reconciliation to take place, the commitment must be evident—and on more than "Access Sunday" occasions. We manifest this energy by recognizing and welcoming persons with disabilities as full members of the church, with gifts and graces that do not differ from the gifts and graces of temporarily able-bodied persons except in the uniqueness of each individual, by literally and figuratively making space for persons with a disability and by inviting their participation and welcoming their gifts.

These gestures give voice to the voiceless; they say, "I hear you; I see you; you are a person who happens to have a disability, not defined nor limited in many ways by that disability." The word companion means, literally, "one with whom one breaks bread." Would that our worshiping, eating, praying, and being together would lead us to companionship. Then all may see that:

God is a God of ease and dis-ease, of ability and dis-ability, of freedom and limitation, movement and stillness, of choices and imperatives, pleasure and pain; of joy and suffering, light and dark, of speech and silence, of running and being carried, giving and receiving help, of calm control and spasticity, of touching and being touched, hearing and quiet.[16]

DISCOVERING A REDEEMING NARRATIVE

The creation of a redeeming narrative requires disabling the narrative of the lie and claiming the power of self-naming. For persons with disabilities, this process demands the creation of a safe, hospitable, and supportive space, both literally in the sense of physical and sensory accessibility, and spiritually in the sense of changes of attitude. When these prerequisites are met, then it becomes possible for persons with disabilities to begin the challenging process of finding the power of "voice" before God.

This process will often include and sometimes even begin with anger and grief. Anger and grief over inhumane treatment by the medical establishment, over rejection by friends and family, over societal and physical barriers may need to be expressed. Internally, this may include anger and grief at the disability itself, at the lost or severely altered hopes, dreams, and plans the individual had, and at herself or himself for giving to the temporarily able-bodied community the power of naming their identity and worth. As Kris Norman wrote in *New Mobility* magazine, "When I really thought about it, I decided I was not so much interested in a cure as a chance to start all over again at being disabled."[17]

In particular, it may be important for persons with disabilities to express anger toward the church for its lack of welcome and its reluctance to adapt to their active presence. There is just cause for this anger. In 1979 the World Council of Churches produced a document entitled *Partners in Life: The Handicapped and the Church*. It is a clarion call to the church to include persons with a disability in all aspects of its life. "To be faithful to the Gospel, the Church must be the place both of the faith that rebels and of the faith that accepts; and it cannot be this unless the handicapped are, and are seen to be, an integral and indispensable part of its life."[18] Few know of the existence of this visionary document.

What most persons with disabilities do recognize is the kind of anger expressed by Sharon Younker-Deatz, a Presbyterian minister who was diagnosed with multiple sclerosis in 1988. When she "only" used a cane, her New Jersey congregation was "very supportive and very loving." But when she needed to use a wheelchair, they refused to build ramps or to make other accessibility modifications. "The congregation said the alterations would either cost too much or spoil the beauty of the sanctuary." Frustrated, hurt, and angry, Younker-Deatz quit. "I didn't want to forgive the people in the church. I didn't want God to forgive them."[19]

This is not an isolated problem involving only a few parishes. Holmes revealed in this same article that

> As the Americans with Disabilities Act made its way through Congress, a coalition of churches, backed by the White House, lobbied for a blanket exclusion on the ground that to include religious institutions would violate the doctrine of the separation of church and state. Further, some denominations worried about the law's costs, and some fundamentalists were concerned that because the law covers people infected with the virus that causes AIDS they might be forced to hire homosexuals.[20]

Again, while few actually know this fact, likewise few have not felt its effects. "If bars are more accessible than altars or theaters more welcoming than churches, more is the shame for us," said Mary Jane Owen, executive director of the National Catholic Office for Persons with Disabilities.[21]

Unfortunately, the Christian prayer tradition has not retained many of the ancient prayer forms that express anger and grief. Lament, curse, exorcism, and excommunication are all prayer forms little used in contemporary prayer, but much needed in order to disable the lie and create a transforming narrative.

Lament is the ritual expression of grief, common in Jewish prayer and prominent throughout the Psalms. It is a form that recognizes that terrible harm has been done and cannot be undone. All that remains to do is to call the world and God to bear witness to the loss and the harm. This act of lament as calling to bear witness is eloquently described by John Weir in his account of the funeral of a young man who died of AIDS:

His memorial service was at the Gay Synagogue in the Village. Gerald had a big, supportive family. They all knew he was gay. The service was in Hebrew. His father got up to read his part. Gerald's father was the kind of Jewish man that Bernard Malamud wrote about—barely assimilated, still with the rough edges, the accent, the conspicuousness of an immigrant. He was a butcher in the Bronx.

He started reading, but then let go of the text, and tipped his head back, and clasped his palms together, and roared. He wailed and shouted in a language that I couldn't understand, but I knew exactly what he meant. I knew exactly what he meant. I think I knew exactly what he meant.[22]

This crying out, calling all to bear witness to pain and loss, is a necessary step in disabling the narrative of the lie.

Anger has been ritualized in curses, excommunications, and exorcisms. These ritual prayer forms are the reverse side of blessings. Where a blessing recognizes and celebrates the goodness in some person or object, a curse or excommunication names the evil and brings it to light. An exorcism goes one step further by working to remove the evil and replace it with goodness. Cursing is a ritual activity much debased and misunderstood these days, often confused with the mere utterance of offensive words. But if a blessing is powerful, then so is a curse.

Of course, persons with disabilities have often been the object of curses, excommunications and exorcisms, when the illness or disability is assumed to be the result of sin or evil of some kind. The illness has often been interpreted by religious people as a curse from God. Persons with disabilities are often excommunicated from church participation, if not "officially," then certainly *de facto,* by the lack of access to most churches. Persons with disabilities have also been subject to exorcism-as-healing. In fact, the power of these rituals of anger has been used by the temporarily able-bodied representatives of the religious community to control and limit the religious activity of persons with disabilities. But when persons with disabilities claim their own anger and are in an environment in which their expression of anger can be received, these prayer forms take on a new life. They become the repository for the expression of power and self-definition of persons with disabilities. They become necessary elements for moving into claiming hope and creating a redeeming and transforming narrative.

Finally, there may be times and circumstances in which it is necessary not only to say no *in* prayer, but to say no *to* prayer. When the sense of betrayal is overwhelming, when God is regarded as complicit in one's suffering, either through failure to act on one's behalf or through failure to live up to God's own promises, then silence may be necessary. There are times when the act of prayer itself, and the trust and self-disclosure it demands, becomes impossible. The knowledge of terrible suffering renders prayer problematic. By intentionally choosing silence, one refuses to further one's own suffering and oppression and identifies oneself with those who are denied voice before God.

Although the expression of grief and anger is not usually encouraged in Christian worship, these expressions need legitimation in order to enable the creation of a redeeming narrative. Expressions of anger and grief are essential to the self-definition of those whose lives and bodies have been and continue to be defined by others. Although such expressions may be painful for the temporarily able-bodied to hear, they ultimately lead to hope. When temporarily able-bodied persons are able to recognize and receive the cry of lament and anger of persons with disabilities as legitimate and meaningful, then a true community is formed. In this community prayer becomes authentic, the narrative of the lie is disabled, and the narrative of redemption and unity is engendered.

PRAYERS OF ANGER AND GRIEF

The freedom to move into the public expression of anger, however well "disciplined" that anger might be, is more difficult to achieve than one might expect. Here feminist ethicist Beverly Wildung Harrison gives wisdom, insight, and empowerment. In her now-classic article "The Power of Anger in the Work of Love," Harrison cites the two functions of anger: indicating that there is a problem with the relationship, and providing the energy necessary to do the work of restoring it.[23] From the outset of this joint project, the work of writing the prayers was the responsibility of the person with an obvious disability. What she found was that the theoretical sections of this chapter came quickly and easily. The constructive part that tapped into her own suppressed anger came at enormous expense, only after days and weeks of avoidance tactics (no distracting project was too

295

small or insignificant) and finally, nightmares. Family, society, and church have all disabled the validity of such prayer and taught us to fear it, our deepest feelings, and the reactions of God and the world.

Perhaps more freedom of expression in prayer resides outside the church, in the world of the playwright, for example. Witness the stunning prayer written by Tony Kushner, author of *Angels in America,* for the Episcopal National Day of Prayer for AIDS at the Cathedral of St. John the Divine in New York City and delivered on October 9, 1994, which began:

> God:
> A cure would be nice. Rid those infected by this insatiable unappeasable murderer of its lethal presence. Reconstitute the shattered, restore to health all those whose bodies, beleaguered, have betrayed them, whose defenses have permitted entrance to illnesses formerly at home only in cattle, in swine and in birds. Return to the cattle, the swine and the birds the intestinal parasite, the invader of lungs, the eye-blinder, the brain-devourer, the detacher of retinas. Rid even the cattle and birds of these terrors; heal the whole world. Now. Now. Now. Now.[24]

Persons with disabilities must be similarly empowered to call God to account for the suffering of the world. Inspired by Kushner's passionate cry, we offer this prayer.

DISABILITY: A LAMENT

Creating God:
You made the sky,
clouds of purest white,
with rays of fuschia and orange and magenta at sunset,
and faces dear with the smiles of loved ones.
Today thousands were born without sight;
thousands more lost vision because of injury or disease.
And it was evening and morning of another day.
Did you call this Good?

You made the finest sands,
snow to crunch under our boots,
fields of green grass,
cool on the soles of our bare feet on a hot summer's day,

and streams to hike alongside with loved ones.
Today thousands were born without feet or legs,
or with legs so twisted or spastic that they would never walk on them;
thousands more lost the use of feet or legs because of injury or disease.
And it was evening and morning of another day.
Did you call this Good?

You made the song of the birds,
the sound of waves lapping against the shore,
the warning wail of the siren,
music, the laughter of children,
and the tender words of loved ones.
Today thousands were born deaf;
thousands more lost their hearing because of injury or disease.
And it was evening and morning of another day.
Did you call this Good?

You made minds,
quick to invent the wheel,
to discover electricity,
to find a way to journey to the Moon,
and to fashion words of poetry for loved ones.
Today thousands were born with mental retardation,
with developmental or learning disabilities;
thousands more were rendered "incompetent" "vegetables,"
because of injury or disease.
And it was evening and morning of another day.
Did you call this Good?

Your hands pushed back the waters
to reveal the dry land,
And fashioned us from clay.
You made our hands to sculpt,
to move with grace like Pavlova or Baryshnikov,
and to caress the bodies of loved ones.
Today thousands were born with no hands or arms,
or with short stumps for arms and flippers where hands should be;
thousands more lost the use of their hands and arms
because of injury or disease.
And it was evening and morning of another day.
Did you call this Good?

You made us to sing,
to shout,
to laugh,
to communicate through important words,
and to speak from our hearts to the hearts of loved ones.
Today thousands were born without speech,
or with speech so difficult that it scarce can be uttered or understood;
thousands more lost the use of their voices
because of injury or disease.
And it was evening and morning of another day.
Did you call this Good?

You made a world of love,
of life shared in community,
of choices and decisions,
safe boundaries,
and relationships with loved ones.
Today thousands were born with autism
or other emotional illnesses;
thousands more entered the fog of emotional illness
because of abuse or injury or disease.
And it was evening and morning of another day.
Did you call this Good?

You breathed into us *ruach,* the breath of life.
You filled the world with the sweet perfumes of flowers.
You made us to breathe the tangy aromas of spices,
the scents of budding trees,
the incense arising from prayers for our loved ones.
You made us to taste the bread and the wine,
Body and Blood of your—and our—Loved One.
Today thousands were born so allergic that they cannot dare smell,
dreading the reaction to what they might suffer if they taste;
thousands more were made allergic
because of injury or disease.
And it was evening and morning of another day.
Did you call this Good?

Where and when can we hold you accountable?
Where are bodies assembled that are guaranteed by the union label?
Where is the card proudly claiming "Packaged for you by Angel 33"?
Where is Quality Control? Customer Service?
Where do we get exchanges?

Where demand parts that work, that hold up under stress,
that permit us to have choices in living our lives?
WE call this Good.

Must we expect less of You than we do of each other?

Hear our prayer.

Where is the mercy you promised us?
Do you remember the Covenant?
Or were these hollow,
mere platitudes?

Does the rainbow mean something to you
or has it become an innocuous icon
for kindergarten teachers and Hallmark cards?

Jeremiah and the Psalmist wailed,
Job raged,
and Jesus wept.
Has God hardened God's own heart?

Hear our prayer.

Are our prayers less valid because we cannot see the candles flickering
on the altar?
Do you ignore us if we cannot kneel to implore you to listen?
Do you choose not to hear us if we cannot hear the Sanctus bell?
Do you demand that we bring a high IQ to this discussion?
Do you judge us insincere if we have no hands to fold in prayer?
Do you get bored and turn away if we speak slowly, or not at all?
Do you sneer at us if we cannot speak to you rationally, in our "right
minds"?
Do you find us unholy if we cannot tolerate the Bread and the Wine?
What, for Christ's sake, would it take for you to hear us?

We are yours, yet we see you distant, irresponsible.
We see you washing your hands of us
just as Pilate washed his hands of your Son.

We see angels taken over by pop culture.
Where are the angels you promised you would give charge over us?
Instead of cute pins on our shoulders

we want angels of mercy.
Mercy to end the unremitting pain,
to stop the infernal, eternal twitching and jerking,
to loose the tongue,
mercy to still the flailing arm,
to open the ears,
to quicken the brain,
mercy to relax the spasm,
to restore the eyes,
to walk and leap and dance,
mercy to touch,
and to feed ourselves with hands of grace,
to extend a greeting to the stranger,
to be free to breathe and taste,
and to soothe the anguished mind.

We want mercy.
Mercy to end Duschenne muscular dystrophy, Down Syndrome, Tourette Syndrome,
ALL Syndromes.
Mercy to halt Huntington's chorea and multiple sclerosis.
Mercy to end birth defects. All of them.
Mercy to stop strokes, and blinding diabetes.
Mercy for healing all in body, mind, and spirit.
Balm in Gilead.
Unction.
Now.
Here is our prayer.

Hear our prayer.

We are weary of trying to name Paul's "thorn in the flesh."
We want to know why you left it there.
We are sick of celebrating Annie Sullivan.

We want to know why Helen Keller became blind, deaf, and mute.
We are angry at fights about whether or not a President can be shown "wheel chair bound."
We want to know why you didn't heal FDR from his polio so he wasn't.
Don't tell us Christopher Reeve is a "true" superman now.
We want to know why you didn't put him back on his horse.

At last, again our prayer

Hear our prayer

Mercy from healing all in body, mind, and spirit
Balm in Gilead.
Unction.
Now.

The empowerment that comes from finally being able to voice this kind of insistent, demanding, frighteningly honest prayer before God leads to also being able to claim one's place in the church community as a place of integrity and of authority. From this place, then, can come the voice that can preside over prayers of exorcism of the demons of ableism, of fear, of superiority, and of indifference.

Holy One, be present now with your legions of angels. Michael and his sword; George who slew the dragon. Christ, be present now; you who knew suffering, you who showed compassion to persons with disabilities, you who dined with blind Bartimaeus. Drive out from ____ (Name of individual, group, or congregation)____ all indifference to the needs of others. Drive out (his/her/their) fear of bodies that are weak, that look different, that don't function as they might. Drive out from (him/her/them) all thoughts and feelings that they are superior, that I am less, that I am foolish, I am insignificant, I am repulsive, I am polluted because I have a disability. Fill them with a sense of their own vulnerability, with kindness, with the spirit of hospitality of which your Son spoke when he said, "When you give a banquet, invite the poor, the crippled, the lame, and the blind" (Luke 14: 13). Then, together at last, we may share the Feast as true sisters and brothers in the faith.

The model for a rite of excommunication can be found in James Lancaster's "Litany for Divine Intervention." Lancaster takes the greater excommunication rite from the *Pontificale Romanum,* the old Roman Catholic rite, and changes it from a prayer designed to suppress "enemies of the church and false teachings" into a "life-giving ritual for our times."[25] The language of oppression specifically directed at homophobia can easily be changed to be directed at ableism. For persons with disabilities to be able to take part in such a ritual means that hope already exists—hope of a church where "isms" and phobias have no place and all find a welcome.

Such a church is living the redeeming narrative. As the Association of Physically Challenged Ministers of The United Methodist Church says in its Creed,

In the name of Christ we are hosts and agents of hospitality. We are the church. We claim our place with others in reconstructing the table of Christ so that all may approach it together as brothers and sisters in Christ, one Body, united and whole.[26]

1. Kat Duff, *The Alchemy of Illness* (New York: Bell Tower Books, 1993), xv.

2. See Hector Avalos, "Disability and Liturgy in Ancient and Modern Religious Traditions," in this volume, and Nancy L. Eiesland, *The Disabled God: Toward a Liberatory Theology of Disability* (Nashville: Abingdon Press, 1994).

3. William W. Rankin, *Cracking the Monolith: The Struggle for the Soul of America* (New York: Crossroad, 1994), 18.

4. *The United Methodist Book of Worship*, 613-14. *The United Church of Christ Book of Worship* includes the services for reconciliation of penitents and healing services in the same section. The distinction between cure and healing is also made by Helen Betenbaugh, in "A Theology of Disability," unpublished paper; she also makes a distinction between moral evil and natural evil in order to interpret the suffering of persons with disabilities. On services of healing, see also Kathy Black, *A Healing Homiletic: Preaching and Disability* (Nashville: Abingdon Press, 1996), 183.

5. See further, Marjorie Procter-Smith, "Contemporary Challenges to Life-cycle Rituals" in Lawrence Hoffman and Paul Bradshaw, ed., *Christian and Jewish Life-Cycle Rituals* (Notre Dame, Ind.: Notre Dame Press, 1996).

6. Kathy Black, *A Healing Homiletic*, 122.

7. In particular, see Andrew Sung Park, *The Wounded Heart of God: The Asian Concept of Han and the Christian Concept of Sin* (Nashville: Abingdon Press, 1993).

8. Joanne Carlson Brown and Rebecca Parker, "For God So Loved the World?" in Joanne Carlson Brown and Carol Bohn, *Christianity, Patriarchy and Abuse* (New York: Pilgrim Press, 1989), 27.

9. Duff, *The Alchemy of Illness*, 77-91.

10. Robert J. Schreiter, *Reconciliation* (Maryknoll, N.Y.: Orbis Books, 1992), 33.

11. Text by Dag Hammerskjold, *Book of Common Worship* (Louisville: Westminster/John Knox Press, 1993), 22.

12. Schreiter, *Reconciliation*, 34.

13. Ibid., 34-36.

14. Ibid., 36-37.

15. For a fuller discussion of the importance of saying no in prayer, see Marjorie Procter-Smith, *Praying With Our Eyes Open: Engendering Feminist Liturgical Prayer* (Nashville: Abingdon Press, 1995) and David Blumenthal, *Facing the Abusing God: A Theology of Protest* (Louisville: Westminster/John Knox Press, 1993).

16. Helen R. Betenbaugh, "ADA and the Religious Community: the Moral Case," in Robert C. Anderson, ed., *A Look Back: the Birth of the Americans With Disabilities Act* (Binghamton, N.Y.: The Haworth Press, 1996), 64-65.

17. Kris Norman, "Starting Over," *New Mobility* 7:33 (June 1996): 8.

18. Lesslie Newbigin, "Not Whole Without the Handicapped," in Geiko Müller-Fahrenholz, ed., *Partners in Life: The Handicapped and the Church* (Geneva: World Council of Churches, Faith and Order Paper No. 89, 1979), 23.

19. Steven A. Holmes, "When the Disabled Face Rejection from Churches That Nurtured Them," *The New York Times* (Sept. 30, 1991): A10.

20. Ibid.

21. Ibid.

22. Quoted in Rankin, *Cracking the Monolith*, 20.

23. Beverly Harrison, *Making the Connections: Essays in Feminist Social Ethics* (Boston: Beacon

Press, 1985), 14. See also Procter-Smith, *Praying With Our Eyes Open,* 50.

24. Tony Kushner, *Thinking About the Longstanding Problems of Virtue and Happiness* (New York: Theatre Communications Group, 1995), 217-18. The full text of this prayer, which runs to seven pages, calls the church and its leaders to account with vivid, pungent imagery.

25. Cherry Kittredge and Zalmon Sherwood, eds. *Equal Rites: Lesbian and Gay Worship, Ceremonies, and Celebrations* (Louisville: Westminster/John Knox Press, 1995), 140.

26. United Methodist News Service (October 1994).

SELECTED BIBLIOGRAPHY

Albrecht, G. L. *The Disability Business: Rehabilitation in America.* Newbury Park, Calif.: Sage Publications, 1992.

Alston, R. C. Russo, and A. Miles. "Brown vs. Topeka Board of Education and the Americans with Disabilities Act: Vistas of Equal Educational Opportunities for African Americans." *Journal of Negro Education* 63:3.

Anderson, R. C., ed. *A Look Back: the Birth of the Americans with Disabilities Act.* Binghamton, N.Y.: The Hayworth Press, 1996.

Aries, P. *Images of Man and Death.* Translated by Janet Lloyd. Cambridge: Harvard University Press, 1985.

Aronowitz, S. and H. Giroux. *Postmodern Education.* Minneapolis: University of Minnesota Press, 1991.

Augustine. *The City of God.* Translated by Henry Bettenson. Middlesex, Eng.: Penguin Books, 1984.

Avalos, H. *Illness and Health Care in the Ancient Near East: The Role of the Temple in Greece, Mesopotamia, and Israel.* Atlanta: Scholars Press, 1995.

Ball, W. B. "Should the Senate Approve the 'Americans with Disabilities Act of 1989'?" *Congressional Digest* 68 (December 1989).

Becker, G. "Stigma as a Social and Cultural Construct." In *The Dilemma of Difference: A Multidisciplinary View of Stigma.* Edited by S. C. Ainlay, G. Becker, and L. M. Coleman. New York: Plenum Press, 1986.

Berkowitz, E. D. *Disabled Policy: America's Programs for the Handicapped.* London and New York: Cambridge University Press, 1987.

Bishop, M. E., ed. *Religion and Disability: Essays in Scripture, Theology and Ethics.* Kansas City: Sheed and Ward, 1995.

304

Black, K. *A Healing Homiletic: Preaching and Disability*. Nashville: Abingdon Press, 1996.

Blumenthal, D. *Facing the Abusing God: A Theology of Protest*. Louisville: Westminster/John Knox Press, 1993.

Bolles, R. N. *Job Hunting Tips for the So-Called Handicapped or People Who Have Disabilities*: A Supplement to *What Color is Your Parachute?* Berkeley, Calif.: Ten Speed Press, 1991.

Bondi, R. *To Love As God Loves*. Philadelphia: Fortress Press, 1987.

_____. *In Ordinary Time: Healing the Wounds of the Heart*. Nashville: Abingdon Press, 1996.

Bowe, F. *Handicapping America: Barriers to Disabled People*. New York: Harper and Row, 1978.

Brock, G. "Liturgical Ministry to the Sick: An Overview." *Journal of Pastoral Care* 45:1 (1990).

Brock, R. *Journeys by Heart: A Christology of Erotic Power*. New York: Crossroads, 1988.

Brown, P. *The Body and Society: Men, Women, and Sexual Renunciation in Early Christianity*. New York: Columbia University Press, 1988.

Browne, S., D. Connors, and N. Stern, eds. *With the Power of Each Breath: A Disabled Women's Anthology*. Pittsburgh: Cleis Press, 1985.

Bush, L. *Health and Medicine Among Latter-Day Saints*. New York: Crossroad, 1993.

Bynum, C. W. *The Resurrection of the Body in Western Christianity, 200-1336*. New York: Columbia University Press, 1995.

Chamberlain, G. L. "Chronicle: Rituals and Healing in the Crisis of AIDS." *Worship* 63:5 (1989).

Cixous, H. and C. Clement. *The Newly Born Woman*. Translated by B. Wing. Minneapolis: University of Minnesota Press, 1988.

Colston, L. G. *Pastoral Care with Handicapped Persons*. Edited by H. J. Clinebell, Jr. Creative Pastoral Care and Counseling Series. Philadelphia: Fortress Press, 1978.

Constantelos, D. J. "Physician-Priests in the Medieval Greek Church." *Greek Orthodox Theological Review* 12:2 (1966-67).

Cooper, B. "The Disabled God." *Theology Today* 49:2 (1992).

Costen, M. and D. Swann. eds. *The Black Christian Worship Experience*. Revised edition. Atlanta: Interdenominational Theological Center Press, 1992.

Cushieri, A. *Anointing the Sick: A Theological and Canonical Study*. Lanham, Md.: University Press of America, 1992.

Davis, L. H., ed. *The Disability Studies Reader.* New York: Routledge, 1997.

DeVries, D. "Creation, Handicapism and the Community of Differing Abilities." In *Reconstructing Christian Theology.* Edited by R. S. Chopp and M. L. Taylor. Minneapolis: Fortress Press, 1994.

Dickson, J. "FDR Memorial Battle Presses On." *Ragged Edge* 18 (March/April 1997).

Dillenberger, J. *A Theology of Artistic Sensibilities: The Visual Arts and the Church.* New York: Crossroad, 1986.

Disability Studies Quarterly. Religion, Spirituality, and Disability Issue. 15 (Fall 1995).

Dolnick, E. "Deafness as Culture." *The Atlantic Monthly* (September 1993).

Donovan, M. S., ed. *Women Priests in the Episcopal Church: The Experience of the First Decade.* Cincinnati, Ohio: Forward Movement Publications, 1988.

Douglas, M. *Purity and Danger: An Analysis of Concepts of Pollution and Taboo.* New York: Hammondsworth, 1970.

Driedger, D. *The Last Civil Rights Movement: Disabled Peoples' International.* New York: St. Martin's Press, 1989.

Duff, K. *The Alchemy of Illness.* New York: Bell Tower Books, 1993.

Durand, J. and D. S. Massey. *Miracles on the Border: Retablos of Mexican Migrants to the United States.* Tucson: University of Arizona, 1995.

Earl, R. "Under Their Own Vine and Fig Tree: The Ethics of Social and Spiritual Hospitality in Black Church Worship." *The Journal of the Interdenominational Theological Center* 14:1.

Eiesland, N. L. *The Disabled God: Toward a Liberatory Theology of Disability.* Nashville: Abingdon Press, 1994.

_____. "Things Not Seen: Women with Physical Disabilities, Oppression, and Practical Theology." In *Grounding the Subject: Feminist Practical Theologies in Context.* Edited by D. Ackermann and R. Bons-Storm. Louvain, Belgium: Peeters, 1998.

Empereur, J. L., S. J. *Prophetic Anointing: God's Call to the Sick, the Elderly and the Dying.* Wilmington: Michael Glazier, Inc., 1982.

Erikson, E. *Childhood and Society.* Second edition. New York: W. W. Norton, 1963.

Farnham, S. G., J. P. Gill, R. Taylor McLean and S. M. Ward. *Listening Hearts.* Harrisburg: Morehouse Publishing, 1991.

Featherstone, H. *A Difference in the Family: Life with a Disabled Child.* New York: Basic Books Publishers, 1980.

Fine, M. and A. Asch, "Disability Beyond Stigma: Social Interaction, Discrimination, and Activism." In *Perspectives on Disability.* Edited by M. Nagler. Palo Alto, Calif.: Health Markets Research, 1988.

Fine, M. and A. Asch, eds. *Women with Disabilities: Essays in Psychology, Culture, and Politics.* Philadelphia: Temple University Press, 1988.

Foley, E. *Developmental Disabilities and Sacramental Access: New Paradigms for Sacramental Encounters.* Collegeville, Minn.: Liturgical Press, 1994.

Fontaine, C. "Disabilities and Illness in the Bible: A Feminist Perspective." In *Feminist Companion to the New Testament.* Edited by A. Brenner. Sheffield: Sheffield Academic Press, 1995.

Foucault, M. *The Birth of the Clinic: An Archaeology of Medical Perception.* Translated by A. M. Sheridan Smith. New York: Vintage Books, 1975.

Fuller, R. *Alternative Medicine and American Religious Life.* New York: Oxford University Press, 1989.

Gallagher, H.G. *FDR's Splendid Deception.* New York: Dodd and Mead, 1985.

Gallop, J. *Thinking Through the Body.* New York: Columbia University Press, 1988.

Gartner, A., and T. Joe, eds. *Images of the Disabled, Disabling Images.* New York: Praeger, 1987.

Gelineau, J. *Liturgy Today and Tomorrow.* New York: Paulist Press, 1978.

Gliedman, J., and W. Roth. *The Unexpected Minority: Handicapped Children in America.* New York: Harcourt Brace Jovanovich, 1980.

Goetze, A. "An Incantation Against Disease." *Journal of Cuneiform Studies* 9 (1955).

Goffman, E. *Stigma: Notes on the Management of Spoiled Identity.* New York: Simon and Schuster, 1963.

Govig, S. *Strong at the Broken Places: Persons with Disabilities and the Church.* Louisville: Westminster/John Knox Press, 1989.

Grimes, R. L. *Beginning in Ritual Studies.* Revised edition. Columbia: University of South Carolina Press, 1995.

Grosz, E. *Volatile Bodies: Toward A Corporeal Feminism.* Bloomington: Indiana University Press, 1994.

Gutierrez, G. *We Drink from Our Own Wells.* New York: Orbis Press, 1984.

Hahn, H. "Politics of Physical Difference." *Journal of Social Issues* 44:39 (1988).

———. "Can Disability Be Beautiful?" *Social Policy* 18:3 (Winter 1988).

Harris, L., and Associates. *The ICD Survey of Disabled Americans: Bringing Disabled Americans into the Mainstream.* New York: International Center for the Disabled, 1986.

Hayum, A. *The Isenheim Altarpiece: God's Medicine and the Painter's Vision.* Princeton: Princeton University Press, 1989.

Heyward, C. *Touching Our Strength: The Erotic as Power and the Love of God.* San Francisco: HarperCollins, 1989.

Hillyer, B. *Feminism and Disability.* Norman, Okla.: University of Oklahoma Press, 1993.

Hogan, G., ed. *The Church and Disabled Persons.* Springfield, Ill.: Templegate Pulishers, 1983.

Holmes, S. A. "When the Disabled Face Rejection from Churches that Nurtured Them." *The New York Times* (30 September 1991).

Ingstad, B. and S. Reynolds Whyte, eds. *Disability and Culture.* Berkeley: University of California Press, 1995.

Irigaray, L. *Elemental Passions.* Translated by J. Collie and J. Still. New York: Routledge, 1992.

———. *Speculum of the Other Woman.* Translated by G.C. Gill. Ithaca: Cornell University Press, 1985.

Irvin, C. "My Own Private Roosevelt." *Ragged Edge* 18 (January/February 1997).

Matthews, G. F., ed. *Voices from the Shadows.* Toronto: Women's Press, 1983.

Jaggar, A. M. and S. Bordo, eds. *Gender/Body/Knowledge: Feminist Reconstruction of Being and Knowing.* New Brunswick, N. J.: Rutgers University Press, 1989.

Kayal, P. M. *Bearing Witness: Gay Men's Health Crisis and the Politics of AIDS.* Boulder: Westview Press, 1993.

Kirkland, G. with G. Lawrence. *Dancing on My Grave.* Garden City, N.Y.: Doubleday, 1986.

Knohl, I. *The Sanctuary of Silence: The Priestly Torah and the Holiness School.* Minneapolis: Fortress Press, 1995.

Kristeva, J. "Stabat Mater." In *The Kristeva Reader,* edited by T. Moi. New York: Columbia University Press, 1986.

Lane, H. *When the Mind Hears: A History of the Deaf.* New York: Knopf, 1984.

Lane, N. J. "Healing Bodies and Victimization of Persons: Issues of Faith-Healing for Persons with Disabilities." *The Disability Rag AND Resource* 14:3.

Lehman, E. C. *Gender and Work: The Case of the Clergy.* Albany: State University of New York Press, 1993.

Lenihan, J. "Disabled Americans: A History." *Performances* (November/December 1976-January 1977).

Lewis, C. S. *The Problem of Pain.* New York: MacMillan Publishing, 1962.

Liachowitz, C. H. *Disability as a Social Construct: Legislative Roots.* Philadelphia: University of Pennsylvania Press, 1988.

Livneh, H. "On the Origins of Negative Attitudes Toward People with Disabilities." *Rehabilitation Literature* 43 (1982).

Longmore, P. K. "The Second Phase: From Disability Rights to Disability Culture." *Disability Rag and Resource* 15 (September/October 1995).

_____. "Uncovering the Hidden History of People with Disabilities." *Reviews in American History* 15.

Luebering, C. "Ministries to the Sick and Well." *Liturgy* 2:2 (1982).

MacIntyre, A. *Three Rival Versions of Moral Enquiry.* Notre Dame: University of Notre Dame Press, 1990.

Mackelprang, R. W. and R.O. Salsgiver. "People with Disabilities and Social Work: Historical and Contemporary Issues." *Social Work* 4 (January 1996).

Madigan, S. "Human Stories that Demand Rituals." *Liturgy* 10:3 (1992).

Mairs, N. *Plaintext.* Tuscon: University of Arizona, 1986.

_____. *Remembering the Bone House: An Erotics of Place and Space.* New York: Harper and Row, 1989.

_____. *Carnal Acts.* New York: HarperCollins, 1990.

_____. *Ordinary Time: Cycles in Marriage, Faith and Renewal.* Boston: Beacon Press, 1993.

_____. *Waist-High in the World: A Life Among the Nondisabled.* Boston: Beacon Press, 1996.

Majik, P. J. "Disability for the Religious." *The Disability Rag and Resource* 15 (November/December 1994).

Makas, E. and L. Schlesinger, eds. *End Results and Starting Points: Expanding the Field of Disability Studies.* Portland, Maine: The Society for Disability Studies and the Edmund S. Muskie Insitute of Public Affairs, 1996.

Marinelli, R. P. and A. E. Dell Orto, eds. *The Psychological and Social Impact of Physical Disability*. New York: Springer, 1984.

Martin, D. *The Corinthian Body*. New Haven: Yale University Press, 1995.

Marty, M. *Health and Medicine in the Lutheran Tradition*. New York: Crossroad, 1983.

May, M. *A Body Knows: A Theopoetics of Death and Resurrection*. New York: The Continuum Publishing Company, 1995.

McClain, W. B. *The Soul of Black Worship*. Multi-Ethnic Center for Ministry, 1979.

McCormick, R. A. *Health and Medicine in the Catholic Tradition: Tradition in Transition*. New York: Crossroad, 1984.

McFague, S. *The Body of God: An Ecological Theology*. Minneapolis: Fortress Press, 1993.

Miles, M. "Disability in an Eastern Religious Context: Historical Perspectives." *Disability and Society* 10 (1995).

Milgrom, J. *Cult and Conscience: The Asham and the Priestly Doctrine of Repentance*. Leiden: Brill, 1976.

Moede, G. F., ed. *Like Trees Walking: Biblical Reflections on Healing*. Princeton, N.J.: Consultation on Church Union, 1988.

Moltmann, J. *The Church in the Power of the Spirit*. New York: Harper and Row, 1977.

Monick, E. *Evil, Sexuality and Disease in Grünewald's Body of Christ*. Dallas: Spring Publications, 1993.

Müller-Fahrenholz, G., ed. *Partners in Life: The Handicapped and the Church*. Geneva: World Council of Churches, Faith and Order Paper No. 89, 1979.

National Organization on Disability. *That All May Worship: An Interfaith Welcome to People with Disabilities*. Washington, D.C., National Organization on Disability, 1994.

_____. *Loving Justice: The ADA and the Religious Community*. Washington, D.C.: National Organization on Disability, 1994.

Ninomiya, A. H. "Japanese Attitudes towards Disabled People: Religious Aspect." *Japanese Christian Quarterly* 52 (1986).

Nouwen, H. *Reaching Out: The Three Movements of the Spiritual Life*. Garden City, N.Y.: Doubleday, 1975.

_____. *The Wounded Healer: Ministry in Contemporary Society*. Garden City, N.Y.: Doubleday, 1972.

O'Day, G. *The Word Disclosed: John's Story and Narrative Preaching*. St. Louis, Mo.: CBP Press, 1987.

Okhuijsen, G., and C. van Opzeeland. *In Heaven There are No Thunderstorms: Celebrating the Liturgy with Developmentally Disabled People*. Collegeville: The Liturgical Press, 1992.

Oliver, M. *Understanding Disability: From Theory to Practice*. London: MacMillan, 1996.

Orsi, R. " 'Mildred, is it fun to be a cripple?': The Culture of Suffering in Mid-Twentieth-Century American Catholicism." *The South Atlantic Quarterly* 93:3 (1994).

Pailin, D. *A Gentle Touch: From a Theology of Handicap to a Theology of Human Being*. London: SPCK, 1992.

Pelka, F. "Fire in the Belly: Just How Independent Is the Independent Living Movement?" *Mainstream* 4 (1994).

Percy, S. L. *Disability, Civil Rights and Public Policy: The Politics of Implementation*. Tuscaloosa: University of Alabama Press, 1990.

Pfeiffer, D. and K. Yoshida. "The Teaching of Disability Studies: Results from a Survey of SDS Members." *Disability Studies Quarterly* 14 (Spring 1994).

Poloma, M. M. "A Comparison of Christian Science and Mainline Christian Healing Ideologies and Practices." *Review of Religious Research* 32:4 (1991).

Procter-Smith, M. *Praying with Our Eyes Open: Engendering Feminist Liturgical Prayer*. Nashville: Abingdon Press, 1995.

Raine, T. "Hooked on Chat and Other Goodies: Adventures On-Line." *Disability Rag* 17 (November/December 1995).

Ramshaw, E. J. "Liturgy for Healing." *Liturgy* 9:4 (1991).

Ransom, J. G. *The Courage to Care: Seven Congregations Are Transformed by Reaching Out to Families with Disabilities*. Nashville: Upper Room Books, 1994.

Rediger, G. L. "Handicapped!" *Church Management: The Clergy Journal* (1982).

Robinson, J. A. T. *The Body: A Study in Pauline Theology*. Bristol, Ind.: Wyndham Hall Press, 1988.

Rothman, D. J. *The Discovery of the Asylum: Social Order and Disorder in the New Republic*. Boston: Little and Brown, 1971.

Rothman, D. J. and S. M. Rothman. *The Willowbrook Wars*. New York: Harper and Row, 1984.

Sacks, O. *Seeing Voices: A Journey into the World of the Deaf*. Berkeley: University of California Press, 1989.

Saliers, D. E. *Worship as Theology: Foretaste of Glory Divine*. Nashville: Abingdon Press, 1994.

Scotch, R. K. *From Good Will to Civil Rights: Transforming Federal Disability Policy*. Philadelphia: Temple University Press, 1984.

————."Disability as the Basis for a Social Movement: Advocacy and the Politics of Definition." *Journal of Social Issues* 44 (1988).

Seybold, K. and U. B. Mueller. *Sickness and Healing*. Translated by D.W. Stott. Nashville: Abingdon Press, 1981.

Shapiro, J. P. *No Pity: People with Disabilities Forging a New Civil Rights Movement*. New York: Random House, 1994.

Sherman, N. *The Fabric of Character*. New York: Cambridge University Press, 1991.

Sider, R. J. "AIDS: An Evangelical Perspective." *Christian Century* 105:1 (1988).

Smith, C. M. *Preaching as Weeping, Confession and Resistance: Radical Response to Radical Evil*. Louisville: Westminster/John Knox Press, 1992.

Smith, Q., L. R., M. Nosek, and L. Gerken. "Education and Training Needs of Independent Living Center Managers." *Rehabilitation Education* 5 (1990).

Soelle, D. *The Suffering God*. Philadelphia: Fortress Press, 1995.

Sontag, S. *Illness as Metaphor and AIDS and its Metaphors*. New York: Doubleday, 1990.

Spencer, J. M. *Protest and Praise: Sacred Music of Black Religion*. Minneapolis: Fortress Press, 1990.

Sullivan, L., ed. *Healing and Restoring: Health and Medicine in the World's Religious Traditions*. New York: Macmillan, 1989.

Sung Park, A. *The Wounded Heart of God: The Asian Concept of Han and the Christian Concept of Sin*. Nashville: Abingdon Press, 1993.

Swain, J., V. Finkelstein, S. French, and M. Oliver, eds. *Disabling Barriers—Enabling Environments*. Newbury Park and London: Sage Publications, 1993.

Taylor, M. C. *Erring: A Postmodern A/theology*. Chicago: University of Chicago, 1984.

Thomson, R. G. "Tenure Battle Questions Legitimacy of Disability Studies." *Ragged Edge* 18 (July/August 1987).

———. *Extraordinary Bodies: Figuring Physical Disability in American Culture and Literature.* New York: Columbia University Press, 1997.

Tiffany, F. C. and S. H. Ringe. *Biblical Interpretation: A Roadmap.* Nashville: Abingdon Press, 1996.

Townes, E. M., ed. *A Troubling in My Soul: Womanist Perspectives on Evil and Suffering.* Maryknoll, N.Y.: Orbis Press, 1993.

Trulear, H. D. "The Lord Will Make a Way Somehow: Black Worship and the Afro-American Story." *Journal of the Interdenominational Theological Center* 13:1.

Tucker, B. P. *The Tiel of Silence.* Philadelphia: Temple University Press, 1995.

Turner, B. S. *The Body and Society.* New York: Basil Blackwell, 1984.

Turner, R. H. "The Theme of Contemporary Social Movements." *British Journal of Sociology* (December 1969).

U.S. Bureau of the Census, Americans with Disabilities: 1991-1992.

Van der Toorn, K. *Sin and Sanction in Israel and Mesopotamia.* Assen, The Netherlands: Van Gorcum, 1985.

Walker, W. T. *Somebody's Calling My Name: Black Sacred Music and Social Change.* Valley Forge, Pa.: Judson Press, 1979.

Warner, P .J. "Congregational Hymns: They're Singing My Song." *Brethren Life and Thought* 33:4 (1988).

Webb-Mitchell, B. *Unexpected Guests at God's Banquet: Welcoming People with Disabilities into the Church.* New York: Crossroad, 1994.

———. *God Plays Piano, Too: The Spiritual Lives of Disabled Children.* New York: Crossroads. 1993.

Weil, A. *Spontaneous Healing.* New York: Knopf, 1995.

Weil, S. *Waiting for God.* Translated by Emma Craufurd. New York: Harper and Row Publishers, 1951.

Welch, S. *Communities of Resistance And Solidarity: A Feminist Theology Of Liberation.* Maryknoll, N.Y.: Marynoll Press, 1985.

———. *A Feminist Ethic of Risk.* Minneapolis: Fortress Press, 1990.

Wendell, S. *The Rejected Body: Feminist Philosophical Reflections on Disability.* New York: Routledge, 1996.

West, C. *Prophesy Deliverance! An Afro-American Revolutionary Christianity.* Philadelphia: Westminster Press, 1982.

White, J. F. *Introduction to Christian Worship.* Second edition. Nashville: Abingdon Press, 1990.

Wilke, H. H. *Creating a Caring Congregation: Guidelines for Ministering with the Handicapped.* Nashville: Abingdon Press, 1980.

Wilkinson, J. J. "Leprosy and Leviticus: The Problem of Description and Identification." *The Scottish Journal of Theology* 30 (1977).

Wink, W. "Holy and Without Blemish Before God: Disability and Normalcy." *Auburn News* 1:1 (Spring 1993).

_____. "Women with Disabilities: A Challenge to Feminist Theology." *Journal of Feminist Studies in Religion* 10:2 (1994).

Woodward, J. R. "The Roosevelt Memorial: Whose Version of History." *The Disability Rag and Resource* 16 (September/October 1995).

Wright, B. *Physical Disability: A Psychological Approach.* New York: Harper and Row, 1960.

Wright, T. J. "Enhancing the Professional Preparation of Rehabilitation Counselors for Improved Services to Ethnic Minorities with Disabilities." *Journal of Applied Rehabilitation Counseling* 19:4.

Young, F. *Face to Face: A Narrative Essay in the Theology of Suffering.* Edinburgh: T&T Clark, 1990.

Ziegler, J. J. "Who Can Anoint the Sick?" *Worship* 61:1 (1987).

Zola, I. *Missing Pieces: A Chronicle of Living with Disability.* Philadelphia: Temple University Press, 1982a.

_____. (ed). *Ordinary Lives: Voices of Disability and Disease.* Cambridge: Applewood Books, 1982b.

_____. "Social and Cultural Disincentives to Independent Living." *Archives of Physical Medicine and Rebilitation* 63.

TOPIC INDEX

abuse, religious, 219-21; in society, 125, 132, 168, 261, 284, 298
access, to Temple, 58, 65-66, 69; limited, 128, 153, 157, 191, 195, 204-6, 215, 218, 288; promote, 215
accessibility, 30, 78, 128, 148, 150, 226, 238, 242-46, 290-93
activism, 200, 209, 212, 228, 251
activist, 16, 165, 200-25, 227, 252-55
advocacy/advocates, 200, 202-3, 205, 208, 214-15, 223, 226-27, 244-45
African American, 207, 209, 212-13, 217, 233-46, 266; music and dance, 241-42; preaching tradition, 236-41; worship space, 242-46
AIDS/HIV: attitude toward, 42, 77, 139; case study, 249-65, 290, 295
Akkadian, 52, 61
Alzheimer's disease, 50
anger, 293-301
animal(s): icons, 43; in liturgy, 46-48; in medical science, 48, 51; sacrifice, 46, 51, 65-67
anointing, 19-20, 38-39, 48-49, 53
Anointing of the Sick, 38-39, 49
appearance: signs of, 62-64; stigma of, 57-59
architecture, 144-47, 158, 163, 267
art, 42-46

baptism, 86, 92, 278
beauty, 118-19
Beloved (Morrison), 132
blind/blindness, 79-86, 89-90, 92, 150-52, 191-96, 220, 225-27, 291, 296
body(ies): of Christ, 124, 271-73; cultural preferences of, 134; diversity of, 128-30, 133; female, 124-25; gestures, 273-75; good, 124-26; resurrected or redeemed, 126-40

caregiving, 109-10
Catholic tradition, 49, 52, 185, 301
Christology, 73, 75, 79, 239
churches: accessibility of, 145-49, 157-58, 267-68, 290-91; architecture of, 145-49, 157-58, 267-68, 290-91; Celtic, 145-46; ordination by, 153-60, 187-99
civil rights, 205-9, 215, 217, 227, 233, 242, 244

clergy, 24, 49, 51, 54, 167, 188-199, 236; *see also priest*
Communion, 143-44, 147, 261, 263, 290
community: attitudes of, 40, 42, 112-14, 150-52; of faith, 23; fear in, 112-14, 150-52; healing, 121-22; inclusive, 128; Internet, 212; place of disabled in, 149-52; Quamran, 67-69; servant, 122; stigma in, 57-58
compassion: of Jesus, 73; in liturgy, 27
Confessions, The (Augustine), 123
congregations, *see* community
Constitution on the Sacred Liturgy, 24
courses, disability studies, 212-13
cross, 93-94, 115, 117, 283
culture: of disability, 209-16; preferences of, 134; unit, 59-60
cure, 38, 50, 74, 78, 115, 282-83, 286, 291, 296, 300

dance, 241-42
Dead Sea Scrolls, 67-68
deaf, deafness, 68, 78, 89, 97, 100, 151, 153, 192-93, 197, 203, 209-10, 214, 225-27, 296
death, 28, 46, 67, 12, 131-32, 140, 162, 242, 255-56, 281; of Jesus, 115-17, spiritual, 262
demon possession, 47, 77, 114-15
denominations, 224-25; Catholic, 38-39, 45, 49; Christian, 46, 47-48, 50, 214; Episcopal,

317

319